HINDUISM

AN INTRODUCTION
Part 1

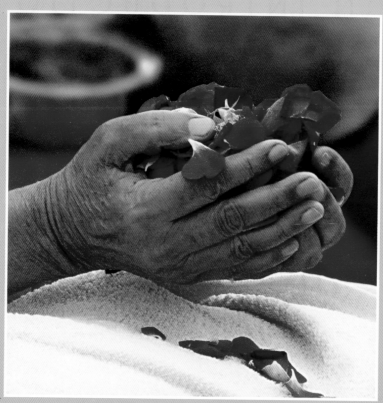

Adoration to the venerable ancient and living traditions of Hinduism

HINDUISM

AN INTRODUCTION

Part 1

By
Sadhu Vivekjivandas

Editorial Consultant
Dr Janakbhai Dave

Swaminarayan Aksharpith
Ahmedabad

HINDUISM, AN INTRODUCTION Pt. 1

Inspirer: HDH Pramukh Swami Maharaj

1st Edition: September 2010
2nd Edition: March 2011
Copies: 7,000 (Total: 12,000)
Price: ₹600/- (Parts 1 & 2)
ISBN: 978-81-7526-433-5

Published & Printed by
Swaminarayan Aksharpith
Shahibaug Road, Ahmedabad-4
Gujarat, India.
Website: www.baps.org

CONTENTS

1

2

3

4

5

6

7

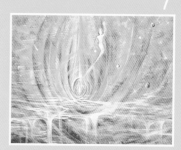

8

9

10

11

12

13

14

15

16

REVIEWS

On perusing 'Hinduism, An Introduction' many prominent spiritual leaders, public figures, scholars and professionals sent their reviews. Some of them are as follows:

The main aspect of Hinduism is that it allows you to participate in the higher experience that it speaks of. One can verify for oneself what it speaks of.

The importance of Hinduism would have slowly faded away in the present day had it not been for several devoted personalities; among them the sadhus of the Swaminarayan *parampara,* who kept it alive.

This book speaks lucidly about the value of our heritage and tradition and also gives an insight into the wisdom of our scriptures.

- Swami Vimalananda

President, The Divine Life Society, Rishikesh

* * *

Since ancient times, the Hindu – Sanatan – Dharma has been the most appropriate and naturally oriented way of life. Beyond the concept of modern secularism, its broadminded global approach offers the scope to every individual to exist, survive and prosper in whatever environment and surroundings he or she may be living.

The publication titled *Hinduism, An Introduction* in two parts, is a quite extensive, informative and elaborate depiction of Hinduism. While going through this publication, the reader is presented with a panoramic view of the Indian ethos. Mostly, people get lost in the outer perceptions of this great religion and get confused about the core notions and concepts. Seen in this light, the author has done a great service to society.

- H.H. Swami Satyamitranand Giri

Bharat Mata Mandir, Haridwar

* * *

The book informs and inspires Hindus worldwide. It ensures Hindus' Unity in Diversity among all sects and lineages. The book also protects, preserves and promotes the sacred values and eternal truths hidden in our Vedas and religious tradition. Anybody who studies this book should be able to feel the mystic nature of ancient Hindu philosophy and rejoice following the rituals of the tradition. *Hinduism, An Introduction* is a storehouse of traditional knowledge and wisdom.

- Jagadguru Sri Sri Sri Dr Balagangadharanatha Swamiji

Sri Adichunchanagiri Maha Samsthana Mutt, Karnataka

This introduction to Hinduism is different from most in a number of important ways. We have chosen to comment on three. Firstly, the whole of Hinduism is presented in all of its grand diversity. Secondly, it shows the reader many facets of modern Hindu temple worship – again a topic often ignored in introductions to Hinduism. The scriptures upon which the ceremonies and architecture are based, the Agamas, are well detailed. Thirdly, though presenting the multiplicity of Deities in Hinduism, the book stresses that Hindus all worship a Supreme Being.

- Satguru Bodhinatha Veylanswami

Head, Kauai's Hindu Monastery, Hawaii (*Hinduism Today* Magazine)

* * *

The book is a beautiful contribution and full of well-articulated thoughts. Hinduism is indeed a natural religion. The book introduces in a clear-cut manner the large body of Hindu canon, divided into revealed (Sruti) and remembered (Smriti) texts.

- Dr A.P.J. Abdul Kalam

Former President of India

* * *

The book strengthens Hinduism by presenting it 'as it is' and 'as it has been'.

To one who believes in Hinduism, this book would elevate the belief to faith, enabled by a better understanding of the subject. To one who is inquisitive about Hinduism, or, is on a journey for searching the souls of several religions on earth, the book would quench one's thirst for knowledge to the extent of Hinduism. Turning over the pages of the book leads one into introspection of self on tenets of Hinduism.

I commend reading of these volumes to all men of faith, to whatever religion they belong, to all seekers of spiritual attainment, and also to those who derive pleasure from digging into historic events or by floating in mysticism.

- R.C. Lahoti

Former Chief Justice of India

* * *

After going through the book I was deeply pleased. Light has been thrown on the backdrop of Hinduism and its importance. Along with the religious aspect the paths of worldly and transcendental elevation have been presented. I myself, and on behalf of the entire Sanskrit world, offer my congratulations for this excellent book.

- Prof. Kutumb Shastri

Vice-Chancellor Sampurnanand Sanskrit Vishvavidyalaya, Varanasi, Uttar Pradesh

* * *

Hinduism is so multi-faceted, so varied in its modes of worship, so rich in its philosophical thoughts, so diverse in its places of worship and rituals that no single book, howsoever voluminous, can describe it in its entirety. Nevertheless *Hinduism, An Introduction* published by Swaminarayan Aksharpith, goes a long way in doing that. It is a very comprehensive and balanced introduction to Hindu beliefs, scriptures, deities, sacred places, festivals, spiritual practices, rituals, sages and thinkers. The book is well-planned and beautifully presented.

- Prof. Swatantra Kumar

Vice-Chancellor, Gurukul Kangri Vishwavidyalaya

Haridwar (Uttarakhand)

* * *

The two volumes on Hinduism are really a wonderful compendium to understand Hinduism or the Sanatana Dharma in its totality and depth. They systematically develop the concept and practice of Hinduism with its entire body of scriptural texts, rituals, methods of worship and its social contexts.

These volumes on Hinduism are very, very useful both to an ordinary curious reader as also to university teachers, students and scholars.

- Dr Mohan Gupta

D.Litt. I.A.S. (Retd.), Vice-Chancellor Maharshi Panini

Sanskrit & Vedic Vishvavidyalaya, Ujjain (M.P.)

* * *

The book is a well researched document that has not deviated from its intention of providing clarity to lots of concepts in Hinduism and removing some of those misconceptions that have been created by the classical Western perspective.

There is no doubt that this book (two parts) would definitely be a guide and inspiration for every student/scholar who wishes to know more about Hinduism in its true magnificence and its grand social perspective.

- Dr Prof. V.S. Vishnupotty

Dean of Faculty of Sanskrit, SCSVMV University,

Enathur, Kancheepuram, Tamil Nadu

* * *

The two volumes of the exquisite and highly informative book written in lucidly clear and simple language is undoubtedly a landmark publication. It provides a kaleidoscopic background of the many different features of this great religion.

Congratulations for providing us such an intellectual extravaganza supported by the many interesting illustrations throughout the book.

— **Professor Ranjit Roy Chaudhury**
MBBS, D.Phil (Oxon), FRCP (Edin),
Member of Board of Governors, Medical Council of India

* * *

I find the book is very exhaustive, giving full details of the religious philosophy, beliefs, rituals and traditions of Hinduism. The beauty of our religious philosophy as written in this book, its general acceptance of each tradition by the others without any criticism is because we see God in every being. The do's and don'ts in social life are also well mentioned and described in this book, which are the basis of harmony, compassion and acceptance of each other. I feel that the book will become popular not only in India but globally.

— **Dr S.K. Sama**
Honorary Physician to the President of India,
Chairman, Sir Ganga Ram Hospital, New Delhi

* **

The book treats the subject of Hinduism in a comprehensive manner and should become a premier primer for the students of Hinduism everywhere. It will help correct many a misconception about Hinduism as it brings out scientific, logical and spiritual foundations of Hindu belief systems. The book maintains historical perspective and spells out the whole range of principles and practices of all major Hindu sects and highlights their systems of philosophy from the ancient to the modern, each one a facet in the fluid mosaic, a note in the eternal symphony of all-inclusive Hinduism.

— **Mahendra Anand**
Senior Advocate, Supreme Court of India, New Delhi

* * *

I can only say that this book should definitely find place in every Hindu house, and it is one single monument of spiritual knowledge. I feel that the book on Hinduism by the author is definitely as a result of great inspiration derived from the life and work of Pramukh Swami Maharaj.

— **Subhash Lakhotia**
Income Tax Practitioner, New Delhi

PREFACE

From the perspective of many Hindus, the history and traditions of Hinduism are both ancient and timeless. This is attested to by the fact that its practitioners traditionally call it Sanātana Dharma, or the Eternal Religion.[1] They believe it was revealed by Paramātmā or God to many enlightened rishis over a period of several centuries. Efforts to establish a historical dating have been subject to continual revision. The majority of Hindus believe that it is the oldest of all world religions.

It is also the world's most diverse religion. Hinduism embraces the worship of many deities, who are believed by many Hindus to be manifestations of the one supreme God. Hinduism is a grand mosaic of various *sampradāyas,* philosophies, mandirs, shastras, sadhus, devotees, holy places, rituals and festivals. It is often referred to by some scholars as a 'family of religions'. Within the rich diversities there are common threads that bind Hinduism into a fascinating and vibrant religion, subscribed to by nearly one-fifth of humankind.

An attempt has been made in this book, *Hinduism, An Introduction,* to explain Hinduism in a progressive series of basic concepts, with each chapter building upon the previous one. The first chapter deals with the meaning and history of Sanātana Dharma. This is followed by a description of the core Hindu beliefs and Hindu sacred texts that contain these beliefs. Next, we explore the expression of these core beliefs in the various philosophies, teachings and traditions of Vaishnavism, Shaivism, Shāktism and Smārtism. Naturally, since each of these four branches of Hinduism has its own mandirs, shastras and gurus, these three pillars of faith are explained next. In all, this publication comprises of two parts, with a total of thirty chapters, that include a description of holy places, festivals, rituals, sacred symbols, sadhana, *āhāra-vihāra,* devotees, rishi-scientists, Hindu concepts and way of life, Hindu reformers, *varnāshrama* dharma,

---

1. Note: In Hinduism the meaning of the term 'religion' differs from its definition in Semitic religions. It is used in the context of 'dharma' in Hinduism. A detailed meaning of 'dharma' is given on pp.17-18, sub-section: Meaning of Sanātana Dharma.

Impressions of India and Hinduism abroad, creation, Swaminarayan Sampradaya,[2] India, FAQs and Selected prayers. Parts one and two have sixteen and fourteen chapters respectively with a total number of 712 pages. To complement the text, volumes one and two contain 397 and 351 photographs, paintings, graphic compositions and maps respectively.

Since relatively little is known about the Swaminarayan Sampradaya to outsiders, the author has included a chapter (in part two) to inform and satisfy the curiosities of those wishing to know about it. Whenever readers come across a Swaminarayan orientation, the author hopes that this will not be taken as an imposition of the Swaminarayan perspective, but rather as an attempt to inform or a natural consequence of his association with and study of this tradition.

This book is the product of reflection and consideration of a wide range of published and unpublished materials. It is written by a Hindu practitioner and BAPS Swaminarayan sadhu. Hence, this book is understandably influenced, to some extent, by the BAPS Swaminarayan understanding of Hinduism. The author has dealt with many beliefs and practices of Hindus, and their participation in Hindu traditions. So, this book is also to a great extent an effort to share the author's appreciation of the many traditions that constitute Hinduism.

The intended readers of this book are Hindu youths and all others who would like to understand Hindu traditions from the perspective of the practitioner, and in this instance, a devoted member of the BAPS Swaminarayan Sanstha. It should be made clear that this book has not been written in a way that scholars and others, who bring different academic skills and modes of critical analysis, would write. In fact, for scholars of Hindu texts, languages, histories, and traditions, perhaps some of the content of this book may appear to be influenced by Vaishnava teachings and practices. I recognize and appreciate that some scholars will have different views and conclusions of their own. Thus, at the cost of repetition, and to avoid misunderstanding, this

---

2. The Swaminarayan Sampradaya was founded by Bhagwan Swaminarayan (1781-1830) over 200 years ago. This religious organization, with several sects today, mainly follows the Vaishnava tradition of Hinduism, worshipping and celebrating Bhagwan Swaminarayan and other Hindu deities.

book is a perspective on Hinduism that comes from the 'inside'.

While care has been taken to avoid an overly academic presentation, references to Hindu shastras and scholars are provided for the benefit of interested readers. Sanskrit words are italicized and their meanings mostly juxtaposed in brackets and also provided in the glossary. One reason why some Sanskrit or Hindi words are not italicized is because they have become a part of the English lexicon and are included in the *Concise Oxford English Dictionary*, eleventh edition (2004). To facilitate pronunciation of names and Sanskrit words, only the long 'a' (as in c*a*r) has been shown in its diacritical form, 'ā'. No diacritic marks are used for anglicized words and names of places, and Indian leaders and spiritual masters of pre- and post- independent India. Another exception has been made by not using the 'ā' and end 'a' for the names of places, sacred objects and people related to the Swaminarayan Sampradaya. This is done to retain the system familiar among BAPS Swaminarayan devotees. A brief bibliography and an index are provided.

Writing this book was a formidable challenge because of the diversity and sheer amount of information about the various philosophies, traditions and practices in Hinduism. Hinduism is so vast, it is impossible to do justice to all of its rich diversity and profound depth in a single publication.

To resolve my fears and feelings of inadequacy for such an enormous undertaking, I sought the blessings of my guru Pramukh Swami Maharaj (Swamishri) in February 2007. I remain forever deeply thankful and indebted to him for his divine grace and guidance in completing this work in three years. I therefore dedicate this book to Bhagwan Swaminarayan and guru Pramukh Swami Maharaj (the fifth spiritual successor of Bhagwan Swaminarayan) for fostering and inspiring the values and traditions of Hinduism in countless Hindus, as well as faith and peace in the lives of many.

My appreciations to Pujya Ishwarcharan Swami, a senior sadhu of BAPS, who first suggested, on the request of Pujya Yogvivek Swami (Head of BAPS Swaminarayan Mandir, London), that we publish a book on Hinduism, and also for prompting and motivating me at regular intervals. His guidance and inspiration were invaluable. I also thank Dr Janakbhai Dave, an erudite scholar who has a master's degree in Sanskrit, ancient history and culture from Bombay University, and PhD in Sanskrit from MS University, Vadodarā, for his meticulous and painstaking effort in providing valuable additions, corrections and references. I express my appreciations to Pujya Shrutiprakash Swami, PhD in Sanskrit and Shad Darshan Āchārya, Dr Narayanbhai Kansara, who has an M.A. in Vedānta and PhD in Sanskrit literature, for resolving many textual questions and doubts.

My gratitude to Pujya Amrutvijay Swami for going through the script and providing valuable suggestions and emendations. I am also grateful to Shri Varanasi Rama Murthy, a veteran journalist who had served on the staff of *Times of India*, Ahmedabad, for reviewing and enriching the text, and Shri G.M. Shah for his patient effort in typing and correcting the text. I remain indebted to the photographers (see p. xii) for the hundreds of photographs used in this publication and to Pujya Mukundcharan Swami for sharing many photos that he has taken in his publications: *Hindu Rites and Rituals* and *Hindu Festivals*. My sincere appreciations to AARSH, Gandhinagar, and the B.J. Institute of Learning & Research, Ahmedabad, for allowing us to scan and use their manuscripts and books as photographs, our departmental staff, Shri Prakash Suthar and artist Shri Jignesh Joshi, for their patient and proficient labour in the design and layout. My sincere thanks to Pujya Shrijiswarup Swami and his team for finalizing the design, layout and for the title cover. My gratitude to the many authors of books, magazines and websites on Hinduism, to Atmaswarup Swami and all those who have helped me in making this publication possible.

I sincerely hope and pray to Bhagwan Swaminarayan, all the divine incarnations, sages and guru Pramukh Swami Maharaj that this publication will inform and enrich all readers about the wisdom and traditions of Hinduism. In addition, may the readers be motivated to study and experience Hinduism further from other books, documentaries and visits to India.

- Author

Acknowledgments for Photographs and Illustrations

Unless otherwise stated photographs and illustrations are by BAPS volunteers and devotees: Yogicharan Swami, Narayanprasad Swami, Harshadbhai Vadodaria, Multimedia Team, Kanubhai Tank, Nayan Shah, Jignesh Joshi and others.

Other contributors who have permitted Swaminarayan Aksharpith to print their photos are:

1. Amar Ujala Group of Newspapers (pp. 246, 246, 252).
2. Anulal V (p. 290).
3. Creative Commons Attribution/Share-Alike License (p. 230).
3. Darshan Thakker (p. 255).
4. Darshanam Sanskrit Mahavidyalaya run by Shree Swaminarayan Gurukul Vishwavidya Pratishthanam (SGVP), Chharodi, Ahmedabad (pp. 16, 55, 58, 116, 136, 228, 344).
5. Hinduism Today (pp. 176, 177, 180, 180).
6. ISKCON Ahmedabad (pp. 5, 174, 318).
7. Kiran Tambat, Nashik (p. 275).
8. Namit Arora (pp. 21, 21, 22).
9. Photographs Cartridge Srinivas Fine Arts (P) Ltd. (pp. 257, 287, 288, 288, 293, 293).
10. Raj Patel, Ahmedabad (pp. 282, 283).
11. Rajendra Rathod, Mumbai (p. 308).
12. Rashtrotthana Sahithya: Keshava Shilpa, Kempegowdanagar, Bangalore-560 019. Trustee: K.S. Narayan, Rashtrotthana Sahithya (pp. 116, 116, 183).
13. Tilak Bisht. www.tilakbisht.com. email@tilakbisht.com (pp. 234, 255).
14. Utkarsh Modi (p. 8).
15. Ved Vignan Maha Vidya Peeth, Bangalore (p. 65).
16. Vivek Desai (p. 302).
17. Vladimir K. www.thezensite.com (p. 12).
18. www.team-bhp.com (p. 277).

We are grateful to all for their generous support.

INTRODUCTION

Sanātana Dharma, commonly referred to as Hinduism, is considered by many of its believers and practitioners to be the world's oldest living dharma or religion that originated from the Indian subcontinent. It has also been described as Vaidika Dharma (religion rooted in the Vedas), Ārya Dharma (dharma of Āryans) and Mānava Dharma (religion of humanity).

Hindu traditionalists prefer to call it Sanātana Dharma. Sanātana means both eternal, and also ancient. And dharma in this case means religion, however, it has a much more deeper meaning than religion. So, Sanātana Dharma means the religion or the tradition of spiritual beliefs, disciplines and practices that are not only ancient but also eternal. In other words Hinduism is a tradition of spiritual, cultural and social disciplines and practices of great antiquity, with its main roots in the Vedas and continuing relevance to our own times.

Hinduism derives its name from the ancient Persians who called the River Sindhu, that flows through modern day Pakistan, as Hindu, because 'S' was pronounced as 'H' in their language. Subsequently, as a result of this linguistic practice, the people living on the eastern banks of Sindhu came to be known as Hindus, and much later the British developed the term Hinduism to describe the various religious traditions they encountered across the country. Thus the name Hindu had a geographical significance. After the Persians, the Greeks called the river Hindu (i.e., Sindhu), 'Indos', and the people, 'Indoi'. In English the words 'Indos' and 'Indoi' became Indus and Indians.

Throughout the course of history, Hinduism has been like a great river that tenaciously moves forward, retaining the ancient while dynamically evolving to meet the present.

WHAT IS HINDUISM?

Sanātana Dharma evolved over a period of several centuries, thanks to hundreds of enlightened rishis or sages. So, it does not have one founder and philosophy. It is often referred to as a family of religious traditions because of its many deities, sacred texts, philosophies, *sampradāyas* and religious leaders. This makes Sanātana Dharma fascinating and rich, yet at the same time difficult for outsiders to grasp.

Hinduism extends the boundaries of the term "religion" beyond that which is described in Western faiths. Dr S. Radhakrishnan, the former President of India and renowned Oxford Professor of Eastern Religions and Ethics, has famously suggested that Hinduism is more than a religion; it is a way of life. Kim Knott, Head of the Department of Theology and Religious Studies at the University of Leeds, writes, "By doing so [that is by saying that Hinduism is a way of life], he [Radhakrishnan] made the point that it was not something separate from society and politics, from making money... and getting an education. And, like other modern Hindus, he suggested that the closest term to be found within Indian thought and practice was Hindu dharma, the law, order, truth, and duties of the Hindu people."[1]

Hinduism is a mosaic of fascinating rituals, festivals, celebrations, sacred texts, beliefs, mandirs and practices

---

1. Knott, Kim. *Hinduism, A Very Short Introduction.* Oxford: Oxford University Press (OUP), 2000, p. 111.

Many other scholars, historians, indologists, practitioners and spiritual leaders have described Hinduism. Pramukh Swami Maharaj, a renowned Hindu leader and head of BAPS Swaminarayan Sanstha, was asked by an Indian industrialist on 6 November 1996 to explain Hinduism in two sentences. Swamiji replied in Gujarati, *"Hindu dharma mānas ne mānava banāve chhe, ane ae mānava ne moksha no mārga shikhvāde chhe."* It means, "Hindu dharma makes an individual into a civilized person, and teaches the person [to attain] the path of *moksha* [liberation]." The words of Swamiji brilliantly summarize Hinduism in brief. One finds them to be true because the basic practice of morality prescribed by the Hindu sacred texts, namely, *satya* (truth), *dayā* (compassion), ahimsa (nonviolence), *brahmacharya* (continence), *asteya* (non-stealing), *aparigraha* (non-possession) and others, transforms an individual into a civilized or noble person. And the idea of *moksha* matches with the ultimate of the four goals (dharma, *artha, kāma* and *moksha*) of human life prescribed by Hinduism.

Hinduism pervades every dimension of the social, cultural and spiritual lives of the Hindus. It is alive and vibrant today in millions of homes and mandirs in India and abroad through its festivals, rituals, spiritual gurus and traditions called *sampradāyas.*

THE ĀRYAN INVASION THEORY

There are two beliefs among scholars about the founders of Vedic civilization. One group strongly propounds that the Āryans[2] came from central Asia, invaded north-western India and established the Vedic culture. The other group says that the Āryans were the original inhabitants of India and thus there was no Āryan invasion of India. Each group argues on the basis of archaeological, linguistic, textual (Rig Vedic accounts) and other sources. However, there is a growing consensus among scholars and researchers that the Āryan invasion and Āryan migration theories are invalid.[3] Lord Colin Renfrew (1988), a British archaeologist writes, "If one checks the dozen references in the Rigveda to the Seven Rivers, there is nothing in any of them that to me implies invasion... Despite Wheeler's comments, it is difficult to see what is particularly non-Aryan about the Indus Valley Civilization."[4] Laurie Patton, Professor of Early Indian Religions at Emory University, Atlanta, USA, notes, "First, very few, if any, archaeologists or linguists embrace the invasion theory, and have not done so for several decades."[5]

Murti-pujā: Worshipping God's image

The Rig Veda says the Vedic civilization flourished in north-western India, known as the land of the Saptasindhu (seven rivers). Scholars, Jim Shaffer and Diana Liechtenstein, in their paper "South Asian Archaeology in the Indo-Aryan Controversy" write, "The excavations at Mehrgarh near Sibri, Pakistan, do demonstrate an indigenous development of agricultural food production by people living there as early as the seventh millennium BC."[6]

Kurma avatar of Bhagwan Vishnu

2. The word Āryan is derived from the Sanskrit word *ārya* which means 'noble'.
3. Poliakov, L. *The Aryan Myth*. New York: Basic Books, 1974, p.4.
4. Renfrew, Colin. *Archaeology and Language: The Puzzle of Indo-European Origins*. New York: Cambridge University Press, 1988, pp. 188-190.
5. *The Indo-Aryan Controversy, Evidence and Inference in Indian History*. Edited by Edwin F. Bryant and Laurie L. Patton. London and New York: Routledge, 2005, p. 16.
6. Ibid. p.82.

CORE BELIEFS AND PRINCIPLES

Hinduism is fascinatingly diverse, yet it has common threads or core beliefs among its many *sampradāyas*. Though not all the core beliefs may be shared by all the *sampradāyas*, a knowledge or understanding of them will help the novice grasp the basics of Hinduism without being confused by its complexity. Hinduism advocates mainly the belief in one Supreme Reality, called Paramātmā, Parameshwara, Parabrahman, Nārāyana or Bhagwan. The majority of Hindus are not polytheists as they have been erroneously branded by many observers throughout history. Hinduism can be said to exhibit its own form of monotheism. Max Müller tried to describe this as henotheism, which means belief in and worship of one supreme God without denying the existence of other 'gods' or forms of the supreme God. Furthermore, Sanātana Dharma includes, among its core principles, belief in the authority of the Vedas, *avatāravāda*, atman, karma, *punarjanma*, *murti-pujā*, *guru-shishya paramparā*, ahimsa, four *purushārthas* and *varnāshrama* dharma. It has also explored and elaborated upon the paths of *shreyas (moksha)* and *preyas* (sensual pleasure), bhakti, dharma, *vidhis* (dos) and *nishedhas* (don'ts), different spiritual and worldly planes and the world of ancestors *(pitru loka)*, *ruta* (cosmic order by God), *satya* (in this case, moral law), sixteen samskaras (sacraments), death, liberation, philosophies, places of pilgrimage and sacred texts.

Most Hindus also believe that God is an all-pervasive reality *(sarva vyāpaka)*, who resides in all *(antaryāmin)* – both in living and non-living things. The Ishāvāsya Upanishad proclaims this in its very first *shloka*, "Ishāvāsyam idam sarvam, yat kincha jagatyām jagat..." It means that "God pervades in all things in the world..." Mahatma Gandhi thought very highly of this *shloka* and declared, "I have now come to the final conclusion that if all the Upanishads and all the other scriptures happened all of a sudden to be reduced to ashes, and if only the first verse in the Ishopanishad [Ishāvāsya Upanishad] were left intact in

A devotee performs abhisheka

Vegetarian food

*Ruta or divine cosmic order
pervades infinite universes*

the memory of Hindus, Hinduism would live forever."[7] That is why for practising Hindus their faith in the all-pervasive power of God leads to the belief that all things are fundamentally rooted in God and not in materialism or atoms. Many Hindus endeavour to observe the ideals of ahimsa, compassion and vegetarianism[8] because of their belief in God's pervasiveness in all living beings.

Two of the important beliefs in Hinduism are the principles of *ruta* (cosmic order by God), which essentially is the law that governs the universe and nature, and *satya* (moral law). Dharma or moral law is prescribed for all humans. It refers to the path of duty, righteousness and morality. When we follow dharma, we are in tune with both God and nature.

All Hindu *sampradāyas* emphasize the need for an ethical life as an essential prerequisite to spiritual realization. Right speech, right thought and right action are promoted by all. They commonly advocate *yama* (restraint) and *niyama* (discipline), which include *satya* (truth), *dayā* (compassion), ahimsa, *brahmacharya* (celibacy), *asteya* (non-stealing) and *aparigraha* (non-greed).

Jnāna: Daily reading of sacred texts

Dhyana: Spiritual meditation

PLURALISM

An outstanding feature of Hinduism is its openness towards multiple pathways or ways of being Hindu. Out of its many traditions four are most prominent: Vaishnavism, Shaivism, Shāktism and Smārtism. They are the main constituents of Sanātana Dharma. Together, they reflect the freedom of thought and the various ways of worship that Hinduism has generously allowed to flourish. Each Hindu aspirant believes and practises according to his or her spiritual leaning, need and karmic disposition. Every person's creed depends upon his *adhikāra* or spiritual eligibility. And it is this eligibility that

7. *Teachings of Mahatma Gandhi*, 1st ed., edited by Chander, Jag Parvesh. Lahore: The Indian Printing Works, 1945, p.295.
8. Neither historically nor in the present are all Hindus vegetarian.

Hinduism

determines the level and type of faith one practises. Hinduism satisfies every aspirant according to his or her spiritual inclinations, needs and merits. Thus, Sanātana Dharma is a fellowship of religious traditions. The fact that the diverse or pluralistic paths of knowledge *(jnāna)*, action (karma), dhyana (meditation) and devotion (bhakti) have formed and flourished into many *sampradāyas* demonstrates Hinduism's inherent flexibility and accommodative nature. And despite its different paths there is an underlying cohesion and common purpose that has sustained Hinduism for thousands of years. The fact that Hinduism has survived many devastating foreign invasions and hegemonies reflects the inner strength of its many traditions.

PART AND WHOLE

Does knowing one of the many traditions of Hinduism (mainly, Vaishnavism, Shaivism, Shaktism and Smartism) mean knowing the whole? The answer is "yes" and "no". "Yes" because all the Hindu traditions have many things in common. And "no" because each of them have their own unique beliefs and practices. Hindus believe that whichever Hindu tradition they follow is related to their emotional and mental inclinations and karmic disposition *(adhikāra)* or spiritual merits *(punya)*. As their spiritual merits increase, through an intensification of sadhanas, they realize higher spiritual levels, and ultimately attain *moksha*.

Bhakti: Bathing God's murti

Yajna: Performing the sacred fire ritual for social and spiritual benefit

BROAD-MINDEDNESS

The sacred Hindu texts introduce and teach many unifying and universal concepts like *"Vasudhaiva kutumbakam"* – the whole world is one family[9] and *"Yatra bhavati vishvam eka nidam"* – the whole world is one nest.[10] They also teach *"Sarve sukhinaha santu"* – let all be happy and blissful,[11] and *"Ā no*

Tableau of a giant nest with different birds to show the world is one family

9. Subhāshitam (collection of popular sayings).
10. Vājasaneya Samhitā 32.8.
11. Subhāshitam (collection of popular sayings).

bhadrāhā kratavo yantu vishvataha" – let noble thoughts come to us from the whole universe.[12] Hindus are also free to choose the path they are most inclined to among the different Hindu *sampradāyas* in realizing Paramātmā or the Ultimate Reality. Hindus do not condemn believers of other religions. Hinduism is tolerant and respects other religions. For a Hindu, respect for other world religions is not considered to be a violation of personal faith. A true Hindu respects those with different religious beliefs, while remaining faithful to his or her own deity, shastra, guru, rituals, festivals and beliefs. For Hindus, a Hindu identity is necessary for the transmission of faith to their children.

TRUE PERCEPTION

Many modern scholars have shown that in the past Hinduism was criticized by colonial scholars due to their own biases and misunderstandings. Even today, when Hinduism is criticized, it might be because of the critic's incorrect perceptions or preset beliefs based upon his or her own religion and culture. Imagine the difficulties one would encounter if one tried to interpret physics from the principles of biology. Hinduism can be fully perceived and experienced by a practising Hindu or a sincere scholar – if they both accept the guidance of a bona fide Hindu guru.

Such gurus, in addition to mandirs and shastras, are the main pillars of Hinduism. Hindu rituals, festivals and spiritual practices revolve mainly around and celebrate these three main aspects.

CLARIFYING HINDU VIEWS

As Hindus there is no need to change or give up one's principle beliefs in order to satisfy other religious and so-called secular viewpoints. And neither should Hindus be swayed

An ascetic engaged in austerity

Utkarsh Modi

A Hindu family

12. Rig Veda 1.89.1.

or be left in doubt about their own principles when people or scriptures of other faiths contradict and criticize them. Some scholars and audiences have misinterpreted some of the principles or practices of Hinduism. One such misconception is that Hinduism is world-negating. Perhaps such conclusions have been derived from observations of Hindu ascetics who wander in society without possessions or personal care, perform severe austerities in remote caves and mortify their flesh. Such conclusions may also have been extrapolated from some philosophical teachings that describe the world to be false or illusory.

Hinduism, however, is not world-negating or non-compassionate, and does not teach to shun one's duty, sympathy and empathy. Renunciation and austerities are a part of spiritual sadhanas or practices, in which an aspirant or ascetic cultivates *vairāgya* or inner indifference to worldly objects and situations. This enables him to eradicate his mundane desires and realize his own atman and God.

Another point to note is that the majority of Hindus are householders leading a normal family life and fulfilling social responsibilities and duties. Furthermore, the Bhagavad Gītā advocates action and doing one's duty, and preaches that work is worship, "Do your own allotted work, (for) work is better than inaction, even the sustenance of your body cannot be accomplished from inaction."[13] The Hindu shastras also prescribe the four *purushārthas* (endeavours or goals), namely, dharma, *artha, kāma* and *moksha*, which are the roadmap of life, prompting all to make efforts to achieve them.

At other times, Hindus have been branded to be fatalistic because of their beliefs in the karma principle (the universal law of cause and effect with regards to one's actions) and God's all-doership. As fatalistic followers, Hindus are criticized as uncompassionate to those who are suffering, physically

---

13. Bhagavad Gita (B.G.) 3.8.

challenged or have lost their lives in natural calamities. Hinduism, however, does not teach fatalism.

Arvind Sharma, Birks Professor of Comparative Religion, McGill University, Canada, asserts, "To think fatalistically about karma is unhelpful when, in fact, as human beings we have the power at any moment to change our own behaviour, and thus its consequences for our future. Free will rather than fatalism characterizes the operation of karma."[14] Hinduism celebrates the karma principle as the individual's freedom to create his or her future state of existence through his or her present actions and thoughts.

Some also think that all Hindus believe in many "Gods". But this is not so. The Hindus mainly believe in one Supreme Paramātmā, who manifests in various human and other forms to reestablish faith and morality.[15] They worship only one or several of his manifestations with the belief that they are worshipping the Supreme Bhagwan.

CASTE SYSTEM

Another aspect that is severely criticised and taught in some textbooks and by some teachers is the caste system. It has been broadcast, written about and taught with such enormity and force as if Hinduism is mostly just about the caste system. But this view is greatly flawed. The caste system is believed to be an aberration of the original Varna System which was based on a person's qualities (gunas) and aptitude for a particular type of work (karma).[16] Some believe that over time, discrimination and class hierarchy crept in due to human imperfections and ego. Recognizing the growing rigidity and injustice of the decaying system, modern reformers of India from the 19th century

Hindus worship different deities, with many believing that they revere the same supreme God

---

14. Knott, Kim. *Hinduism – A Very Short Introduction.* Oxford: OUP, 2000, p.39.

15. B.G. 4.8: "For the deliverance of the good and the destruction of the wicked and for establishing righteousness I come into being age after age."

16. Ibid. 4.13 *(varnas).* "According to the differentiation of *guna* and karma, the four divisions of human society are created by Me."

 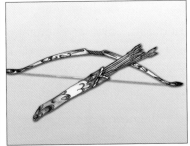

Top left, clockwise: A symbolic representation of the ancient Varna System which comprised of the Brahmins (spiritual mentors), Kshatriyas (rulers and protectors), Shudras (weavers and labourers) and Vaishyas (farmers and businessmen)

onwards like Bhagwan Swaminarayan, Raja Ram Mohan Roy, Dayananda Sarasvati, Swami Vivekananda, Mahatma Gandhi and others made great efforts to eradicate discrimination based on caste.

Every society has its problems and issues. Many Hindus have recognized their problems and have taken steps at many levels to rectify them. Although sati, dowry and caste discrimination continue to exist in some places, they are officially banned by the Indian Penal Code.[17] Many Hindu and social organizations have been making active efforts to eradicate these inequities. The rapid urbanization and spread of education in India in the last century has also mitigated caste discrimination. But there are those who believe in the caste system for several reasons; one of which is to ensure their idea of an ideal or compatible marriage.

SCIENCE AND LITERATURE

For many Hindus, religion and science, faith and rationality

---

17. Prohibition of Sati Act (1829), Untouchability Offences Act (1955) and Dowry Prohibition Act (1961).

Remains of Nālandā – an ancient Indian university, now in Bihar, India

are not viewed as incompatible. In Hinduism, spirituality does not reject reason, and reasoning does not deny faith. Sages like Sushruta, Charaka, Āryabhatta, Varāhamihira, Nāgārjuna and others made pioneering discoveries and inventions in science. They established some of the most popular sciences like ayurveda, yoga, *sthāpatya* shastra (science of architecture), *artha* shastra (science of economics), mathematics, astronomy, surgery, etc.

India is also the land where great works of literature and epics like the Rāmāyana, Mahābhārata and others were written by enlightened rishis. Great rishis and teachers taught in Takshashilā (c. 500 BCE) and Nālandā (500-1300 CE), its premier universities, to over 10,000 students from India and abroad in about 68 different branches of knowledge. The Indian rishis and masters endeavoured in nearly all domains of spiritual and secular knowledge to understand the universe, life, soul and God in a holistic way.

ANCIENT CIVILIZATION, MODERN RELEVANCE

As the ancient Hindus ventured abroad and outsiders visited India, there was a natural transmission of the vast knowledge, wisdom, traditions, practices and experiences of Hinduism.

Today, Hinduism is a representative of not only India but the ancient wisdom of humanity. In our age of globalization, the scourges of fanaticism, terrorism, sectarian violence, exploitation of human beings and the environment, and a plethora of social and moral ills are ever burgeoning and causing untold damage, anxieties and dismay. The inspiring values of Hinduism effect a positive change and provide lasting solutions to our growing conflicts and problems.

Dr Arnold J. Toynbee (1889-1975), the noted British historian, expressed, "It is already becoming clear that a chapter which had a Western beginning, will have to have an Indian ending, if it is not to end in self-destruction of the human race. At this supremely dangerous moment in human history, the only way of salvation is the ancient Hindu way."[18]

After reading the Bhagavad Gitā, Ralph Waldo Emerson, (1803-1882), Lecturer in Theology at Harvard University and a Unitarian minister, wrote, "I owed a magnificent day to the *Bhagavat Geeta*. It was the first of books; it was as if an empire spake to us, nothing small or unworthy, but large, serene, consistent, the voice of an old intelligence which in another age and climate had pondered and thus disposed of the same questions which exercise us."[19]

Sanātana Dharma is basically a holistic religion that inspires morality, faith, peace, love, service to God and mankind. Hence, it has the capacity to nourish and liberate people of different spiritual inclinations and natures, and provide valid answers to individual problems and global crises. The more one learns about and experiences Hinduism, the more one comes to appreciate its richness, depth, comprehensive approach, celebratory spirit, magnanimity and capacity to relieve people from all types of bondage and suffering and elevate their souls to the height of eternal joy and happiness.

Dr Arnold J. Toynbee

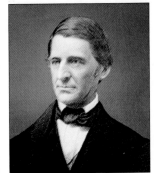

Ralph Waldo Emerson

---

18. Toynbee, Arnold. J. *A Study of History*, published in 12 volumes.

19. *Journals of Ralph Waldo Emerson, Vol.7*, edited by Edward Waldo Emerson and Waldo Emerson Forbes. London: Constable & Co. Ltd., and Boston and New York: Houghton Mifflin Company, 1913, p.511.

1

Sanātana Dharma

The magnificent Himalayas have spiritual vibrations because of the austerities of hundreds of ancient rishis and the divine revelations graced upon them by Paramātmā. (Inset) In Hinduism the sound of the conch shell is considered to be auspicious

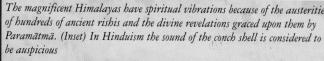

Divine Revelation, Sanātana Dharma, History, Artefacts, Āryan Invasion Theory

INTRODUCTION

In ancient times the Hindus were known as Āryas[1] (meaning the 'noble' ones). The Āryas called their religion[2] the 'Ārya Dharma' – 'Religion of the Āryas'. Later, it was also known as 'Mānava Dharma' – the religion of humankind based on human values; 'Sanātana Dharma' – 'The Eternal Religion'; and 'Vaidika Dharma' – the religion rooted in the Vedas.

The term Hinduism was unknown to the ancient Āryas or Āryans. It came much later and much after the Persians coined the word Hindu. Persia (now Iran) had a common border with ancient India or Āryāvarta[3] – the land of the Āryans. The common border was the River Sindhu (called Indus in English) that runs down from the north in the Himalayas. The ancient Persians pronounced 'S' as 'H' and thus Sindhu became Hindu. And they named the Āryans, living on the eastern side of the River Sindhu, Hindus. Several millennia later the religion of the Āryans became known as Hinduism, the term first used by orientalist scholars in the early nineteenth century, and the entire country came to be called Hindustan (the land of the Hindus). Taking the cue from the Persians, the Greeks called the Sindhu as 'Indos' and the people as 'Indoi', and later in English the river came to be known as 'Indus' and the people 'Indian'.

1. The English distortion of the Sanskrit word Ārya is Āryan.
2. Note: the meaning of the term 'religion' is dharma in the context of Hinduism. For meaning of dharma see pp.17-18.
3 Ancient India was also known as Brahmarshidesha, Brahmāvarta, Madhyadesha, Jambudvipa and Bhāratavarsha.

Guru teaching the Vedic mantras in a gurukula

In the Rig Veda, the Indian sub-continent or Bhārata, as it was popularly known later, is called the region of Saptasindhu, i.e., the land of the seven great rivers.[4]

DIVINE REVELATION

Sanātana Dharma was not founded by any mortal person. For many Hindus the Supreme Reality or Paramātmā revealed the spiritual truths to different enlightened sages or rishis while they were in a state of samadhi.[5] The sages then transmitted this wisdom to their disciples through recitations.[6] These revealed truths are called the Shruti or Veda. Shruti means "that which is heard" or revealed. The name Veda comes from the Sanskrit root word 'vid' which means 'to know'. The Vedas or the Shruti shastras are the fundamental sacred texts of the Hindus.

The Vedas are *apaurusheya*, meaning not man-made. Since

---

4. Seven great rivers: Sarasvati (Sarsuti), Sindhu, Vitasta (Jhelum), Parushni (Rāvi), Askini (Chenāb), Vipāsha (Beās), and Shutudri (Satlaj).

5. The final state in yoga, wherein one experiences the presence and bliss of God.

6. Jean Le Mée, the author of *Hymns from the Rig-Veda,* writes, "Precious or durable materials – gold, silver, bronze, marble, onyx, or graphite – have been used by most ancient peoples in an attempt to immortalize their achievements. Not so, however, with the ancient Aryans. They turned to what may seem the most volatile and insubstantial material of all – the spoken word – and out of this bubble of air fashioned a monument which more than thirty, perhaps forty, centuries later stands untouched by time or the elements. For the Pyramids have been eroded by the desert wind, the marble broken by earthquakes, and the gold stolen by robbers, while the Vedas remains, recited daily by an unbroken chain of generations, travelling like a great wave through the living substance of the mind." Published by Jonathan Cape Ltd, London, 1975, p. ix.

the truths were divinely revealed by God they are also eternal like God himself, hence the name Sanātana Dharma – The Eternal Dharma. Many Hindus and scholars believe that they were transmitted through the ages to the present day with very little changes. The noted Orientalist and Sanskrit scholar, A.A. Macdonell (1854-1930 CE) wrote about the Rig Veda, "Excepting single mistakes of tradition in the first, and those due to grammatical theories in the second period,[7] the old text of the Rigveda thus shows itself to have been preserved from a very remote antiquity with marvellous accuracy even in the smallest details."[8] Hindus believe that the Vedas are the most ancient of the world's sacred texts. Even today they are regularly recited and applied in almost all sacred ceremonies in countless mandirs and homes.

Hinduism has no single author because the revelations are considered by Hindus to have been made to many rishis, none of whom claimed to be the author or sole receptor of the revelations by God.

MEANING OF SANĀTANA DHARMA

Sanātana means eternal. Dharma is often translated to mean 'religion'. The Concise Oxford English Dictionary defines religion as, "The belief in and worship of a super human controlling power, especially a personal God or gods."[9] It also includes belief in tenets and practice of rituals.

The term 'dharma', however, has a multi-layered meaning. It is derived from the Sanskrit root word *dhru,* which means 'to hold'. Dharma means that which 'upholds', 'supports' or 'nourishes' the existence of a thing or being. Dharma also means the essential nature or the defining characteristic of something.

---

7. The first period refers to existence of the Rig Veda alone before the other Vedas came into being, and the second period refers to when the Rig Veda appeared in the phonetically modified form called the Samhitā text.

8. Macdonell, Arthur A. *A History of Sanskrit Literature.* New York: D. Appleton and Company, 1900, p. 48.

9. *Concise Oxford English Dictionary.* Oxford: OUP, 11th edition, 2004, p. 1215.

Everything in the universe has its dharma, because all things owe their very existence to it. For example, the dharma or essential nature of fire is its power to burn and give light and heat. The dharma or principal nature of water is its quality to wet and flow. And, for inanimate objects, they share the dharma or principle of inertness.

Man also has a core nature that sustains his existence; which is distinct from that of the rest of creation. Hindus believe that the essential dharma or nature of man is humaneness (*mānushyam*), discernment *(viveka)* and the power to become divine. Man's essential nature differentiates him from all other living things because it gives him the power to choose between right and wrong and to attain divine qualities.

Sanātana Dharma therefore means that which eternally 'supports' or 'nourishes' everyone and everything, i.e., all life and the entire creation. It is in this context that Hindus describe Sanātana Dharma or Hinduism as the 'eternal religion'. 'Dharma' in its simplest form also means truth, law, duty and obligation. Sanātana Dharma is popularly known as Hinduism.

From the perspective of the Semitic religions (Judaism, Christianity and Islam), religion is defined as having one transcendent God, a sole founder, one scripture, one governing institution or church, priests and other dimensions such as a single set of tenets, ethics and rituals. From the perspective of Sanātana Dharma, religion has a much broader concept, since Sanātana Dharma believes in one Supreme Reality called Paramātmā or Bhagwan and his manifestations. It does not have a single founder or a central institution. So, Sanātana Dharma, which is treated as a religion, is a religion that has a different connotation from the Western meaning. In fact, Sanātana Dharma comprises of many *sampradāyas* or religious traditions.

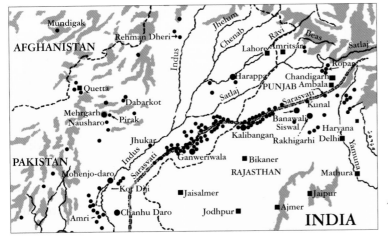

The Harappan sites (in bullet points) along Rivers Sarasvati (now extinct) and Indus (Sindhu)

HISTORY

The ancient civilization of India developed between two great rivers – the Sindhu[10] (also known as Indus, now in Pakistan) and the Sarasvati[11] (now not visible and believed to have dried up around 1900 BCE). The Sarasvati River, once ran parallel to the Sindhu, roughly 300 km east of it.

Both the rivers are believed to have been in existence since Vedic times. The Rig Veda describes the Sarasvati[12] as a mighty river flowing from the "mountains to the sea" (Rig Veda 2.

---

10. The Sindhu or Indus River originates in the Tibetan plateau in the vicinity of Lake Mānasarovar in Tibet. Today the river travels through the Ladākh district of Jammu and Kashmir and then enters Northern Areas (Gilgit-Baltistan), flowing through the north in a southerly direction along the entire length of Pakistan, to merge into the Arabian Sea near the port city of Karachi in Sindh.

11. The Sarasvati River had originated from the Kapāla Tso (lake) in the Himalayas to the southeast of Kailāsa, and probably flowed southward to Mānasarovar. From there it is believed to have descended through Rāksashatāl, Plaksha Prasravana lake, Ādibadri (presently Dhuling Math in Tibet), Mānā Pass, Kedārnātha, Rishikesha, Haridwāra, Merut, Delhi, Mathurā, Bharatpur, between Pāli and Jodhpur and flowed up to Panchpadrā in Rajasthan. From here it entered into Gujarat and flowed through Siddhapur, Pātan and finally met the Arabian Sea near Prabhās Pātan. In its long journey, the Sarasvati is believed to have been joined by the rivers Shatadru (Satlaj) originating from Mount Kailāsa, Drishadvati from Siwālik Hills and the old Yamunā. Through the millennia the river had changed its course many times. (Thakker, P.S., Probable Course of River Vedic Sarasvati Through Remote Sensing Data. In *Rasik Bhārati*. Gandhinagar: Sanskrit Sahitya Akademi. 2005)

12. In 1978, satellite images from earth sensing satellites launched by NASA and ISRO (Indian Space Research Organization) showed traces of an ancient river course on the very route of the River Sarasvati. They clearly showed the dried bed to be six to eight kilometres wide, and at some places to be 14 kilometres, which is larger than the River Ganga today. (Source: Dr J.R. Sharma and his colleagues A.K. Gupta and G. Shreenivasan of the Remote Sensing Centre of ISRO, Jodhpur, Rajasthan, mapped the course of the once mighty River Sarasvati.)

River Indus (Sindhu) flows through mountainous terrain in Pakistan

41.16, 7. 95.2).[13] Archaeological and sacred textual evidence shows that there was significant religious activity in the proto-historic (ancient) period of the Indus and Sarasvati civilizations. The Indus valley civilization developed on the River Sindhu, and Harappa and Mohenjo-daro (excavated in Pakistan) were two cities of this highly developed urban civilization. Dholavira and Lothal (in Gujarat, India) are remnants of the same civilization. H.D. Sankalia, a veteran Indian archaeologist and indologist, states, "While Mehergarh serves as an excellent preface to the rich Indus civilization, this civilization itself has now been found all over Gujarat, Kutch, Saurashtra, and seen to have crossed Madhya Pradesh and reached Maharashtra."[14] The Vedic civilization developed on the banks of River Sarasvati; it is also known as the Sarasvati civilization, which is geographically depicted in the Rig Veda.

The Sarasvati River is mainly mentioned in literary sources, i.e., the Rig Veda, having no other proof until recently. Through Satellite imagery scientists have discovered paleo-channels (geological formations indicating an ancient dried river bed) along a path through which the Sarasvati flowed. On the other hand the Indus civilization left behind hundreds of archaeological relics like towns, ports, figures, figurines, jewellery, seals, etc. The seals found here have a script, which has remained undeciphered till this day. Therefore it is difficult to make a definite statement about their authors, cultures and time frame. But both the Indus and the Sarasvati civilizations can be seen as having contributed to the development of Hinduism.

Recent scholars have concluded that Indian culture is at least over 9,000 years old. "The excavations at Mehrgarh (Jansen et

---

13. Similar references are found in the Aitareya Brāhmana (2.19.1,2), Panchavimsa Brāhmana (25.10.7) and Shatapatha Brāhmana (7.2.1,4). The great epic Mahābhārata declares that various Vedic sacrifices were performed on the banks of this river (Ādiparva 95.26 and Vanaparva 36.41). Expert geologists, Puri and Verma, (1998) express the same view about the River Sarasvati in 'Glaciological and Geological Source of Vedic Sarasvati in the Himalayas' in *Itihāsa Darpan*, ix (2): pp. 7-36.

14. Sankalia, H.D. Down the Corridors of Indian Archaeology. In *Indian Heritage*, edited by Vasanti Mazumdar. Bombay: Indian Council of Social Welfare, 1980, p.2.

al. 1991; Jarrige et al. 1995) near Sibri, Pakistan, do demonstrate an indigenous development of agricultural food production by people living there as early as the seventh millennium BC. As a cultural occupation, Mehrgarh Period 1A[15] dates to the seventh millennium BC period (Shaffer 1992); because of the essential cultural complexity in that occupation stratum, some scholars posit an even earlier period for the cultural innovation there of achieving plant and animal domesticates."[16]

The discovery of some vestiges of the Indus valley civilization occurred by accident. When two British engineers who were in charge of constructing a railway line had the mounds at Harappa dug, they discovered burnt bricks which could be used as ballast. Little did they know that they were digging up a past and hitherto unknown facet of the history of India! The bricks turned out to be more than 4,000 years old! After this initial discovery and excavation, large scale excavations were carried out by British and Indian archaeologists, Sir John Marshall and E.J.H. Mackay at Mohenjo-daro and M.S. Vatsa at Harappa in 1921-22. These two highly advanced cities were discovered to be about 600 km apart.

Ruins of Mohenjo-daro, 300 km north of Hyderabad (Sindh), Pakistan

The society and culture of these cities are referred to as the Indus valley civilization or the Harappan civilization. Some other important sites of this civilization are Kalibangan in Rajasthan, and Dholavira, Lothal and Rangpur in Gujarat, India.

From the evidence found[17] it has been proved that India had

Dholavira site, Gujarat

Lothal site, Gujarat

---

15. Period 1A indicates the first excavation at Mehrgarh. The second excavation is noted as 1B, and so on.

16. Shaffer, Jim G. and Lichenstein, Diane A. South Asian Archaeology and the Myth of Indo-Aryan Invasions. In *The Indo-Aryan Controversy*, edited by Bryant and Patton. London: Routledge, 2005, p. 82.

17. Recently, divers of the National Institute of Ocean Technology (NIOT) have discovered an ancient city submerged in the gulf of Khambhāt (Cambay) in Gujarat. Sonar mapping of the site revealed it to be 10km by 2km, or the size of Manhattan. Radiocarbon dating of a wooden object from the site showed it to be 7500 BCE. Glenn Milne of the University of Durham, using inundation maps and sea level curves estimates that the city may have been submerged 10,000 or even 12,000 years ago. Considering that it is vast and sophisticated, a long period of development must have preceded it. This means the urban culture to which it belonged must have been much older. Source: Gupta, H.K. (2002) Oldest Neolithic settlements discovered in Gulf of Cambay. *Journal* of the Geological Society of India, v.59(3), pp.277-278.

a highly advanced civilization in other areas of the subcontinent. Several hundreds of towns and sites existed near the banks of the Sindhu and Sarasvati Rivers and other neighbouring regions.

FACTS AND ARTEFACTS OF INDUS CIVILIZATION

The well-planned cities of Harappa, Mohenjo-daro and others of the Indus civilization had two-storey houses of brick and stone, large community baths, properly planned drainage and sewage systems, and well-built roads, which in some places were sixty-feet wide. Wood was generously used, not only for construction purposes, but also for making a variety of furniture like cots, chairs, stools and tables. Its people cultivated wheat, barley and dates; domesticated animals from the camel to the humped zebu; and had invented the wheel and yoked buffalo or oxen to their carts. They used gold, silver, lead, tin, copper, bronze and garments of spun and woven cotton more than 3,000 years ago.

One of the most noteworthy features of Harappa was its big granaries. There were twelve granaries arranged in two parallel rows, with ventilation and passages of approach. The distinctive feature of Mohenjo-daro was "the great Bath". It was built of brick set in gypsum mortar with a damp-proof layer of bitumen. The bath is 54 by 33 metres (177 by 108 ft). The outer walls are 2 to 2.5 metres (7 to 8 ft) in thickness. In the centre of the paved quadrangle is a large swimming bath, 11 by 7 metres (39 by 23 ft).

Let us consider some common aspects typical to all the sites of the Indus Civilization. "People were mostly vegetarians and ate fish also. Apart from wheat, barley and rice they also grew fruits and vegetables like pumpkin, dates and coconuts. The ornaments they used were girdles, earrings, bangles, necklaces, nose-rings, anklets, hairpins and beads. Weights and measures had been standardized. Trade and commerce by land and by sea with Sumeria, Babylonia and Egypt were flourishing.

Namit Arora

The 'Great Bath' at Mohenjo-daro

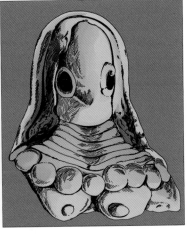

Left: An illustration of a male terracotta figurine offering namaste, Harappa
Right: An illustration of a female terracotta figure testifies to the use of vermilion in circa 2800-2600 BCE, Harappa.

People were good at arts and crafts. Music and dancing were also known to them, as can be guessed through figures found on seals. Worship of Shiva-Pashupati, goddess Durgā, *lingas* and certain animals and trees like bison, fish, serpent, tulsi and peepal tree seem to have existed."[18]

Many of the artefacts and relics found from these cities include seals, statues, female figurines, beads, pottery, tools, jewellery, games and children's toys such as small carts. More than 3,000 seals and artefacts have been found so far.

Some of the symbols and illustrations are *swastika*-like figures (symbol of auspiciousness and good fortune), a one-horned animal (that probably represents the Varāha avatar of Bhagwan Vishnu), objects similar to Shiva *lingas,* figures in dancing poses, and the most discussed of all the Harappan seals depicting a deity in a yogic posture surrounded by animals is believed to be Bhagwan Shiva called Pashupati – the Lord of Animals. The inscriptions on the seals have still remained elusive to experts who are unable to decipher their script. But the symbols and illustrations reflect distinct highly developed and planned urban civilization of the Indus valley.

Illustration of Harappan seal: The so-called unicorn bull, believed to represent the Varaha avatar (divine boar)

Pashupati Harappan seal: A three-headed figure in a yogic posture. Many have identified it to be Bhagwan Shiva as Pashupati

---

18. Swami Harshananda. *A Concise Encylopaedia of Hinduism, Vol. 2.* Bangalore: Ramakrishna Math, 2008, pp. 70-71.

Countries of Central Asia (circled) from where the Aryans are believed to have come to India, according to some Western scholars

THE ĀRYAN INVASION THEORY

As mentioned earlier in the 'Introduction', there are two hotly argued views among scholars about the Āryan invasion of or migration to India. This controversial topic is not intended to distract readers from learning about Hinduism. Rather, bringing up this issue about the history of ancient India is to provide some historical context for the texts and traditions that are the primary focus of this introductory book. The following text explains briefly about the two theories. The case for the invasion/migration theories will be understood from the arguments given against the Āryan invasion theory.

But first, let us briefly understand what the Āryan invasion theory is. Many scholars and books of Indian history teach about the Āryan invasion of India, describing that the Āryans were people who came from Central Asia or Europe. According to these scholars they invaded India around 1500 BCE. After overpowering and killing some of the inhabitants of the Indus valley who had built the cities of Harappa and Mohenjo-daro, they established themselves over north India. They are said to have composed the Rig Veda and other Vedic literature and founded the Vedic civilization.

Max Müller, an Oxford University scholar and German-born Indologist of the 19th century, strongly propagated the Āryan

German-born Indologist, Max Müller

Invasion theory and announced that the Vedas were composed in 1200 BCE. Prof. B. B. Lal, former Director General of ASI and former Head of the School of Studies in Ancient Indian History at Jivaji University, Gwalior, in his chapter *Āryan Invasion of India – Perpetuation of a Myth*[19], argues that Müller arbitrarily assigned the Vedas to have been composed in 1200 BCE. B.B. Lal says that Max Müller accepted the time of Buddha, i.e., 600 to 500 BCE, and then he gave a period of 200 years to each of the successively preceding periods of Vedic literature, namely, Āranyakas, Brāhmanas and Vedas. When, however, he was criticized by a host of his contemporaries such as Theodor Goldstucker (1821-1872, a German Sanskrit scholar), William D. Whitney (1827-1894, an American linguist and philologist) and H.H. Wilson (1786-1860, an English orientalist), Müller admitted that he had hypothetically assigned 200 years to each period of Vedic literature. Prof. B.B. Lal quotes Max Müller, "All I have claimed for them has been that they are minimum dates, and that the literary productions of each period which either still exists or which formerly existed could hardly be accounted for within shorter limits of time than those suggested...

"If now we ask as to how we can fix the dates of these periods, it is quite clear that we cannot hope to fix a *terminun a qua {sic}*. Whether the Vedic hymns were composed [in] 1000 or 2000 or 3000 years BC, no power on earth will ever determine."[20] Later in life, Max Müller had second thoughts about his estimate on the date of the Vedas and admitted, "Whatever may be the date of the Vedic hymns, whether 1500 or 15000 BC, they have their own unique place and stand by themselves in the literature of the world."[21]

The descriptions in the Vedas, archaeological excavations and other scientific facts also prove otherwise. Some of the

19. *The Indo-Aryan Invasion Controversy*. Edited by Bryant and Patton. London: Routledge, 2005, pp. 50-51.

20. Müller, Max. *Physical Religion*. New Delhi: Asian Educational Services, 1890 (1979), p. 51.

21. Müller, Max. *The Six Systems of Philosophy*. Reprint Varanasi: Chowkhamba, 1962, p.35.

arguments as to why the Āryan invasion never happened are as follows:[22]

- There is no memory of an invasion or of a large-scale migration in the records of ancient India – neither in the Vedas, in Buddhist or Jain records, nor in Tamil literature.

- The Rig Veda describes the landscape, fauna, flora and climate of northern India, but does not mention the countryside in the Caucasus near the Caspian Sea or other parts of Central Asia that some Western scholars assert as the original home of the Āryans.

- There is cultural continuity between the archaeological findings of the Indus-Sarasvati civilization and subsequent Indian society and culture: a continuity of religious ideas, arts, crafts, architecture, and system of weights and measures. If there was an Āryan invasion then there would not have been a cultural continuity.

- The archaeological discoveries of relics at Mehrgarh reveal a culture similar to that of the Vedic Indians. The Rig Veda shows not a nomadic but an urban culture. The supposed Āryans who invaded India and wrote the Vedas had a nomadic culture.

- The racial diversity found in skeletons in cities of the Indus civilization is the same as in today's India; there is no evidence of a new race from outside India.

- The Indus cities were not destroyed by invaders but deserted by their inhabitants because of desertification of the area due to the change in course of River Sindhu or Indus. Strabo, a Greek historian, reports (Geography xv.1.19) that Aristobulas had seen hundreds of villages and towns deserted because the Indus had changed its course.

- The battles described in the Rig Veda were not fought

Illustrations of vessels of clay relics from Mehrgarh

22. Klostermaier, K.K. *Hinduism, A Short History.* Oxford: One World, 2000, pp.37-39.

between invaders and natives but between people belonging to the same culture.

❖ Archaeologically there are no ruins, remains, or settlements of any invading Āryans that existed apart from the indigenous developments.

❖ The Āryan invasion theory was based on the assumption that a nomadic people (the supposed Āryans from abroad) possessing horses and chariots defeated an urban civilization (the Indus or Harappa civilization) that is believed to not have had any horses. And in the Rig Veda horses are described to be of great importance, both as secular and sacred objects. This supposedly proves that there was an Āryan invasion. But archaeological evidence demonstrates that the Harappan knew the use of horses. Horse teeth have been found in Amri on the Indus and Rana Ghundai on the Baluchistan border which is dated to 3600 BCE. Bones of the domesticated horse have been found in early layers of excavations in Harappa, so this precludes the possibility that they were left by the 'invaders'.

From 1944 to 1946, Mortimer Wheeler, Director General of ASI, worked on excavating the Indus Valley sites. He strongly advocated the Āryan invasion from the skeletal remains he found at Mohenjo-daro. His account is found in history textbooks.[23] But, later archaeologists disproved Wheeler's interpretation with the fact that the skeletons showed no evidence of violent deaths and no Harappan sites have been found to be destroyed by outside invaders. There are, to date, no ruins, remains of encampments or settlements and relics clearly indicating any invading Āryans apart from indigenous developments.

Prof. B.B. Lal, former student of Mortimer Wheeler, argues against his mentor's theory, saying that, "There is no evidence of attacks on the citadels of the Harappan cities, which would

An illustration of Mortimer Wheeler who advocated the Āryan invasion theory

---

23. *The Indus Civilization: Cambridge History of India.* Cambridge University Press, 1953, p.92.

have been the first structures to be destroyed in the case of an attack." Further, Lal adds that the thirty-seven skeletal remains are from a lower level of the site. If these skeletons did really represent the massacre by invaders, then they should have been on the uppermost level of the site. And lastly some vestiges of the invaders would have been found, but that is not the case. Professor of Archaeology at University of California Berkeley, George F. Dales (1964) very aptly described this so-called massacre as "The Mythical Massacre at Mohenjo-daro."[24] At the end of the introduction in *The Indo-Āryan Controversy* (2005: pp. 16-17), Ms. Laurie Patton, joint editor and professor of Early Indian Religions, writes, "Very few, if any archaeologists or linguists embrace the invasion theory and have not done so for several decades."

In recent years, with the near collapse of the Āryan Invasion Theory, some scholars have proposed the Āryan Migration Theory – the Āryans migrated to India instead of having invaded it. This theory has also become a hotly debated issue. Prof. J.G. Shaffer, a renowned archaeologist, says that modern archaeological evidence of artefacts found in Harappa and Mohenjo-daro do not support the idea of Āryan migration into India. He says, "It is possible to document archaeologically a series of cultural changes reflecting indigenous cultural development from prehistoric to historic periods."[25]

CONCLUSION

Many Hindu practioners and scholars believe that Sanātana Dharma or Hinduism is the oldest, non-proselytising religion. It is practised today by over 800 million Hindus in India and 20 million Hindus abroad.

With its holistic views and catholicity of approach, Hinduism

---

24. Lal, B.B. Aryan Invasion of India – Perpetuation of a Myth. In *The Indo-Aryan Controversy*, edited by Bryant and Patton. London: Routledge, 2005, pp.52-53.

25. Cited by Flood, Gavin. *An Introduction to Hinduism*. New Delhi: Cambridge University Press, Foundation Books, First South Asian Edition, 2004, p. 33.

Jnāna-mārga: Reading a spiritual text

Bhakti-mārga: Devotional rituals

Karma-yoga: Service to society

Dhyana-yoga: Meditation

expands the narrow boundaries of the term 'religion'. It is a mosaic of different *sampradāyas* or faiths, each adding new colour to the original. It is both very simple, i.e., a devotee can please God with a single leaf, a flower, a fruit or water as explained in the Bhagavad Gitā 9.26, and very elaborate, i.e., a royal sacrifice or Rājasuya *yajna* is recorded to have lasted for months, if not years. It touches the life of a Hindu before birth (*garbhādhān* samskara) and is carried on even after his death (*antyeshti*). The great philosopher and President of India, Dr S. Radhakrishnan (1888-1975), calls Hinduism a way of life with defining rules of dos and don'ts. At the same time, it gives options to reach the highest Hindu goal of life, namely, *moksha* (liberation of soul). A person may follow the paths of knowledge, action or devotion in accordance to his or her aptitude and interest. This democratic approach in matters of faith and practice is truly a distinctive feature of Hinduism. For many Hindus it is reflected in the belief in one Supreme Reality or God who is described and worshipped in many ways. It is also reflected in its tolerance and respect for people who subscribe to other belief systems. There have been almost no organized attempts of conversion to Hinduism by inducement or force.

Hinduism's history is rich, varied and stretches back to several millennia. It is surprising that many ordinary and educated Hindus are ill-informed or ignorant of the basic tenets and traditions of their wonderful religion. The following chapter will explore some of the prominent Hindu beliefs held by one-sixth of humanity.

SUMMARY

1. The ancient Persians called people living by the eastern side of the River Sindhu as Hindu.

2. Greeks called the River Sindhu as 'Indos', and later in English it became 'Indus'. Subsequently, the country and its people came to be known as 'India' and 'Indians' respectively.

3. Hindus were originally known as Āryas. Their religion was called Ārya Dharma, Mānava Dharma, Sanātana Dharma, Vaidika Dharma, and today, Hinduism.

4. Sanātana Dharma was revealed by God to rishis. The Vedas are called Shrutis because they were revealed by God to the rishis. They heard the Vedas in their samadhi condition and learned them by heart. They then orally transmitted them to their students.

5. Many Hindus believe that the Vedas are the most ancient sacred texts in the world, which are recited even today. The name is derived from the Sanskrit root word 'vid', which means 'to know'.

6. The civilization that developed along the banks of the Rivers Sindhu and Sarasvati came to be known as the Sindhu (Indus) and Sarasvati civilization. The River Sarasvati was roughly 300 km east of Sindhu.

7. The advanced cities of Harappa and Mohenjo-daro of the

Indus Valley civilization were discovered in 1921 and 1922 respectively. They had broad roads, sewage and drainage systems, two-storey houses, seals with the *swastika*, and illustrations believed to be of Shiva in yogic posture and others.

8. Max Müller propounded the Āryan Invasion theory in 1890, saying that the Vedas were written in 1200 BCE. In 1944, Mortimer Wheeler interpreted an Āryan invasion from the skeletons found at Harappan sites. But many scholars have argued against the Invasion Theory with archaeological and sacred Hindu textual evidences. Still, the issue is being hotly debated by both sides.

2

Core Beliefs of Hindus

Mandir, bell and lotus are important elements of Hindu tradition.
(Inset) Atman or soul is a fundamental entity in all life

One Supreme Bhagwan, Authority of the
Vedas, Avatāravāda, Atman, Karma,
Punarjanma, Murti-pujā,...

INTRODUCTION

What defines a Hindu? One who is born in Bharat (India) is a geographical definition of a Hindu. One who is born to Hindu parents is a familial statement. And one who is born into the fourfold caste system is a genetic inheritance description.

All these are partial definitions, because a Hindu born abroad is also a Hindu, so is a foreigner who accepts Hinduism and also one born outside the fourfold caste system. The traditional defining principles of most Hindus are the belief and faith in one Supreme Divine Reality or Paramātmā and the acceptance of the authority and infallibility of the Vedas.

While Hinduism is famously diverse, it also has common threads, or core beliefs, that are generally accepted by many of its practitioners. Exploring such prominent beliefs can help us get a clearer picture of the basic elements of Hinduism. These core Hindu beliefs generally include the principles of:

1. **One Supreme Divine Reality:** The Supreme Divine Reality or Paramātmā manifests in various forms. The Rig Veda says, *"Ekam sat viprāhā bahudhā vadanti,"* which means "Truth is one, but the wise describe it in many ways."[1] The belief in one supreme God is called *Ekeshwaravāda*.

2. **The Authority of the Vedas:** The Vedas are the ancient shastras revealed by Paramātmā or Bhagwan to the enlightened rishis of India. They include the four Vedas (Samhitās) and their respective appendices, namely,

---

1. Rig Veda 1.164.45.

Brāhmana, Āranyaka and Upanishad texts. The scholar Bryan K. Smith in *Reflections on Remembrance, Rituals, and Religions* (1989), writes, "Hindus are those who use the Veda as a reference point for creation, maintenance and transformation of their traditions."[2] For many Hindus the Veda is a divine revelation, and as such, its principles have not originated at a particular time in history but are eternal and of divine origin.

3. **Avatāravāda:** The principle that Bhagwan or God himself takes birth on earth in human and other forms. Avatar means "descent of God", i.e., he manifests on earth. He comes to liberate his devotees, establish dharma and destroy evil.[3]

4. **Atman:** It is unborn, eternal and indestructible inner self[4] that is the essence of life in all animate things. The atman is *sat* (eternal), *chitta* (consciousness) and *ānanda* (bliss). The nearest English word for atman is soul or self. The Supreme Bhagwan is believed to reside in all atmans as *antaryāmin,* inner-controller and guide.

5. **Karma:** The universal law of cause and effect according to which a person is responsible for his or her actions and their effects. God gives the appropriate fruits of a person's good or bad actions.

6. **Punarjanma:** The principle of reincarnation or rebirth (*punarjanma*)[5] in which the atman (soul) passes through many births to attain spiritual enlightenment or *moksha*. *Punarjanma* is linked to the karma principle.

7. **Murti-pujā:** A belief that God manifests in a *murti* (image) through which he can be worshipped and adored through acts of devotion. This tradition believes that God has a form, and the worship of God's *murti* is

---

2. OUP, 1989, p.13.
3. B.G. 4. 7-8.
4. Ibid. 2.20.
5. Ibid. 4.5.

Hinduism

essential for spiritual elevation of the self.

8. **Guru-shishya Paramparā**: This tradition is very significant for the majority of Hindus. Through the God-realized living guru the disciple realizes the highest spiritual wisdom and attains *moksha*. A *sampradāya* is defined as *guru-shishya* tradition – "*Sampradāyaha Guru Kramaha.*"[6] This means, "Succession of gurus is called a *sampradāya*."

9. **Four Purushārthas**: Hindu sacred texts state that there are four *purushārthas* or endeavours or goals of life, namely, dharma (staying faithful to one's moral duties), *artha* (acquiring wealth), *kāma* (fulfilling one's desires) and *moksha* (acquiring final liberation). The ultimate goal of life is *moksha* – freedom from the cycle of births and deaths through self-realization and God-realization. Out of the four *purushārthas, artha* and *kāma* are relevant for householder devotees and dharma and *moksha* are relevant for both householders and ascetics.

10. **Ahimsa**: Hindus believe that God pervades all living and non-living things. This means that God pervades humans, animals, plants, mountains and the whole of creation. Hence, the Hindus love and respect all life forms and generally practise ahimsa or nonviolence.

11. **Varnāshrama Dharma**: Dharma is generally explained as *varnāshrama* dharma. This means the duties and responsibilities of Hindus in relation to their varnas (classes) and ashramas (stages of life). Note that the varna system is not the same as the Indian caste system. The Indian caste system is a distortion of the varna system, as the caste system is purely based on one's birth. The *varnāshrama* system provided Hindu society with an organized social structure for the development and elevation of society and individuals.

---

6. *Halāyudha* Dictionary, Bhumikānda. p. 402. And, Monier Williams. *A Sanskrit-English Dictionary*. Oxford: Clarendon Press, 1988, p.1,175.

An artist's impression of the Divine who is both immanent in and transcendent to the infinite universes

Narayanprasad Swami

Besides these eleven core beliefs there are others to which some Hindus give importance and subscribe to. Furthermore, as long as Hindus accept the belief in one supreme God and the authority of the Vedas, even if they reject some of the other core beliefs, they can still traditionally be considered Hindus. For example, certain Hindus believe that God has a form and thus they practice *murti-pujā*, while at the same time, others believe God to be formless and thus do not perform *murti-pujā*. Despite such differences, both are considered to be Hindus.

DETAILS OF EACH BELIEF

We shall now try to understand in some detail each of the eleven core beliefs that generally qualify a Hindu.

1. ONE SUPREME BHAGWAN OR GOD

Hinduism has often been misinterpreted as a religion of innumerable 'Gods'. Many Hindus believe in one Supreme Paramātmā or Bhagwan (God) who manifests in many forms. The Rig Veda clearly states *"Ekam sat viprāhā bahudhā vadanti"* – "Truth is one, but the wise describe it in many ways." Bhagwan is *sat-chit-ānanda* (eternal, consciousness and bliss). He is supreme, all-powerful, the all-doer and the all-pervading. Bhagwan is the giver of the fruits of karmas to all souls (karma

One of many minor gods: Indra, the rain-god

phala pradātā). He is also known as Parabrahman, Paramātmā, Parmeshwara and by other names.

Bhagwan has a divine, personal form *(sākāra),* however he is also believed by a section of Hindus to be formless or impersonal *(nirākāra).* He comes on earth in human and other forms to liberate the pious souls, fulfil their devotional wishes and faith, and to destroy evil.[7] According to different Hindu Vaishnava traditions there have been 39 or 24 avatars (incarnations) of Bhagwan, out of which 10 (Dashāvatāra) are revered as the principal avatars. In the Shaiva and Shākta traditions there have been ten avatars in each. It is because of the many manifestations and forms of God in Hinduism that others have come to believe it to be polytheistic. But principally many Hindus believe that the different forms of God are manifestations of the one Supreme Bhagwan. He possesses infinite divine qualities, out of which six are prominent: *jnāna* (knowledge), *aishwarya* (lordship), *shakti* (ability), *virya* (power), *teja* (brilliance) and *bala* (strength).

Many Hindus, especially the Vaishnavas, believe that understanding the glory of Bhagwan and worshipping him with the belief and faith that he is supreme *(sarvopari),* the all-doer *(sarva kartā),* always having a divine form *(divya sākāra)* and is ever present *(prakat)* on earth through a God-realized guru, liberates one from the bondage of *māyā* and blesses one with *moksha.*

Devas or *devatās* are the minor gods (namely, Indra, Agni, Surya, Varuna, Vāyu, Yama and many others), of whom there are 330 million according to the Purānas. They are all minor deities who do their duties in accordance with the authority and instructions of the supreme God.

With regard to the common features of Bhagwan in all Vaishnava *sampradāyas,* Gavin Flood, Professor of Hindu Studies and Comparative Religion, Oxford University, explains, "The

Varuna, the ocean-god

7. B.G. 4.7-8.

The Vedas are the ancient sacred texts of the Hindus. Veda Vyāsa compiled them into four texts

Lord is the 'Supreme Person' *(Purushottama)* with personal qualities *(saguna)*, rather than an abstract absolute *(nirguna)*; the Lord is the cause of the cosmos, he creates, maintains and destroys it; the Lord reveals himself through sacred scriptures, temple icons, in his incarnations (avatar) and in saints."[8]

2. AUTHORITY OF THE VEDAS

Spiritual faith cannot be wholly imbibed in one's life in a matter of days or a couple of years. It requires a lifetime or even many lifetimes of sadhana or spiritual endeavours. But the important question is: What is required to develop absolute faith in God? How should one exert oneself? What are the pitfalls and dangers that one should be aware of? What are the practices or sadhanas required to consolidate one's faith? Is there one path or are there many? Should one follow or believe what one's mind says or take the word of any person?

The answer is that one should not follow any non-standard means or unauthorized ways. Following an authorized shastra or the bona fide guru is the Hindu tradition. The Vedas are the ancient sacred texts of the Hindus. For Hindus there is no higher scriptural authority than the Vedas. All orthodox Hindu texts derive their source and authority from the Vedas.

---

8. *An Introduction to Hinduism.* 2004, p.118.

Hinduism

The orthodox Hindu schools of philosophy and *sampradāyas* are called *āstikas,*[9] mainly because they base their beliefs and practices on the Vedas, Brāhmana, Āranyaka and Upanishads. This gives them spiritual legitimacy and provides cohesion to sustain their schools of philosophy and religious traditions. Those who do not accept the Vedas are generally termed as *nāstikas* or non-believers.

3. AVATĀRAVĀDA

Avatāravāda is the principle that God assumes a human or other forms to liberate countless *jivas* from material bondage and the cycle of births and deaths. It is of prime importance in Hinduism. Avatar literally means 'one who descends.' The term incarnation, is considered to be an English equivalent of avatar. However, it fails to capture the exact meaning of avatar, i.e. the belief by many Hindus that God is totally divine, despite him assuming a living form and exhibiting all the traits of a living being. Even though in a human or any other form his hunger, thirst, sleeping, eating and all other actions appear similar to humans or other living beings, yet they are divine. God's body and his actions are therefore absolutely divine and liberating.

The doctrine of *avatāravāda* or incarnation is an important feature of the Bhagavad Gītā (B.G. 4. 5-8). Some of the ten main avatars (Dashāvatāra)[10] of the Purānas are mentioned in the Vedic literature. For example, the Shatapatha Brāhmana[11] mentions the descent of God as Matsya (fish) and its story of liberation in 1.8.1.1-16, Kurma (tortoise) in 1.8.5.15, Varāha (boar) 14.1.2.1-11 and Vāmana (dwarf) 1.2.5.1.

One may ask as to why God should assume an avatar? Can

Shri Rāma and Krishna are worshipped by many Hindus as avatars of Bhagwan Vishnu

---

9. Astika schools of philosophy are Sānkhya, Yoga, Nyāya, Vaisheshika, Uttar Mimānsā and Purva Mimānsā.

10. The ten avatars (Dashāvatāra): (1) Matsya (fish), (2) Kurma (tortoise), (3) Varāha (boar), (4) Nrusimha (man-lion), (5) Vāmana (dwarf), (6) Parshurāma, (7) Rāma, (8) Krishna, (9) Buddha and (10) Kalki (will ride on a white horse – yet to manifest).

11. The biggest of all Brāhmana texts. It belongs to the Shukla Yajur Veda. The work, almost entirely, deals with various aspects of Vedic *yajnas*.

he not liberate souls from his divine abode with his infinite powers? Yes he can, but the two main reasons why he incarnates in a human and other forms are: (1) To fulfil the wishes and accept the love and devotion of his devotees and countless other spiritually inclined souls, and (2) to destroy *adharma* or evil on earth.[12] The first reason allows devotees to develop deep bonds of love and glory through their personal association with God. Eventually this deep love or attachment to God liberates them from the trammels of *māyā*.

4. ATMAN OR JIVA

The nearest translation of atman or *jiva* is self or soul. Hindus believe that all living things have a *jiva* or atman. It is the fundamental principle of all life which pervades the body and experiences.

The ancient rishis of India turned their thoughts inward to discover their inner self. They had a unique experience of a metaphysical entity, i.e., self, that was beyond the external, physical world they were living in. They found it to be eternally existing *(sat)*, having consciousness *(chit)* and infinitely blissful *(ānanda)*. This self is luminous, pure and bodiless; beyond sorrow and decay. The rishis discovered that what they experienced was their true self and the very essence of their life. They called it atman or *jiva* or *jivātmā*, which is pure, immortal and untouched by evil. The Bhagavad Gita describes the nature of atman in chapter 2.19-25. It says that atman is not born, nor does it die. It casts off worn-out bodies and enters into other new ones. No weapons can split it, nor fire burn it. No waters can wet it, nor wind dry it. The atman is invisible, unthinkable and unchanging.

According to the Advaita philosophy of Shankarāchārya a *jiva* is in bondage, goes through transmigration, and when free from *māyā*, it is identical to Brahman (Ultimate Reality).

The atman is sat-chit-ānanda

---

12. *"Yadā yadā hi dharmasya..."* B.G. 4. 7-8.

Hinduism

Shankarāchārya differentiates between *jiva* and atman, where one bound by *māyā* is called *jiva* and when that *jiva* becomes free of *māyā,* it is called atman. The bhakti Vedānta schools (founded by Rāmānujāchārya, Nimbārkāchārya, Madhavāchārya and others) consider *jiva,* atman or *jivātmā* to be atomic in size and innumerable, to pervade the physical body in which it resides and to be totally separate from and subservient to Brahman or God. Furthermore, it is important to note that the bhakti schools do not differentiate between *jiva* and atman as Shankarāchārya does. These schools understand the words *jiva,* atman and *jivātmā* to be synonymous, and by nature the *jiva* is pure and unbound by *māyā.* But when the *jiva* is bound by *māyā* (due to I-ness and My-ness) and goes through the cycle of births and deaths, they call it a *baddha* (bound) *jiva,* and when it is liberated, they call it a *mukta jiva.*

Hinduism believes that the *jivas* or atmans pervade the physical body it resides in *(sarva-gataha).*[13]

5. KARMA

Karma means action or deed. Any physical, mental or emotional action is called karma. No living being can remain without performing actions for even a moment.[14] For every action there is a result or consequence. Hindus believe that karma is the universal law of cause and effect which governs life. It is a natural law of human life, just as gravity is a law of matter.

Hinduism teaches that a person's karma, past or present, is responsible for good or bad consequences in his or her life. It is also responsible for the disparities in life: rich and poor, high and low, intelligent or ordinary, good and bad. Hindus believe that nothing in our world is merely accidental or a chance happening.

---

13. B.G. 2. 24.
14. B.G. 3. 5-8.

Good deeds like charity confer merit (punya)

The common wisdom, "As you sow, so shall you reap" succinctly sums up the Hindu law of karma. Good actions produce happiness and bad actions lead to suffering and misery in the present or future lives. Understanding the principle of karma can encourage a person to make moral and spiritual choices in his or her daily activities.

A prominent and early mention of the karma principle is found in the Brihadāranyaka Upanishad 3. 2.13, in which Sage Yājnavalkya tells Ārtabhāga, "Meritorious action leads to merit *(punya)*, while evil action leads to further evil." The Shvetāsvatara Upanishad 5.7 clearly states, "One who performs actions wanders in the cycle of transmigration according to his [good or bad] actions."

The law of karma is a moral principle that explains the circumstances and incidents in the present life to be the consequences of a person's deeds in the past or present lives. Nothing in one's life or in this world happens without a cause or reason. So a person's present or past governs his present and his present actions also shape his future. This means that every person is to some extent an architect of his own future.

There are two types of karmas that a person performs, namely, *nishkāma* and *sakāma*. *Nishkāma* karma means actions performed without any expectation of material gain, ego and

Bad deeds like violence, molestation and others incur sin (pāpa)

material desires, but solely done to perform one's duty (dharma) and please God. *Sakāma* karma means acts done for a specific material desire or purpose.

Karma is also categorized into three types:

i. *Kriyamāna* karma: The karma or action being performed every moment. The consequences or fruits of these karmas may be attained in this, the next or future lives.

ii. *Sanchita* karma: The vast accumulation of karma containing the sum total of all karmas done in one or many lives. The fruits of these karmas are being experienced or yet to be experienced.

iii. *Prārabdha* karma: The portion of one's *sanchita* karma that one is presently experiencing in this birth. For example, the attributes and conditions of one's physical body, mental capacities and circumstances are due to one's *prārabdha* karmas.

Hindus believe that God gives the fruits of one's good and bad karmas, that is, he is the karma *phala pradātā*. Karma or deed does not by itself produce or give results; it is only when God decides what to give as the fruits of one's karma that one actually experiences their positive or negative effects. It is worth noting that the karma principle is not applicable to animals because their actions are instinctual and they lack discrimination between right and wrong.

The principle of karma is not antithetical to the concept of human effort. As mentioned earlier, *kriyamāna* karma, that is doing karma every moment, is a part of the karma principle. Without daily action or deeds how can one hope to experience the result of present or past deeds! So karma does not negate the importance of human effort in any way.

Kim Knott mentions in her book[15] how Prof. Arvind Sharma deals with karma in his book *Hinduism for Our Times*, "To think fatalistically about karma is unhelpful when, in fact, as human beings we have the power at any moment to change our own behaviour, and thus its consequences for our future. Free will rather than fatalism characterizes the operation of karma." Karma is thus not fate, because a person acts out of free will and is thus responsible for shaping his or her own destiny.

To dissolve or overcome the burden of karmas one has to perform good karmas, moral karmas and spiritual karmas with no desire for material gains *(nishkāma),* and with the aim of pleasing God and the guru. Performing selfless karmas like service to mankind, praying, doing bhajan, reading or listening to shastras, performing bhakti of God, serving one's guru, etc. elevates one's soul. Through the performance of *nishkāma karmas,* one finally attains *moksha* by the grace of God or guru.

Karma is further discussed in Part 2, Chapter 7, Hindu Way of Life.

6. Punarjanma or rebirth

Punarjanma or reincarnation or rebirth is the natural process of birth, death and rebirth. Hindus believe that the *jiva* or atman (soul) is intrinsically pure. However, because of the layers of I-ness and My-ness, the *jiva* goes through transmigration

---

15. Knott, Kim. *Hinduism, A Very Short Introduction*. p. 39.

Reincarnation is the natural process of birth, death and rebirth

in the cycle of births and deaths. Death destroys the physical body, but not the *jiva*. The *jiva* is eternal. It takes on another body[16] with respect to its karmas. Every karma produces a result which must be experienced either in this or some future life. As long as the *jiva* is enveloped in ignorance, it remains attached to material desires and subject to the cycle of births and deaths. According to the Purāṇas, every *jiva* passes through 8,400,000 life forms. The four categories into which the *jiva* is born are: *udbhija* (born of seed, i.e., plants), *jarāyuja* (born of womb, i.e., mammals), *swedaja* (from sweat, i.e., bugs) and *andaja* (born of egg, i.e., birds and reptiles). Hindu texts such as the Purāṇas teach that the regression of a soul into animal bodies is due to its base karmas; similarly, the progression of the soul into human and divine bodies is due to its meritorious karmas. Birth in a human body is the highest and rarest of all births, because it provides the *jiva* an opportunity to achieve its main purpose: *mukti* or liberation.

Understanding *punarjanma* eliminates the fear of death. One realizes that one is not the body, but the immortal soul which takes on many bodies in its evolutionary sojourn through samsara. Reincarnation ends when one's karmas are resolved, God is realized and the fruit of *moksha* is attained.

---

16. B.G. 2. 22.

What are the Reasons for Punarjanma?

There are several reasons why the *jiva* takes on different physical bodies:

i. To experience the fruits of one's karmas

This is the main reason for rebirth. A person's karmas influence his or her life and destiny. *Sāttvika* karmas i.e. good or righteous deeds, reward one with the pleasures of *swarga* (abode of the devas). *Rājas* karmas or pleasure-seeking material actions reward one with *mrutyuloka* (mortal realm or earth). And *tāmas* karmas, actions related to inertia, laziness and evil, condemn one to *pātāla-loka* (the lowest realm or the nether world). When the *jiva* exhausts its *sāttvika* karmas in *swarga*, it gets a human birth on earth.[17]

ii. To satisfy one's desires

When a person indulges in material pleasures, he or she subsequently develops a stronger desire to enjoy more of it *(vāsanās)*. This unending craving to satisfy one's desires causes the *jiva* to assume new physical bodies.

iii. To complete one's unfinished sadhana

When an aspirant making spiritual efforts for liberation from *māyā* dies without attaining his goal, the *jiva* gets another human body to complete its sadhana.

iv. To fulfil a debt

When a *jiva* is indebted to another *jiva,* it gets a human birth to fulfil its debt and receive what is owed to it. The *jiva* comes in the form of a relative, friend or an enemy.

v. To undergo sufferings because of a great soul's curse

A person's grave error or sin may incur the wrath or displeasure of God or a rishi. This results in the *jiva* of that person getting

---

17. B.G. 9.21.

another birth, not necessarily into a human body.

vi. To attain *moksha*

By the grace and compassion of God or a God-realized guru, a *jiva* gets a human body to purge itself of the layers of base instincts or moral and spiritual weaknesses.

When the *jiva* takes on another body, it is God who gives it an appropriate one in keeping with its karmas. When the *jiva* enters the new body it does so with its subtle *(sukshma)* and causal *(kārana)* bodies.

Sometimes the enlightened person (a *mukta*) takes birth by God's wish to carry out a special mission.

7. MURTI-PUJĀ

The worship of a sacred image of God, or his manifestations, or guru is known as *murti-pujā*. In Vedic times, the Indian rishis worshipped the forces of nature, namely, Varunadeva (sea-god), Indradeva (rain-god), Suryadeva (sun-god), Agnideva (fire-god), Vāyudeva (wind-god) and others. They revered and appeased these devas for their contributions in mankind's existence and happiness, by chanting various prayers in the form of mantras and by performing *yajnas*. Over time, they developed elaborate rituals of devotional worship for those devas and for the supreme God.

To facilitate their concentration on and worship of God, the rishis made *pratikas* (symbols) and *pratimās* (*murtis* or images) of clay, stone, metal and wood.[18] With consecration ceremonies,

---

18. In the Rig Veda (8.29) there is a beautiful description of the bodies, limbs and weapons of deities, and, according to it, Tvashtā is an artisan for the devas or deities as well as an architect. He is called *devashilpi* (1.20.6). It means that there must have been competent sculptors at that time. Later in the Vishnu Purāna (3.2.11) he is identified with Vishvakarmā – the famous sculptor, architect and engineer of the devas.
In the Kāthaka branch of the Krishna Yajur Veda (22.11) there is the mention of sage Devala who lived by preparing images. There is a reference to an image in the Sāma Veda (1.9.5) and the Atharva Veda refers to a temple (2.2.2.). The Sadvimsha Brāhmana text (5.10) not only mentions images but even the sculptor like Tvashtā. By the time of the Shrautasutras and Grihyasutras the worship of deities through images in temples were well established (Gautam Grihyasutra 3.7). Swami Harshananda. *A Concise Encyclopaedia of Hinduism, Vol.2.* Bangalore: Ramakrishna Matha, 2008, p.343.

| Stone | Wood | Metal | Sandalwood |
| Painting | Sand | Conceived by mind | Precious stone |

Hindu sacred texts describe eight forms of God's murtis

God was invoked (*prana-pratishthā*) into a *murti*. Then the rishis regarded such a *murti* as God himself and not a statue. The *murti* became the focus and object of worship. The *murti* helps the aspirant to withdraw his mind and senses from material objects and concentrate on it. When the aspirant reaches the pinnacle of his sadhana, he realizes God, and he sees, speaks with and touches him.

The Shrimad Bhāgvata Purāna (11.27.12) describes eight types of God's *murtis*:

> *"Shaili dārumayi lauhi lepyā lekhyā cha saikati,*
> *Manomayi manimayi pratimā ashtavidhā smrutā."*

"A sacred image is made of one of eight materials: stone, wood, metal, sandalwood paste or clay (or other material that can be moulded), sand, precious stones, conceived by mind and through painting or etching."

Professor Gavin Flood states, "Many Hindus believe in a transcendent God, beyond the universe, who is yet within all living beings and who can be approached in a variety of ways. The transcendent is mediated through icons in temples, through natural phenomena, or through living teachers and saints. Devotion [bhakti] to deities mediated through icons and holy persons provides refuge in times of crises and even final liberation [*moksha*] from action [karma] and the cycle of reincarnation [samsara]."[19]

In Bhakti Yoga the aspirant associates with the *murti* of God through devotion and love. He expresses his love through *sevā* and worship of God's *murti*. *Murti-pujā* has been practised for several centuries in India. Mandirs are built for darshan, worship, pilgrimage and service of God's *murti*. The worshippers of *murtis* and proponents of mandirs are followers of the Bhakti *sampradāya,* believing in God who always has a divine form (*sākāra*) even in his divine abode.

The Bhakti *sampradāyas* in Vaishnavism believe that the consecrated *murtis* of the supreme God and his manifestations in mandirs are not symbols but realities. Service of God means *seva* of his *murti*, which is an indispensable part of devotional practice for all Vaishnava devotees. Almost all Vaishnava, and many Shaiva, Shākta and Smārta shastras, called Āgamas, contain elaborate sections on rules, regulations and methods of *murti-pratishthā* and daily worship. One of the great teachers of Shri Vaishnavism, Shri Pillai Lokācharya, in his work *Mumukshupadi* states, "The extreme limit of the easy accessibility that is mentioned here is the worshipped image. This form of the Lord [as *murti*] is our refuge. He holds the divine weapons in his hands. He keeps one of his hands in a posture asking us not to fear. He wears a crown. His face is smiling. His sacred body reveals that He is the protector and an object of enjoyment. "[20]

For many Hindus who practice *murti-pujā* the devotional rituals provide joy and peace. Many also experience a sense of being near to God and understanding the futility of worldly pleasures.

---

19. Flood, Gavin. *An Introduction to Hinduism.* New Delhi: Cambridge University Press, Foundation Books, First South Asian Edition, 2004, pp. 10-11.
20. Klostermaier K.K. *Hinduism, A Short History*, 2000, p.133.

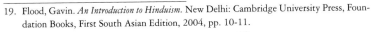

Devotion to God means adorning the image with clothes, jewellery and flowers

Guru-shishya tradition: A guru blesses a disciple in his gurukula (tableau)

8. GURU-SHISHYA PARAMPARĀ

The Guru and *Guru-shishya* (master-disciple) tradition is a unique feature of Hinduism. Since Upanishadic times the guru has played the role of imparting spiritual *(parā)* and mundane *(aparā)* knowledge *(vidyā)* to the disciple. The guru guides, inspires and also engages the disciple in the rigours of spiritual sadhana and worldly knowledge. Through spiritual disciplines he aids the disciple in realizing the Divine and in fulfilling the four *purushārthas* of human life.

For an aspirant bound by *māyā,* self-realization and God-realization are not possible without an adept guru. The guru must be *brahmanishtha* (God-realized) and *shrotriya* (one who knows and has realized the true meaning of the shastras) in order to liberate the aspirant. The *shishya* or disciple must be humble and totally obedient with unflinching faith in the guru.

The Hindu shastras and traditions speak glowingly of the guru as the form of God. The "God-realized" guru represents God, but he is not God. He purifies the disciple to make him eligible to experience the eternal bliss of God. So, by seeing, hearing, serving and thinking of the guru, one perceives and serves God. In this way, the guru is the bridge to and means of realizing God.

Ahimsa teaches love and compassion for all living beings

The guru *paramparā* or disciplic succession is central to the transmission of worldly and spiritual knowledge for most Hindus. Many Hindu traditions put great emphasis on two factors for transmission of knowledge: (1) its continuity or unbroken line of transmission and (2) importance of guru or teacher. Through the true spiritual guru, any given Hindu tradition is able to adhere to its core principles. The guru plays the role of a judge in interpreting those longstanding principles of Hinduism for new contexts and emerging conditions.

9. AHIMSA

Hindus believe in and practice the principle of ahimsa or nonviolence and non-killing. Ahimsa does not mean nonviolence in action alone, but also in thought and speech. Firstly, it is based on the Hindu beliefs that all living and non-living things are created by God and pervaded by him – "*Ishāvāsyam idam sarvam*" (i.e., "God pervades all things") – as stated in the Ishāvāsya Upanishad. Therefore everything is sacred. Secondly, the majority of Hindus also believe there are separate and independent atmans in each living body, and God resides within all of them. From these two beliefs was born the principle of ahimsa and compassion for all living things.

*The four goals of human life:
Dharma (righteousness),
Artha (prosperity),
Kāma (worldly desires) and
Moksha (liberation)*

Thirdly, the law of karma also deters one from violent and cruel actions or killing of any living being because of the adverse consequences to oneself.

Fourthly, the principle of *punarjanma* or rebirth operates in relation to good and bad karmas. A person who performs good karmas is rewarded with a happier and higher next life, whereas one who sins faces punishment, misery and degradation in this life or future lives.

Devout Hindus are generally vegetarian and abstain from killing or violence in any form. Ahimsa is one of the pillars of morality in Hinduism. Mahavir, Gandhiji and others were great apostles of ahimsa.

10. Four Purushārthas

All human beings have certain common desires to fulfil during their four stages of life. The ancient Indian seers recognized the four *purushārthas* or goals of human life to be basic and ideal. They are: (1) Dharma (righteousness, duty and moral order) to be performed, (2) *Artha* (wealth and prosperity) to be acquired, (3) *Kāma* (worldly desires) to be fulfilled and (4) *Moksha* (liberation) to be attained. In this way the ancient Hindus maintained a holistic perspective to human life and thus never neglected any aspect of it. The four goals or endeavours are the roadmap for a happy life on earth and beyond. The householders are guided to pursue all four goals, while the ascetics are ordained to focus on only two goals: dharma and *moksha*. Let us try to understand the goals briefly:

i. Dharma

Dharma is the foundation and first of the four principal human goals. It has its source in (1) Vedas (also known as Shruti), (2) tradition (also known as Smruti) and (3) customs of virtuous people. It is based on *ruta* (cosmic law) and *satya* (moral law). Dharma also refers to moral duties, obligations and conduct, namely, *vidhis* (dos) and *nishedhs* (don'ts). It includes *satya* (truthfulness), *saucha* (purity), *dayā* (compassion), ahimsa, *brahmacharya* (celibacy), *asteya* (non-stealing), *aparigraha* (non-possession), and *akrodha* (non-anger). Following dharma as prescribed by the Hindu shastras brings one *punya* (merit), success, fame and happiness. Furthermore, imbibing *ekāntika dharma*, which is superior to Varnāshrama Dharma because it consists of the virtues of dharma, *jnāna, vairagya* and bhakti, merits one with final liberation or *moksha*.

The Mahābhārata states, "If dharma is destroyed, it will destroy humanity and the world; If dharma is protected [i.e. practiced], it will protect them."[21] It further declares, "Where there is dharma, there is victory."[22] In brief, dharma is the upholder, supporter and sustainer of society. It is the very essence of one's being.

ii. Artha

For progress and the fulfilment of dharma and *kāma,* wealth or *artha* is essential. Therefore the second life endeavour for

---

21. *"Dharma eva hato hanti, Dharmo rakshati rakshitah."* (Mahābhārata, Vana Parva, 313.128)
22. *"Yato dharmastato Krushno."* (Mahābhārata, Bhishma Parva, 43.60 and Shailya Parva, 62.32)

the householder is the acquisition of wealth and material prosperity. The efforts and means to realize this goal must have a righteous and moral basis. They must be based on dharma or lawful means. Any wealth acquired through unethical ways does not give peace, happiness and prosperity. So, the basis of earning a living rests upon the foundation of dharma.

iii. Kāma

Fulfilment of biological, physical and material desires is the third goal. This mainly includes getting married and having a family. The householder is ordained by the shastras to legitimately fulfil his or her worldly desires in accordance to the canons of dharma.

Artha and *kāma* are important goals for the householder for the growth and progress of society.

iv. Moksha

Moksha means liberation from the web of *māyā,* freedom from the cycle of births and deaths, and the eternal experience of divine happiness. This is the ultimate and final goal of human life. The atman within the human body is imperishable and eternal, unlike the body. But because of a person's ignorance, worldly desires and sinful karmas his or her atman goes through the cycle of births and deaths. The final objective of human life is to be liberated from mundane bondage and the cycle of births and deaths. This is achieved through refuge in God or a God-realized guru. Thereafter, through the guru's grace one becomes free from the bondage of *māyā*, and is blessed with self-realization and God-realization. Most of the Bhakti *sampradāyas* believe that when a devotee dies, his or her atman is blessed with a divine body, and it ascends to the supreme divine abode of God *(videha mukti)*. Here, it forever resides, remaining blissfully absorbed in the darshan and *sevā*

Darshanam

Brahmins: Priests and teachers

Kshatriyas: Rulers and protectors

Vaishyas: Businessmen and farmers

Shudras: Weavers and labourers

The varna system (social order) of India included the Brahmins, Kshatriyas, Vaishyas and Shudras

of Paramātmā. Some *sampradāyas* believe in being blessed with *mukti* while alive *(jivan-mukti)*.

11. VARNĀSHRAMA DHARMA

Hindu society had an organized social structure for the harmonious progress and development of individuals and society. It was called the *varnāshrama* system, which classified people into four classes (varnas) and stages (ashramas). Varna included the Brahmins, Kshatriyas, Vaishyas and Shudras; and ashrama meant the four stages of life, namely, Brahmacharya (student wedded to celibacy), Gruhastha (householder), Vānaprastha (retired life) and Sannyās (ascetic life).

The system, not practiced now, was originally based upon the personal qualities *(gunas)* and aptitudes for types of work (karmas) of individuals. It was not birth-based, i.e., caste system, as it later deviated to become.

The observance of *varnāshrama* dharma credited the individual with *punya* and thus the attainment of *swarga*. For details refer to Part 2, Chapter 9, Varnāshrama.

SUMMARY

1. Two of the many fundamental beliefs that qualify a Hindu are that he or she believes in one Supreme Paramātmā who manifests in many forms, and the authority of the Vedas.

2. The other important principles are *avatāravāda*, atman, karma, *punarjanma, murti-pujā, guru-shishya* tradition, ahimsa, four *purushārthas* and *varnāshrama dharma*.

3. *Avatāravāda* is the principle that God comes in human and other forms to liberate souls and eradicate evil.

4. Atman is the essence in all living things. It is *sat* (eternal), *chit* (consciousness) and *ānanda* (bliss).

5. Karma means any physical, mental or emotional deed. It is not a self-operating system but is governed by God. God dispenses the fruits of one's karmas (as karma *phala pradāta*). Rebirth is a direct consequence of one's karmas.

6. *Punarjanma* means rebirth. The soul gets different life forms according to its karmas. Birth in a human body is the greatest and most precious of all births.

7. *Murti-pujā* is a tradition based on the belief that God has a divine human and other forms. Since creation comprises shapes and forms, similarly, the creator too has a form. *Murti- pujā* enables the aspirant to focus his or her senses and mind on God.

8. The God-realized guru guides and liberates the *shishya* from the bondage of *māyā* and prepares him to lead a meaningful life in this world and the next. The *guru-shishya* tradition is an important facet of Hinduism.

9. Ahimsa means nonviolence in thought, speech and deed. Hindus believe that all things are created by God and pervaded by him. Therefore everything is believed to be sacred. Devout Hindus are generally vegetarian and abstain from killing in any form.

10. The four *purushārthas* are the four goals of human life. The rishis fully considered the needs of *brahmachāris* (celibate students), householders and ascetics by providing a roadmap of life. They guided householders to aspire for four *purushārthas* or goals of human life, namely, dharma, *artha, kāma* and *moksha*, while encouraging the ascetics to focus on dharma and *moksha*.

11. *Varnāshrama* dharma means duties and responsibilities of Hindus in relation to their varnas (classes) and ashramas (stages of life).

Hindu Shastras

(Sacred Texts): Part I

Top left, clockwise: Sacred manuscripts of Rig, Yajur, Sāma and Atharva Vedas. (Inset) Rushikumars of 'Darshanam' chanting Vedic mantras

The Vedas, Content of Vedas,
The Upanishads

INTRODUCTION

The sacred texts or scriptures that contain the tenets of Hindu Dharma are called shastras. The word shastra literally means a treatise that commands and protects the person who obeys it. Furthermore, shastra also includes works on the life stories and teachings of the avatars of Paramātmā or God.

Hinduism has a rich collection of shastras, namely, the Vedas or Shruti shastras, Smruti shastras, Agamas and Tantras, Vedāngas, Upavedas and Sutra literature. For many Hindus the holiest and the most ancient of shastras are the Vedas or Shrutis. Shruti means "that which is heard" or revealed. They were revealed by Paramātmā or God to the ancient rishis in their deep meditation. Then the Vedas or the revealed knowledge was handed down by an oral tradition. They include the four Samhitās, Brāhmana texts, the Āranyaka texts and the Upanishads. The four Samhitās are, the Rig, Yajur, Sāma and Atharva Samhitās. The Samhitās primarily comprise of prayers to personified natural forces like fire, rain, water, thunder, etc., and the Ultimate Reality. They deal with prayers for prosperity, progeny, matrimony, domestic rites and more. The Brāhmana texts provide guidance about performance of *yajna* rituals and the Āranyakas include spiritual contemplation and meditation. The Upanishads contain philosophical discourses on Brahman (Ultimate Reality) and its relation to souls and the material world. Traditional schools of Hinduism consider the Vedas to be the most authoritative sacred texts.

In addition to the Shruti shastras, there are texts known as Smruti. Although they are secondary in authority to the Vedas, the Smruti shastras also play a very important role in Hinduism. Smruti means "that which is remembered". Smruti shastras are the written accounts of rishis who remembered what they had heard from their great spiritual masters. As opposed to Shruti shastras, Smruti shastras were composed through human agency. They deal with moral and social laws, rites and rituals and history. They include the body of texts known as Dharma Shastras such as Manu Smruti, Yājnavalkya Smruti, etc., Itihāsa or epics, namely, the Rāmāyana and Mahābhārata (with the Bhagavad Gitā as its core), and the 18 Mahā-Purānas, 18 Upa-Purānas and other literature.

Both the *shrutis* and *smrutis* deal with the ritual, philosophical, spiritual, moral and social aspects of Hinduism. They answer questions like who is God; where does he reside; what does he look like; how are we related to him; and how should we strive to realize him? They prescribe various means of realizing God, overcoming obstacles and the dos and don'ts of social and spiritual life.

The Āgamas or sectarian literature are exclusive to some *sampradāyas*. Their followers consider them to be divinely revealed *(shruti)* and equal in authority to the Vedas. The three Hindu traditions of Vaishnavism, Shaivism and Shāktism have their own Āgamas or Tantras (literature primarily devoted to Shakti or the Divine Mother). Even Buddhists and Jains have their own Āgamas or Tantras. The Vaishnava texts are called Vaishnava Āgamas, Shaivite texts are called Shaiva Āgamas and the Shākta texts are called Shākta Āgamas. The Āgamas deal mainly with the concept of God and the means to attain him through bhakti, rituals, ceremonies, construction of mandir, installation of sacred images, yoga and philosophy.

The Vedic sciences include the Vedāngas (limbs of the Vedas) and the Upavedas (subsidiary Vedas).

The Sutra literature is also a part of the ancient Sanskrit literature that contains concise statements of wisdom called *sutras* or aphorisms. It includes the Kalpasutras, Gruhyasutras and Brahmasutras.

According to the Purva Mīmānsā (a school of philosophy which deals with the dos and don'ts, Vedic rites, rituals and sacrifices) and Uttara Mīmānsā (or Vedānta, which deals with the topics of *ātmā*, Paramātmā, *jnāna* and *moksha*) a shastra should have four basic factors, viz:

1. *Vishaya* or a designated subject to discuss and inform.
2. *Prayojana* or purpose or goal to be gained by its study and practice.
3. *Sambandha* or connection with other related subjects.
4. *Adhikāri* means a competent student or person. So, a shastra is meant for one who is spiritually competent. The incompetent may misunderstand and misinterpret the shastra.

We shall now deal briefly with the Shruti texts – the Vedas, Brāhmanas, Āranyakas and the Upanishads. The other texts mentioned above will be dealt with in the subsequent chapters.

1. THE VEDAS (SHRUTI SHASTRAS)

The foundational shastra for all *āstika* Hindus are the Vedas. A practising Hindu is generally defined to be one who believes in the authority and sanctity of the Vedas.

The name Veda comes from the Sanskrit root word 'vid', which means 'to know'. Thus, the Vedas mean knowledge. They contain both spiritual and worldly knowledge. The Vedas are considered by Hindus to be the oldest sacred texts in the world which continue to be recited and studied to this day. Hindus consider the Vedas to be *apaurusheya*, i.e., not man-made, but revealed by God. It is difficult to assign a time frame for the Vedas. The dates given by different scholars range from

A Hindu believes in the authority and sanctity of the four Vedas and other sacred literature

Murti of Veda Bhagwan worshipped at Veda Mandir, Ahmedabad

Veda Mandir, Ahmedabad

25000 BCE to 1000 BCE. Hindus regard the Vedas to be eternal.

Traditionally, the single large Veda was later classified by Veda Vyāsa into four texts, namely, the Rig Veda, Yajur Veda, Sāma Veda and Atharva Veda. He taught one of them to each of his four disciples – Rig Veda to Paila, the Yajur Veda to Vaishampāyana, the Sama Veda to Jaimini and the Atharva Veda to Sumantu.[1]

For millennia, the Vedas have been handed down to posterity by word of mouth. The Shruti texts or the Vedas, as traditionally defined, include the Samhitās, Brāhmanas, Āranyakas and Upanishads. Conventionally, it is the Samhitā (collection of mantras or hymns) that is indicated by the word Veda. There are four Samhitās, namely, Rik Samhitā or Rig Veda, Sāman Samhitā or Sāma Veda, Yajus Samhitā or Yajur Veda and Atharvan Samhitā or Atharva Veda. The Brāhmanas, the Āranyakas and the Upanishads of each of the four Vedic Samhitās have different names.

Each Samhitā has its own associated texts in prose called the Brāhmanas (which are ceremonial handbooks), Āranyakas (deal with profound interpretations of rituals) and Upanishads (give metaphysical explanations). The Brāhmanas deal mainly with rules and regulations laid down for the performance of rites and

1. Mahābhārata, Ādi Parva, 60.5 and Shrimad Bhāgavata, 12.6.50.

rituals of various *yajnas* (fire rituals, also known as sacrifices) as well as application of hymns in them. It also has interesting dialogues, myths and stories, but very little philosophy. The Samhitā and Brāhmana texts form the karma or ritual part (*karma-kānda*) of Vedic literature.

The Brāhmanas were followed by the Āranyaka texts, which were the result of contemplations of yogis and rishis in the forest. They mark the transition from ritualism to spiritualism, i.e., they discuss the spiritual significance of Vedic *yajnas* and devas. Finally, the Upanishads contain the very core of Indian philosophy (*jnāna-kānda*) and focus on the nature and relation between *jagat* (world), atman, Brahman (God) and *mukti* (liberation). They are the creative part of Indian Philosophy. They are also known as Vedānta because chronologically they form the "end" or "concluding" part of the Vedas, and philosophically they teach the highest spiritual knowledge. As their authority is unquestioned the Upanishads form the first of the three basic treatises of Vedānta called Prasthāntraya. Since the Upanishads are part of the Vedas they are also called Shrutiprasthāna. The Āranyaka and the Upanishad texts together form the *jnāna-kānda* or the knowledge section of the Vedas.

THE FOUR VEDAS OR VEDIC SAMHITĀS

I. RIG VEDA

The Rig Veda or Rig Veda Samhitā is the oldest and the most important of the four Vedas. It consists of ten *mandalas* (books), which have 1,028 *suktas* or *ruchās* (hymns) comprising of 10,552 mantras known as *ruks* (verses) that were revealed to various rishis at different periods of time. The mantras are prayers mainly to the nature gods to grant riches, progeny, long life, peace, and eternal happiness; and some mantras refer to victories of princes and kings in wars, subjects like marriage, generosity and other mundane things. The main

A manuscript of the Rig Veda. It contains rituals for yajnas, prayers, philosophy, cosmology, process of creation,...

devas or gods of the Rig Veda were Agni (the fire-god), Indra (rain-god), Varuna (ocean-god), Mitra (sun-god), Vāyu (wind-god), Prajāpati (creator) and the Ashwins (divine physicians). The Rig Veda also has mantras like the Nāsadiya and Purusha *suktas* that are concerned with cosmology and creation. The Rig Veda contains philosophical ideas that form the basis of later philosophies derived and developed by the rishis. Bhakti or devotion also has its origin in the Rig Veda Samhitā. It contains monotheism or belief in one Supreme Reality who is called by different names. The worship of the Supreme Reality having a form and qualities *(saguna upāsanā)* is also referred to in the Rig Veda. The Aitareya and Kaushitaki Āranyakas and Upanishads were a development from the Rig Veda.

The Vedic rishis were both male and female. Some of the prominent male rishis included Angiras, Agastya, Vasishtha, Vishwāmitra, Grutsamada. The main female rishis were Ghoshā, Godhā, Apālā, Kuhu, Sarama and others.

The special priest of the Rig Veda is called a *hotā*. He is an expert who recites the mantras of the Rig Veda to invoke the devas for receiving the oblations.

The mantras of the Rig Veda are in Vedic Sanskrit. For thousands of years these mantras have been meticulously transmitted orally, and finally when they came to be first written in the last few millennia, they were inscribed on dried palm leaves. Consequently, for thousands of years up to the present, there has been almost no change or corruption in the chanting and meaning of the Vedic mantras. There are, however, very minor variations in the written versions and even in oral versions owing to regional differences, transcription mistakes, and what might fall into the category of "human error".

A Yajur Veda manuscript. It deals mainly with rituals of worship

II. Yajur Veda

The Yajur Veda mantras deal with the rituals of worship or the ceremonial aspect of Hinduism. There are about 1,975

Students in a gurukula reciting Vedic mantras, Ved Vignan Maha Vidya Peeth, Bangalore

mantras known as *yajus* that explain the significance of the performance of sacrificial rites. Many of the Yajur Veda mantras are found in the Rig Veda. The two branches of Yajur Veda are Krishna Yajur Veda and Shukla Yajur Veda. The former has both prose and poetry while the latter has only poetry. The language of the Yajur Veda and its descriptions of devas and society are very similar to that of the Rig Veda. There are a large number of mantras connected with *yajnas* like Ashvamedha, Vājapeya and Rājsuya. There are also mantras related to devotion in the Yajur Veda.

The special priest of the Yajur Veda is known as *adhvaryu*. He is an expert in reciting mantras for specific rituals in *yajnas.*

The Taittiriya and Shatapatha Brāhmanas and Brihadāranyaka and Ishāvāsya Upanishads were a development from the Yajur Veda.

III. SĀMA VEDA

'Sāman' means 'tune', and in this case it refers to the tunes in which the Vedic hymns are chanted. The *sāmans* are essentially Rig Vedic mantras set to music. The Sāma Veda is also known as the Veda of music because all the mantras are set to the seven basic notes of Indian music known as the *sapta svara* system. The Sāma Veda is the smallest of the Vedas, but it

A part of Sāma Veda manuscript. It is the Veda of music

is most appealing because of its sweet music, poetic expression and touching sentiments of devotion. It is believed that the birth of Indian classical music can be traced to the Sāma Veda.

The Sāma Veda has 1,875 mantras, the majority of which are from the Rig Veda. The Panchavimsha, and Shadvimsha Brāhmanas, the Tāndya, Chāndogya and Kena Upanishads were a development from the Sāma Veda.

The Sāma Veda gained importance and prominence because Bhagwan Krishna said in the Bhagavad Gitā (10.22), "I am Sāma Veda among the Vedas."

The special priest of Sāma Veda is known as an *udgātā*. He is an expert singer who invites the devas by singing the mantras to entertain and please them.

IV. ATHARVA VEDA

The Atharva Veda was not included as the Fourth Veda up to the time of the Bhagavad Gitā[2], because its mantras had little to do with the main *yajna* rituals as in the other three Vedas. It has information on aspects that are not found in the other three Vedas. The Atharva Veda contains 736 hymns or *suktas* with a total of 6,077 mantras. They deal with health, medicine, victory, friendship, progeny, black magic, and charms and chants used for offensive and defensive purposes. The Atharva Veda also contains mantras that deal with building construction, trade and commerce, statecraft, penances, long life, harmony in life and mantras to ward off evil spirits. This Veda also refers to *swarga* (heaven) and *naraka* (hell), virtue and sin, and qualities like *satya* (truth) and *tapas* (austerity), and ceremony like *diksha* (initiation) that help a person attain perfection.

The Atharva Veda is also called Brahmā Veda because the priests who specialise in its recitation are called the Brahmā priests. Furthermore it is also called Bhaishajya Veda (the Veda of medicines and treatment of diseases) and Kshattra Veda

A part of Atharva Veda manuscript. It deals with health, victory, friendship, and charms and chants used in warfare

2. The Bhagavad Gitā mentions the three Vedas as *traividya* or *trayi* (B.G. 9. 20-21).

(the Veda of the warrior class). So, unlike the other Vedas, the Atharva Veda touches a wider scope of worldly subjects.

The Gopatha Brāhmana and three important Upanishads, Prashna, Mundaka and Māndukya, developed from it.

2. CONTENT OF VEDAS

The Vedas predominantly deal with prayers to the nature gods and the Ultimate Reality, the means to attain desirable objects and avoid undesirable ones. They generally elaborate upon devas (gods), and sometimes upon devis (goddesses), man, morality, rituals to propitiate devas, unity of all beings and *moksha*. They also deal with matrimony, friendship, prayers, progeny, longevity, prosperity and medicines.

Chanting of mantras as prayers by individuals was the first stage in the Vedic period (Samhitā period). During this time an individual himself chanted prayers for his spiritual and secular progress. He himself was both the host and the priest for all his rituals, prayers and worship. The *yajna* rituals represented the second stage (Brāhmana period) wherein a householder performed different and elaborate *yajna* rituals under the guidance and instruction of specialist priests. The third stage (Āranyaka period) emphasized meditation and contemplation on the concept of *yajna* rituals. In this there was almost no actual performance of the rituals. This stage was a link between the ritualism of the Brāhmana period and the philosophy of the Upanishadic period. And, the final and fourth stage was the Upanishadic period wherein the guru taught his disciples the esoteric doctrine of Paramātmā, *ātmā*, creation of world, *moksha* and other metaphysical subjects. This constituted the *jnāna-mārga* or path of knowledge for *moksha*.

The gradual shift in focus from ritualism to spiritualism through the Vedic periods thus sought to satisfy all the needs and wants of man, whether mundane or transcendental.

Some very important concepts and rituals are given in the

The Rig Veda is revered and recited by Hindus

Vedas, including *ruta* (cosmic order), *satya* (here: moral order), *runa* (obligation), hymns of creation *(Nāsadiyasukta)* and the Ultimate Reality *(Purushasukta)*. They are briefly discussed below.

I. RUTA (COSMIC ORDER)

Ruta is the universal principle of cosmic order or laws of nature that prevail over or govern all the universes. *Ruta* is mentioned in the Rig Veda and Krishna Yajur Veda, and it is one of the important concepts of Sanātana Dharma. *Ruta* pervades all of creation, and must be observed by all the devas and humans. The whole universe is founded on *ruta* and moves in it. Prof. Gavin Flood writes, "This integration of society and cosmos, of body and society, is sacred order or law *(ruta)* of the universe, which is eternal and unchanging, brought to life in vedic ritual, expressed in the songs of the vedic seers, and elucidated in the Brāhmanas [texts]."[3] Varuna deva is both the custodian of *ruta* and *satya*.

Ruta is the principle of cosmic order

Prayers being offered to the sun-god

II. SATYA (MORAL ORDER)

Satya or truth is the universal moral order that applies to all human beings. It is the essential characteristic of Paramātmā and therefore *satya* stands for God. *Satya* is unchanging and unaffected by time and place; it is eternal. Abiding by *satya* one always triumphs and attains spiritual elevation. *Satya* helps a person progress towards God. The Mundaka Upanishad states, "*Satyam eva jayate na anrutam*" – "Only truth triumphs not untruth."[4] The first half, "*Satyam eva jayate,*" is the motto of the Government of India.

III. RUNA (OBLIGATION)

Another important concept is that of *runa*, which means

3. Flood, Gavin. *An Introduction to Hinduism.* New Delhi: Cambridge University Press, Foundation Books, First South Asian Edition, 2004, p. 49.
4. Mundaka 3.1.6.

indebtedness or obligation. Sanātana Dharma believes that man is indebted to the devas (gods), rishis, *pitrus* (forefathers), people and animals in many ways. *Runa* is hinted at in the Rig Veda (8. 32.16 and 6. 61.1), and stated clearly in the Taittiriya Samhitā (6. 3.10.5) of the Krishna Yajur Veda and the Shatapatha Brāhmana text of Shukla Yajur Veda (1. 7.2.11). The concept is first described as *runa-traya* (three-fold debts or obligations), namely, *deva-runa* (debt to gods), *rishi-runa* (debt to sages) and *pitru runa* (debt to ancestors). Later two more obligations were added to form the five *runas*, i.e., *nru-runa* (debt to human beings) and *bhuta-runa* (debt to all living beings including birds, animals, etc.).[5] It is to be noted that the five *runas* or obligations are fulfilled through the practice of *panchamahāyajnas,* namely, *deva-yajna, rishi-yajna, pitru-yajna, nru-yajna* and *bhuta-yajna.* The word *yajna*, with the exception of *deva-yajna*, does not refer to performance of fire sacrifices, but alludes to selfless religious and charitable services performed to repay one's debts. Hence, the Hindu shastras prescribe the performances of *panchamahāyajnas* by all householders. Let us consider each of the *runas* briefly.

1. **Deva-runa** means indebtedness to the devas (gods). The devas give us many things in the form of nature, like light, water, fire, air and wind. By offering oblations in a *yajna kunda* (fire altar) an aspirant expresses his appreciation to the devas and seeks their blessings for happiness, prosperity and protection. This is called *deva-yajna.* When the devas are pleased by the offerings, they make the natural forces helpful to the worshippers and also fulfil their worldly desires.

   Deva-runa: Offering oblations to the devas in a yajna kunda

   Thus *deva-runa* is repaid by properly performing Vedic sacrifices or *deva-yajnas.*

2. **Rishi-runa** means indebtedness to the rishis or sages, who gave us the legacy of spirituality, culture and education.

Rishi-runa: Studying and teaching the sacred texts

5. Hiriyanna. M. *Outlines of Indian Philosophy.* London: George Allen & Unwin Ltd, 1951, p.45.

This debt can be repaid by studying the sacred texts, teaching them to the next generation, practising them and performing the samskaras and austerities prescribed by sages. This is called *rishi-yajna* or *brahma-yajna*.

3. ***Pitru-runa*** means obligation to one's forefathers. This is fulfilled by getting married, i.e., becoming a householder. One appeases one's ancestors by offering rice balls (*pindas*) and water (*arghya*) daily. Furthermore, it also includes performance of funeral rites and subsequently the annual *shrāddha* or rite to propitiate one's ancestors. The practice of these rites and rituals is known as *pitru-yajna*.

Pitru-runa: Offering rites to propitiate one's ancestors

4. ***Nru-runa*** is the fourth obligation. It refers to charity to mankind and serving human beings who are ailing, needy, in difficulty and in pain. Serving society in times of calamity and need is the fulfilment of *nru-runa*. It also includes the preservation of social, cultural and moral values by practising truth, kindness to fellow humans, and love for neighbours and friends. God blesses those who fulfil *nru-runa* with peace, happiness and progress. The practice of these rituals is called *nru-yajna*.

Nru-runa: Charity and service to humankind

5. ***Bhuta-runa*** is the last of the five human debts. In this, people are expected to repay it daily by setting apart a portion of their meals for the birds and animals. This ritual practice is called *bhuta-yajna*. Furthermore, the Mahābhārata mentions an important aspect of *bhuta-runa:* not to be cruel but to be kind to all living beings.[6]

The first and third (*deva-runa* and *pitru-runa*) deal mainly with sacrificial rites (*yajnas*), and the last two (*nru-runa* and *bhuta-runa*) deal mainly with acts of charity, sympathy and nonviolence. The *rishi-runa* deals with self-study, practising austerity and transmission of sacred texts to the next generation. Collectively these *runas* are known as *ishtāpurta,* which means

Bhuta-runa: Offering food and service to animals

6. Ādi Parva, 120. 17-20.

the cumulative result of performance of sacrificial rites and good works for others.[7]

Through the principle of *runa* and the ritual of repaying debts, people learn to rise above self-centredness and to be grateful to all those from whom they obtain and inherit many things.

IV. HYMNS OF CREATION AND THE ULTIMATE REALITY

The Rig Veda has some of the best mystical poetic hymns, like the *Nāsadiyasukta* (hymn of creation: 10.129.1-7), and the *Purushasukta* (hymn of the Ultimate Reality: 10.90.1-16). The *Nāsadiyasukta* deals with the difficult topic of creation. It describes what existed before creation and how creation came about through the Ultimate Reality. Briefly, the hymn says that the Ultimate Reality willed the creation of this world and the living and non-living forms got manifested. The whole secret of creation is known perhaps only to Him. The hymn states, "It is Positive Being from whom the whole existence arrives. The Absolute Reality is at the back of the whole world."[8] With regards to the origin of the universes the *Nāsadiyasukta* describes creation to have been willed by an external agency, i.e., the Ultimate Reality.

The *Purushasukta* in the Rig Veda shows the organic and social unity of the universes. In this hymn, all existence — earth, heavens, devas, planets, living and non-living objects, four varnas, time and other aspects of society — originated from the Ultimate Reality (Purusha), who pervades the world and yet remains beyond it. So the Ultimate Reality is shown to be immanent and transcendent (For details see Part 2, Chapter 11, Concept of Creation).

The belief in the one Ultimate Reality is the principle of these two hymns.

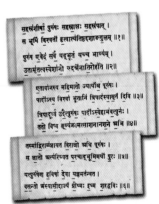

Purushasukta hymn in praise of the Supreme Person, from the Rig Veda

---

7. Monier-Williams, Monier. *A Sanskrit-English Dictionary.* Clarendon, UK: OUP, 1988, p.169.

8. Radhakrishnan, S. *History of Indian Philosophy, Vol.1.* London: Allen & Unwin, 1948, p.101.

The Upanishads explain spiritual truths through dialogues, anecdotes, allegories and stories

3. THE UPANISHADS

The Upanishads, also known as Vedānta, are the culmination of the Vedas, both philosophically and chronologically. The Upanishads form a part of the Shruti shastras. They have inspired and sustained Hindus over the millennia. Swami Harshananda, a senior sanyasi and scholar of the Ramakrishna Order, writes, "By advocating the ultimate triumph of the spirit over matter, of man over nature, the Upanishads have created, strengthened and preserved a great tradition of spirituality.... No school of thought, no religious movement, of the subsequent periods in the history of India has remained untouched by their influence, if not pervaded by them."[9] The Upanishads are philosophical dialogues that contain the core of Vedic philosophy and thus form the fundamental *jnāna-kānda* of Hindu philosophy. They are independent and unique works by themselves in thought and sentiment despite their being the end-part of the Vedas. The emphasis from rituals and ceremonies prominent in the Brāhmanic period shifted to philosophy and spiritual wisdom from the Upanishadic period. Tradition asserts that there are more than 200 Upanishads. Among them ten are the oldest and prominent, on which

Sacred manuscripts traditionally wrapped in cloth

9. Swami Harshananda. *A Concise Encyclopaedia of Hinduism, Vol.3.* Bangalore: Ramakrishna Math, 2008, pp. 439-440.

Hinduism

Ādi Shankarāchārya had written his commentaries. They are Isha, Kena, Katha, Prashna, Mundaka, Māndukya, Taittiriya, Aitareya, Chāndogya and Brihadāranyaka. Some also add three other ancient Upanishads, the Shvetāshvatara, Kaushitaki and Maitri, to this list of principal Upanishads.[10] The Upanishads explain the spiritual truths through dialogues, anecdotes, allegories and stories.

The word Upanishad is derived from the root 'sad' which means 'to sit', with the prefixes 'upa' and 'ni' meaning 'very near'. Upanishad thus means 'to sit devotedly very near the guru' to listen to the sublime spiritual truths. The guru, through verbal instructions or mere presence, dissolves the doubts and ignorance of his disciples.

Four brief statements, considered by some Vedāntins to be the gist of the Upanishads, are known as the *mahāvākyas*. They are:

1. *"Prajnānam Brahma"* – "Divine Consciousness is the Supreme Reality" (Aitereya: 5.3).

2. *"Aham Brahmāsmi"* – "I am Brahman" (Brihadāranyaka: 1.4.10).

3. *"Tat tvam asi"* – "You are That (Brahman)" (Chāndogya: 6.8.7).

4. *"Ayam ātmā Brahma"* – "This indwelling self is Brahman" (Māndukya:2).

These four statements contain, in a nutshell, very important elements of Upanishadic philosophy. Then, through discussions, these philosophical statements later developed into many works of Vedānta, like the Mahāvākya Upanishad.

The Upanishadic knowledge of Brahman and Parabrahman, *jiva*, *jagat* and *mukti* was transmitted from generation to generation, in which each disciple after graduating was bound by duty to disseminate it to his sons or disciples.

In the long tradition of Vedic literature, the Upanishads represent the most earnest and sincere efforts of the profound

Manuscript of Ishāvāsya Upanishad

---

10. Hume, Robert Ernest. *The Thirteen Principal Upanishads*. New York: OUP, 1975.

thinkers (sages and seers) to solve the problems of the origin, nature and destiny of man and the universe, and the meaning and value of 'knowing' and 'being'.

TEACHINGS

The Upanishads describe that our world (samsara) is ever changing and perishable. However, the Supreme Reality or Parabrahman, that pervades the world, is eternal and unchanging. He is the bedrock and essence of all things. The Mundaka Upanishad describes the pervasive nature of Parabrahman. The Upanishads confirm that though sages worshipped many manifestations of the Divine, there is only one underlying Parabrahman described variously by wise men as mentioned in the Rig Veda 1.164.45: *"Ekam sat viprāh bahuddhā vadanti."* Everything comes from that Supreme Reality or through his will.

The Katha Upanishad states that the body is destroyed but not the *ātmā* and Paramātmā (God) that reside within it. The Chāndogya Upanishad says *"Tat tvam asi"* – "That thou art" (6.8.7), meaning, you are Brahman. Another interpretation is the idea of the same Parabrahman or Ultimate Reality residing in all atmans (or *ātmās)*. This means that we are all the children of one Reality.

Another feature of the Upanishadic teachings is to be free from the fear of death. It perceives death of the body as a natural process wherein the atman never dies. The atman is inherently pure, always existing and joyful *(sat, chit* and *ānanda)*.

The principle of karma is another significant teaching of the Upanishads. A person is bound by his karmas, and when he becomes free from them, his atman attains liberation.

The Upanishads contain several instructive stories and dialogues between gurus and disciples that teach about the Ultimate Reality and other metaphysical aspects.

The Katha Upanishad describes the story of Nachiketā,

Satyakāma Jābāla gains brahmavidya through obedience to guru

Hinduism

a precocious child. He wanted to know the secret of eternal life from Yama, the lord of death. Despite Yama's offerings of riches and material joys, Nachiketā remained undeterred in his desire to know the secret of eternal life. Finally, Yama imparts to him the immortal knowledge.

In the Chāndogya Upanishad, one also finds stories that explain the nature of Ultimate Reality. One such story describes Satyakāma Jābāla's earnest aspiration to attain *brahmavidyā* (divine knowledge). His unquestioning obedience to the guru's word by tending to cows earns him his grace and subsequently *brahmavidyā*.

Another story from the Chāndogya Upanishad describes guru Dhaumya, who commanded his disciple, Āruni, to stop the water from leaking out of his fields. Āruni lay across the breach and stopped the water from flowing out. The guru was pleased with him and blessed him with *brahmavidyā*.

A third story from the Chāndogya Upanishad is related to Shvetaketu, the son of Āruni. On returning from his guru's ashram after completing his Vedic studies, he was filled with pride. Āruni asked, "Have you attained the knowledge whereby all the unknown becomes known?" Shvetaketu said no. Then his father made him dissolve salt in water and taste it, and said that, like salt Brahman or God is all pervading. With the dawning of this knowledge, Shvetaketu shed his ego.

Prince Dara Shukoh, son of Shah Jahan, translated some of the Upanishads into Persian

The Upanishads are replete with many such stories and dialogues that deal with spiritual knowledge.

World interest in the Upanishads was awakened after their translations into other languages. The Mughal Prince Dara Shukoh's[11] (1613-1659 CE) spiritual longing and quest for reality inspired him to study the Upanishads. He translated some of them from Sanskrit into Persian in 1657 CE. The French scholar and traveller, Anquetil du Perron (1773-1805), introduced Hindu philosophy to the West by translating some of the Upanishads.

Anquetil Du Perron, a French scholar, published a Latin translation of the Upanishads

---

11. Son of Emperor Shah Jahan.

Raja Ram Mohan Roy (1775-1833), a Bengali social activist and founder of the Brahmo Sabhā, which was later renamed as Brāhmo Samāj, made the first English translation. In 1876, Max Müller published a German translation.

The Upanishads have been known as the Himalaya of Indian thought. The German philosopher Arthur Schopenhauer (1788-1860) stated, "In the whole world there is no study so beneficial and so elevating as that of the Upanishads. It has been the solace of my life, it will be the solace of my death."[12]

Paul Deussen (1845-1919 CE), Professor of Philosophy at the Universities of Berlin and Kiel, wrote of the Vedānta as, "And so the Vedānta, is the strongest support of pure morality, is the greatest consolation in the sufferings of life and death."[13]

There are many other great scholars who have appreciated and written copiously about the Vedas, Upanishads and other Hindu Shastras.

Raja Ram Mohan Roy, founder of Brāhmo Samāj, made the first English translation of some of the Upanishads

Arthur Schopenhauer, a German philosopher

SUMMARY

1. The Vedas are the foundational shastras of the Hindus. Hindus believe them to be the oldest sacred texts in the world, revealed by God to the enlightened rishis of India. They are known as the Shruti shastras. Shruti means "that which is heard" or revealed. They include the Vedas (Samhitās), Brāhmanas, Āranyakas and Upanishads.

2. There are four Vedic Samhitās, or collections of mantras or hymns that are commonly referred to as the four Vedas: the Rig Veda, Yajur Veda, Sāma Veda and Atharva Veda. The Rig Veda is the oldest and deals with propitiating the devas (gods of nature) through prayers and rituals.

3. The Samhitās contain hymns for simple rituals. The Brāhmana texts explain the meaning and application of the mantras for performing rites and rituals in *yajnas.*

12. *A Cultural History of India,* edited by A.L. Basham. New Delhi: OUP, 2008, p.474.
13. Deussen, Paul. *The Elements of Metaphysics.* London & New York: Macmillan and Co. 1894, p.337.

The Āranyakas encompass spiritual contemplation and meditation. They mark a shift from ritualism (*karma-kānda*) in the Brāhmana texts to the realm of philosophical ideas in the Upanishads. Thus, the Āranyakas are the links between the Vedas and the Upanishads. Finally, the Upanishads contain the knowledge of Parabrahman, atman, universe and liberation.

4. Some of the concepts dealt with in the Rig Veda are *ruta* (cosmic order), *satya* (moral order), the seeds of *runa* (obligation), hymns of creation and the Ultimate Person or Purusha.

5. The Upanishads are the end parts or culmination of the Vedas, both chronologically and philosophically, so they are known as the Vedānta. In all, there are over 200 Upanishads, of which thirteen are the most ancient and prominent. They reveal the core of Vedic philosophy and comprise the *jnāna-kānda* of the Vedas.

Hindu Shastras

(Sacred Texts): Part II

Veda Vyāsa narrates the Mahābhārata while Shri Ganesha writes. (Inset) Bhagwan Krishna imparts the divine knowledge (Bhagavad Gitā) to Arjuna

Smruti Shastras:
Dharma Shastras, Itihāsas and Purānas

INTRODUCTION

The Vedas are the primary sacred texts of the Hindus which command the highest authority. Since they were not authored by man but revealed by God to the enlightened rishis they are self-authoritative, needing no external endorsement or legitimacy. Next in importance are the Smruti shastras. Smruti means "remembrance". The Smruti shastras were written by great seers based on the teachings they remembered from their spiritual masters. The authority of these shastras is derived from the spiritual standing of their authors and their congruence with the Vedas. Yet, since the Smruti shastras are man-made, they are considered secondary to the Shruti shastras.

The Smruti shastras include a large number of heterogeneous works like the Dharma Shastras, the Itihāsas or epics (Rāmāyana and Mahābhārata), and the Purānas.

The source of the Dharma Shastras lies in one of the six Vedāngas (limbs of Veda). Among the Vedāngas, the Kalpasutras deal with the correct performance of rituals. The Kalpasutras include the Shrautasutras, which focus on the performance of public rituals; the Gruhyasutras, which focus on domestic rites; the Dharmasutras, which explain laws and social ethics; and the Sulvasutras (or Sulba), which outline the geometrical rules of construction for *yajna vedis* or fire-altars, etc. The Dharmasutras, of which the Baudhāyana, Gautama, Vashishtha and Āpastamba are important, are the source of the Dharma Shastras. The Dharma Shastras elaborate upon the

Dharmasutras and are of a later age. The Dharmasutras are entirely in prose whereas the Dharma Shastras are in verse.

The Dharma Shastras are typically named after their authors. Thus, the Dharma Shastras written by Manu (according to Paurāņic tradition he is the forefather of the human race) is called Manu Smruti, by Sage Yājnavalkya the Yājnavalkya Smruti, and by Sage Nārada the Nārada Smruti. These and many other Dharma Shastras prescribe a moral and social code of conduct for individuals, communities and states that encompass the religious, social, political, economical and legal realms.

Another branch of the Smruti shastras are the Itihāsas, which include the Rāmāyana and the Mahābhārata. They are renowned as the great epics of India. A third type of Smruti shastras are the Purānas, which are an invaluable source of religious and historical literature extolling the avatars of God, devas, creation and dissolution of worlds, and royal dynasties. Because it is said that the meaning and purport of the Veda can be understood with the help of the Itihāsa and Purāna shastras,[1] cultivating a proper understanding of these shastras is essential for understanding Hinduism.

We shall now deal with the Dharma Shastras, Itihāsas and Purānas in some detail.

1. DHARMA SHASTRAS

The principle of dharma (morality) and its application in all areas of life is of great importance in Hinduism. Dharma is explained by the Vedas, the Smrutis, and the teachings and conduct of one who is *brahmanishtha* (God-realized) and *shrotriya* (one who knows the true meanings of the sacred texts).

The Dharma Shastras are the primary texts of Hindu law and code of conduct. They often start with creation narratives and conclude with advice on how to attain final liberation

Hindu law is based on the Dharma Shastras

1. *"Itihāsapurānābhyām Vedam Samupabrumhayet."* Mahābhārata 1.67.

or *mukti.* Many of the Dharma Shastras or Smrutis, such as Manu Smruti, Yājnavalkya Smruti, Nārada Smruti, Pārāshara Smruti, etc., cover three major topics: (1) *Āchāra,* i.e., code of conduct for all varnas (classes) and ashramas (stages of life); (2) *Vyavahāra,* i.e., social and financial dealings and interactions which involve civil, criminal and religious regulations and (3) *Prāyashchitta,* i.e., atonement for moral lapses. The Smrutis also deal with rules of inheritance, laws of marriage and families, the duties of kings and ministers, worship of God, sacraments from birth till death, *yajna* rituals, and customs and manners to be observed in daily life. The moral law consists of *vidhi* (prescriptions or dos) and *nishedha* (prohibitions or don'ts). The Dharma Shastras contain principles of dharma as a universal and all-encompassing law, which applies to different circumstances.

We shall briefly consider the three main Dharma Shastras, namely, the Manu Smruti, the Yājnavalkya Smruti and the Nārada Smruti.

I. MANU SMRUTI

Manu formulated the Hindu code of conduct (social, moral and spiritual) from the Shruti shastras in an organized way. He gave the Manu Smruti, which is the earliest and most important of all the Dharma Shastras or moral texts available. It is believed to have taken final shape between 200 BCE and 200 CE. It has twelve chapters and 2,694 *shlokas* or verses dealing with *āchāra, vyavahāra,* and *prāyashchitta.* The Manu Smruti describes in detail the duties of the four varnas (classes) and ashramas (stages), the duties of the king, council of ministers and chief justice, civil and criminal law, and other aspects of society. Manu explicitly states that, of the four stages, the householder *(gruhasthāshrama)* stage is the most important to society, because it supports the other three ashramas and also allows the fulfilment of the four goals of life (four *purushārthas*).

Manu Smruti: The Hindu code of conduct

To understand the Manu Smruti clearly, the commentary by Medhātithi (c. 825-900 CE) is considered to be very useful and important.

Gavin Flood writes, "Schopenhauer's philosophical heir, Friedrich Nietzsche (1844-1900), also admired Hindu ideas and referred to the 'Laws of Manu' as a text far superior to the New Testament."[2] Many others have admired the depth of the Hindu shastras.

II. YĀJNAVALKYA SMRUTI

The second of the Smruti shastras is the Yājnavalkya Smruti (finalized between 100 BCE and 300 CE), which has 52 chapters and 1,010 *shlokas*. It deals with the three main aspects of human life: *āchāra*, *vyavahāra* and *prāyashchitta*. It agrees with Manu Smruti in many aspects and makes clear distinctions between civil and criminal law. In its section on *āchāra* or code of conduct (having 13 chapters), it deals with ceremonies of initiation, duties of the four varnas and ashramas, domestic and social duties and rites of purification and *yajna*. In its section on *vyavahāra* (having 25 chapters) it defines the social rights and duties of the householder. Three hundred and seven verses outline legal procedures and titles of litigation. In its section on *prāyashchitta* or atonement (having 14 chapters), it deals with penalties and means to purge sins. The Yājnavalkya Smruti has an important commentary called the Mitāksharā by Vijnāneshwara (c. 1100 CE). India's current code of Hindu law is mainly based on the Yājnavalkya Smruti and the Mitāksharā. The Mitāksharā was first translated into English in 1810 by the English orientalist Henry Thomas Colebrooke.

III. NĀRADA SMRUTI

The Nārada Smruti deals only with the *vyavahāra* aspect,

A manuscript of Yājnavalkya Smruti

Sage Nārada: The author of Nārada Smruti

---

2. Cited by Flood, Gavin, *An Introduction to Hinduism*. New Delhi: Cambridge University Press, Foundation Books, First South Asian Edition, 2004, p.269. From Nietzsche, *The Twilight of the Idols and the Anti Christ*. Harmondsworth: Penguin, 1968, pp. 56-9.

i.e., social dealings and interactions that involve civil, financial, criminal and religious rules and regulations. It has 21 chapters and 1,028 verses and is believed to have been composed between 100 and 300 CE. It is considered to be an important legal text with reference to ancient criminal laws and court procedures. This text mainly follows the Manu Smruti but differs in some aspects, particular in the area of juristic principles. It is known for its detailed treatment of ordeals called *'divya'*[3] that were employed in courts of law. Manu mentions two forms of ordeals, Yājnavalkya five, and Nārada states nine ordeals.

IV. CONCLUSION

The Dharma Shastras emphasize the practice of dharma for all Hindus for their material, social, moral and spiritual advancement and happiness. They clearly define the duties of the four varnas and ashramas. They also discuss the very important concept of *runa* or obligation to society, family and one's own self. Manu and many others believed that the systems of the four varnas and ashramas were most appropriate for the development and harmony of both the individual and society. In the case of the four ashramas, the first ashrama dictates the observance of *brahmacharya* (celibacy) and dedication to academic study; the second is *gruhasthāshrama* or the life of a householder, during which one fulfils one's desires to raise a family and discharge one's duty to society; the third is *vānaprasthāshrama,* in which one retires from active life to focus completely on spiritual matters; and the last is *sannyastāshrama,* in which one completely renounces the world to fully engage oneself in meditation and other spiritual sadhanas.

The Dharma Shastras play an important role in preserving the character, unity and strength of Hindu society

---

3. *Divya* generally means divine, but when it is used in the Dharma Shastras it means "that which decides a matter in dispute not determined by human means of proof" in a court of law. The suspect could be subjected to an ordeal when eye witness accounts or circumstantial evidence is not available or is not conclusive. The *divyas* range from two to nine, such as, *visha* (administering poison), *koshapāna* (drinking holy water used for bathing an image of worship), *phala* (licking a red-hot ploughshare), *tāndula* (swallowing of specially prepared rice grains) and *taptamāsa* (taking out heated gold pieces with one's bare fingers).

A thoughtful study of the Dharma Shastras or Smrutis shows them to be a source of profound ethical guidance, inspiration and moral strength. Also, while the Smrutis have their roots mainly in the Vedas, they have allowed for necessary adjustments in their codes of conduct in light of continuing societal changes. Because of this flexibility, Hinduism remains a flourishing religion with continuing relevance to the world.

The Dharma Shastras have played a very important role in preserving the character, unity and strength of society. They preserve dharma or the basic values of life, emphasize more so upon duties and responsibilities of people towards society rather than mere individual rights and privileges, and make necessary changes to suit the needs of changing times.

2. ITIHĀSAS

The Rāmāyana (the story of Bhagwan Rāma's life) and the Māhābharata (the story of the Pāndavas and Kauravas) are two great epics that constitute the Itihāsas (histories) of ancient India. Through the narration of incidents that took place in ancient days, the Itihasas stress the importance of the four *purushārthas:* dharma (virtue), *artha* (wealth), *kāma* (worldly desires) and *moksha* (liberation). The Mahābhārata is known as the fifth Veda, even though it is classified as a Smruti (text of human authorship) and not a Shruti (revelation) text. All castes had access to the Itihāsas. The Rāmāyana and Mahābhārata were written by two great sage-poets, Vālmiki and Veda Vyāsa, respectively. Both the epics have played, and are still playing, a significant role in enriching and shaping the lives of Hindus and Hindu society. Formerly, the Vedas were accessible to only the learned Brahmins, but the epics, which portray the teachings of Hinduism in simple language, were available to all. They describe the history of the royal dynasties, and teach moral and spiritual values. The two epics became the sources of poetry, dance, drama, art, architecture and folk songs that have been sung and

Sage Vālmiki scribes the Rāmāyana

enacted in all Indian languages for thousands of years.

There are a few regionally and linguistically different versions of the Rāmāyana and Gitā, but the moral implications and ideals in them are not different.

I. RĀMĀYANA

Sage Vālmiki's Rāmāyana is a poetic description of Bhagwan Shri Rāma's life. It is in Sanskrit and is known as the *ādikāvya* – first poem. It contains 24,253 *shlokas* in seven books *(kāndas)*: Bālakānda, Ayodhyākānda, Aranyakānda, Kishkindhākānda, Sundarakānda, Yuddhakānda and Uttarakānda. The language of the Rāmāyana is simple, beautiful and vivid. It has become so famous that it has become a source of all later Sanskrit epic poems. Like the Māhabhārata, it is recited and enacted in all languages and regions of India as well as in countries like Indonesia, Thailand, and other places where Hinduism has spread.

The story of Rāma[4] is traditionally older than that of the war between the Pāndavas and Kauravas in the Mahābhārata. The Mahābhārata also contains the story of Rāma in brief.

---

4. According to *Ancient World – A New Look*, edited by N. Mahalingam, published in Madras, 1981, some important dates from Rāma's life in accordance to astronomical descriptions in the Rāmāyana and Purānas have been calculated, namely, Rāma's birth – 4439 BCE, his exile – 4414 BCE and his coronation – 4400 BCE.

Murtis of Bhagwan Rāma, Sitā and Hanumān at Swaminarayan Akshardham, New Delhi

Hinduism

The city of Ayodhyā on the bank of River Sarayu, where Bhagwan Rāma was born

Bhagwan Krishna says in the Bhagavad Gita that he is Rāma among the wielders of weapons.[5]

Bhagwan Rāma, in the Rāmāyana, is shown as a perfect being, an incarnation of virtue to emulate. He lived, ruled and remained within the bounds of propriety, and hence he is called Maryādā Purushottama. The main characters of the epic include King Dasharatha of Ayodhyā and his three wives and sons: Kaushalyā, Sumitrā and Kaikeyi. Kaushalyā was the mother of Rāma, Sumitrā gave birth to two sons, Lakshmana and Shatrughna, and Kaikeyi gave birth to Bharata. Rāma, the eldest, became the crown prince of Ayodhyā. The night before Rāma's coronation Kaikeyi demanded of Dasharatha the fulfilment of two wishes he had promised many years earlier. The request came as a shocking surprise for the king. Kaikeyi demanded that Rāma be exiled to the forest for fourteen years, and her son, Bharata, be given the throne instead.

Rāma, his wife, Sitā, and Lakshmana spent their years of exile in the forest, patiently bearing discomforts and trials that came their way. In the final year, Sitā was abducted by the evil Rāvana, the king of Lankā. Then with the help of Sugriva, Jāmbavān, Hanumān and the *vānaras* (monkeys), Rāma killed Rāvana and his army and rescued Sitā. Rāma thus destroyed

---

5. *"Rāmaha shastra bhrutām aham."* B.G. 10.31.

adharma and re-established dharma. Finally, Rāma and Sitā were crowned as the king and queen of Ayodhyā.

The Vālmiki Rāmāyana portrays the glory of Rāma as an ideal man, son, brother, husband and king, possessing virtues of truthfulness, nobility, valour and kindheartedness. Sitā is an ideal of fidelity and devotion. The sacrifice, dedication and allegiance of Lakshmana and Bharata to Rāma are incomparable. Hanumānji's humility, devotion and sacrifice to Rāma are extolled in the Rāmāyana.

The Rāmāyana depicts the picture of an ideal man, family and kingdom (Rāma *rājya*). The emphasis is on virtuous conduct, annihilation of evil *(adharma)* and establishment of righteousness (dharma). It has provided enough ideas and ideals to inspire countless to rise from the human level to divine heights.

In the Rāmacharitamānas, the Hindi version of the Rāmāyana text, Tulasidāsa portrays Rāma as an incarnation of Bhagwan Vishnu. His edition of the Rāmāyana inspires devotion and glory of Rāma as God. The verses *(chopāis)* from the Rāmacharitmānas are very popular and sung with devotion in India and abroad. Notably, it is used as the main text for the Rāmalilā, the famous annual dramatic enactment of Rāma's life in North India.

Out of several other vernacular editions of the Rāmāyana Kamban's Rāmāyana in Tamil, Krittivāsa's Rāmāyana in Bengali, Cherman's 'Rāmāyanam' in Malayalam, Ranganātha's 'Rāmāyanam' in Telugu, Giradhara's 'Rāmacharitra' in Gujarati and Madhav's Rāmāyana in Assamese are popular in their respective states. If the worth of a literary work has to be evaluated by the impact it has had on each succeeding generation, then the Rāmāyana of Vālmiki stands out as supreme in world literature. Its influence and effect on Hindu religion, social values, literature, music, dance, drama, paintings, sculptures, in fact, on so many facets of Indian life, is immense and enduring. It has been said that as long as the mountains

The Kauravas cheat the Pāndavas during a game of dice

stand and rivers flow on this earth, the story of Rāma's divine adventures will remain famous in the world.

II. MAHĀBHĀRATA

There are few other works whose influence on all aspects of life in India has been as profound and perpetual as that of the Mahābhārata. Amidst vast diversities in language, culture and philosophical beliefs, Hindus have been brought together by their shared heritage of the Rāmāyana and the Mahābhārata.

The Mahābhārata is an epic account of the people of greater Bhārata (India) written by Veda Vyāsa. With 18 books (*parvas*) containing about 100,000 Sanskrit *shlokas*; it is eight times the size of Homer's *Iliad* and *Odyssey* combined. The Mahābhārata is a story of triumph of good over evil, that is dharma over *adharma*. In it, Veda Vyāsa has brilliantly described all the shades of human nature – good, bad and evil – and Bhagwan Shri Krishna's divine role in protecting and preserving dharma.

The popular epic begins with the two brothers, Dhritarāshtra and Pāndu. The younger brother, Pāndu, was appointed as the king, but due to a curse he retired to the forest and died. Subsequently, the blind Dhritarāshtra became the regent and administrator. Pāndu's five sons were known as the Pāndavas and Dhritarāshtra's one hundred sons were called the Kauravas. The

Mahābhārata is centred around a feud between these cousins. Duryodhana, the eldest son of Dhritarāshtra and leader of the Kauravas, schemes with his sly maternal uncle, Shakuni, to deceptively win the kingdom of the Pāndavas in a game of dice. Yudhishthira, the eldest of the Pāndavas, loses the game and his kingdom, and he and his brothers are exiled to the forest for thirteen years. After returning, Duryodhana refuses to return their share of the kingdom. Subsequently, a devastating 18-day war follows, leading to the defeat and death of the Kauravas, including that of Duryodhana, Bhishma, Dronāchārya, Karna and many other great warriors. Yudhishthira becomes the king of Hastināpura.

From a mundane perspective, the Mahābhārata was a fierce conflict between cousins. From an ethical standpoint, it was a war between good and evil, justice and injustice; in which the two sides pitted against one another are considered to be analogous to the devas and demons. The war concluded with the victory of dharma. From a metaphorical perspective, the war was not only fought on the grounds of the Kurukshetra, but it is still being fought in our own minds today. It is a battle between the higher and the lower self in man. The Pāndavas, with the help of Shri Krishna (Super-Self), emerged victorious in the conflict against the lower self in man in the form of the Kauravas. The events and teachings of love, war, morality and sacrifice convey powerful moral, social, political and spiritual lessons to one and all and for all times to come.

The Mahābhārata reflects the fundamental lesson of what one can attain through faith and refuge in God. Against great odds, the Pāndavas were victorious because of Shri Krishna's grace and divine intervention. It also conveys the message of *"Yato dharmastato Krushno, yataha Krushnastato jayaha"* – "Where there is dharma there is Krishna, and where there is Krishna there is victory."[6]

---

6. Mahābhārata, Bhishma Parva, 43.60 and Shalya Parva, 62.32.

Bhagwan Krishna reveals his divine cosmic form to Arjuna on the battlefield

The essence of the Mahābhārata lies in the Shrimad Bhagavad Gitā. The Gitā is a part of the Bhishma Parva of the Mahābhārata and contains the teachings of Shri Krishna to Arjuna on the battlefield. It is a perennial source of social, moral and spiritual inspiration for mankind. The essence of the Shrimad Bhagavad Gitā lies in its last *shloka, "Yatra Yogeshwarah Krushno..."* – "Where there is Krishna and Arjuna (God and his ideal devotee) there certainly will be wealth, victory, power and morality."

The Mahābhārata is more than just a history or *itihāsa* narrated as a poem. It is considered to be an authoritative Dharma Shastra – an encyclopaedia of law, morality, social and political philosophy, that lays down principles for the attainment of dharma, *artha, kāma* and *moksha*. It embraces every aspect of life. Hence it is popularly believed, "Whatever there is in the Mahābhārata one will find elsewhere; and what is not in it cannot be found anywhere else".[7] The fact that many Hindus revere the Mahābhārata as the "fifth Veda" is a testament to its vast scope, profound wisdom and spiritual authority.

The Mahābhārata describes many men and women who shine as beacons of ideal moral conduct and spirituality for humanity. The actions of its heroes have been sung uninterruptedly for

---

7. Mahābhārata, Swargārohana Parva, 5.50.

centuries by sages, political thinkers, poets, dramatists and devotees around the world. Bhagwan Krishna and Arjuna are worshipped as Nārāyana and Nara. Their sacred images, known as Nara-Nārāyana, are installed in many mandirs throughout India.

India's glorious culture and civilization have survived and progressed partly because of its shastras, mandirs, divine incarnations, sages, festivals, social customs and leaders. For centuries, the ideals of the Rāmāyana and Mahābhārata have been the soul of India's people, sustaining them in painful and challenging times.

III. BHAGAVAD GITĀ

Authored by Veda Vyāsa, the Bhagavad Gitā is a part of the Bhishma Parva (chapters 25 to 42) of the Mahābhārata, containing 700 *shlokas* in 18 chapters. The Bhagavad Gitā is believed to be the essence of the Upanishads.

"Sarvopanishado gāvo dogdhā gopālanandanaha,
Pārtho Vatsaha sudhir bhoktā dugdhām gitāmrutam mahat."[8]

"All the Upanishads are like cows, Shri Krishna is the cowherd and Arjuna is the calf, the wise person is the drinker, and the nectar-like milk is the Gitā itself." The Gitā mainly contains the dialogue between Bhagwan Shri Krishna and Arjuna on the battlefield of Kurukshetra more than 5,000 years ago.

The Gitā is one of the three texts of Indian philosophy known as Prasthānatrayi. The other two are the Upanishads and the Brahmasutras.

The Bhagavad Gitā, literally means "divine song", was born out of the *vishāda* (sadness) of Arjuna. The battle of the Mahābhārata was about to commence when Arjuna told Bhagwan Krishna, his charioteer, to take his chariot in front of the Kaurava army. On seeing his gurus, elders, kith and kin on the battlefield, Arjuna suddenly became sad and distressed and

The Bhagavad Gitā

8. Bhagavad Gitā (Gitā Māhātmya: 6).

Murti of Shri Gitā Devi, Ahmedabad   *Shri Gitā Mandir, Ahmedabad*

dropped his bow. He felt it would be impossible for him to kill those to whom he was so attached.

Shri Krishna urged him to fight because it was his duty as a Kshatriya (warrior). He then elaborated upon the fleeting attributes of the body and the eternality of the soul.

The Gitā encompasses religion, ethics, metaphysics and the ideal way of living. The enquiries and doubts posed by Arjuna and the solutions given by Shri Krishna are valid even today. A reading of the holy text confers great religious merit, guidance and inspiration in life. The main teachings in the Gitā are: (A) Yoga, (B) Doctrine of Avatar, (C) Cosmic form of God, (D) Doctrines of Karma and Rebirth and (E) *Guru-shishya* Relationship. We shall now deal briefly with each of them.

A. Yoga

The Gitā has shown three main ways to realize God, namely, Jnāna Yoga, Karma Yoga and Bhakti Yoga.

- ❖ **Jnāna Yoga (Chapters 1-6):** The path of spiritual wisdom is called Jnāna Yoga. Knowledge or *jnāna* means discrimination between the real and the unreal. It also means realization of one's soul to be imperishable and immortal, and the body to be perishable and mortal. Shri Krishna explains this immortality of the atman by saying that it cannot be slain, burnt or destroyed in any manner. It is the body which is destroyed and not the atman. One who is born dies and one who dies is born again.[9] Jnāna Yoga also encourages the realization that God resides in all atmans,[10] and therefore every individual possesses divine consciousness.

To attain God-consciousness one needs to discipline the senses, perform spiritual practices and have firm faith. The Gitā praises the *jnāni* or, one who has realized Jnāna Yoga, as being dearest to God.

- **Karma Yoga (Chapters 7-12):** The path of action is known as Karma Yoga, where ideally all activities are to be performed without any attachment and expectation (*nishkāma* karma) for their fruits or results. The Gitā does not preach the renunciation of action but renunciation of the fruit of action.

- **Bhakti Yoga (Chapters 13-18):** Having profound love for God is Bhakti Yoga. It is total surrender to God through absolute devotion.

B. Doctrine of Avatar

The Gitā states that God is born on earth in human form to eradicate *adharma* and establish dharma, i.e., to destroy evil elements and protect the pious. In this way, God is the sustainer of the moral order.[11]

C. The Cosmic Form of God

In the eleventh chapter of the Gitā, Arjuna requests Shri Krishna to reveal his cosmic form (Vishwarupa). The Lord blesses Arjuna with divine sight and he sees the effulgent, infinite and awe-inspiring form of Shri Krishna. His Vishwarupa form has infinite arms, and countless faces radiant with the light of

Bhakti Yoga: Offering food to an image of God

9. B.G. 2.27.
10. B.G. 18.61.
11. B.G. 4. 7-8.

Guru imparts spiritual knowledge to his disciples

innumerable suns and universes. Arjuna also sees the Kaurava army, including Dhritarāshtra, Bhishma, Drona, Karna and its chief warriors being consumed as they enter into the mouth of Shri Krishna's cosmic form. Arjuna is overwhelmed by the immensity of this divine vision, and thus prays to Shri Krishna to revert to his original, serene and beautiful human form. For Arjuna, this incident revealed Shri Krishna's divinity.

D. Doctrines of Karma and Rebirth

The Gitā explains that every karma or action produces a corresponding result. The good and bad karmas are rewarded or punished by God with good or bad fruits. One's karmas are responsible for birth and rebirth, and hence, they are the root cause of suffering. To be liberated from the effects of suffering from karma and rebirth, one has to perform *nishkāma* karma — actions with no desire for their fruits.[12]

E. Guru-shishya Relationship

The Gitā exemplifies a key aspect of the *guru-shishya* relationship,[13] where Bhagwan Krishna, the teacher, imparts knowledge to Arjuna, the disciple. He teaches Arjuna that true

---

12. B.G. 2.51; 3.19; 5.20-21.

13. B.G. 2.7.

knowledge can be obtained by surrendering *(pranipāta)* to the guru, by questioning and asking for clarification of principles *(pariprashna)* and through dedicated service *(sevā)*.[14]

The message of the Gītā is universal. Its aim is to remedy the conflicts that arise from misidentification with the body *(dehabhāva)*, inordinate attachment to kith and kin *(moha)* and base instincts (vāsana: lust, anger and greed) through absolute refuge in God and selfless performance of one's own karmas.

3. PURĀNAS

The Vedas are the foundational sacred texts of Hinduism. But the language and content of the Vedas were difficult for the common people to grasp. To present its wisdom in an easily understandable manner to the masses, Veda Vyāsa wrote the Purānas, which are a valuable source of ancient religious and historical literature. The Purānas help one understand and interpret the Vedas. Its language is simpler and the principles and concepts are explained in a more understandable manner. Thus, the Purānas effectively address the religious, social and moral needs of man.

We are indebted to the Purānas for providing us with the Hindu religious practices like meditating on God, *murti-pujā*, *shrāddha* (rites to propitiate one's ancestors), and duties of varnas and ashramas which embrace the sacred and social aspects of human life. Furthermore, they explain the importance and necessity of building mandirs, consecrating the sacred *murtis* of God, and performing daily rituals. They also emphasize the merits of *tapas (austerity)*, *tirtha-yātra* (pilgrimage), *dāna* (donations), and the need for celebration of festivals and many other aspects of daily life and relations.

The Purānas consist of 18 Mahāpurānas ('great Purānas') and 18 Upapurānas ('secondary Purānas'). They deal predominantly with the glory of avatars of God, devas,

---

14. B.G. 4.34.

The devout read, listen to and revere the Purānas

creation *(sarga)*, dissolution and re-creation *(pratisarga)* of the universe, dynasties of devas *(vamsha)*, the eras of the 14 Manus *(manavantaras)* and the histories of the Solar and Lunar dynasties of kings *(vamshānucharitra)*.[15]

The 18 Mahāpurānas are: (1) Brahma (2) Padma (3) Vishnu (4) Shiva (5) Bhāgavata (6) Nārada (7) Mārkandeya (8) Agni (9) Bhavishya (10) Brahmavaivarta (11) Linga (12) Varāha (13) Skanda (14) Vāmana (15) Kurma (16) Matsya (17) Garuda and (18) Brahmānda. Traditionally, they are divided into three groups of six, out of which one group focuses upon Bhagwan Vishnu, another on Bhagwan Brahmā and the third on Bhagwan Shiva. The six Vaishnava Purānas are the Vishnu, Nārada, Bhāgavata, Garuda, Padma, and Varāha Purānas. The six Purānas related to Brahmā are the Brahma, Brahmānda, Brahmavaivarta, Mārkandeya, Bhavishya and Vāmana Purānas. And the six Shaiva Purānas are the Matsya, Kurma, Linga, Shiva, Skanda and Agni Purānas.

Among all the Mahāpurānas, the Shrimad Bhāgavata is the most popular and widely expounded by religious gurus and proponents of the Bhakti tradition. It has about 18,000 *shlokas*, referring to the ten avatars of Bhagwan Vishnu and

Gurukula students listen to stories from the Purānas

---

15. Swami Harshananda, *A Concise Encylopaedia of Hinduism*, *Vol. 2*. Bangalore: Ramakrishna Math, 2008, p.571.

emphasizing Bhagwan Krishna's life and work. The Bhāgavata Purāna gives importance to bhakti towards God, which is reflected through austerity, charity, tolerance and faith in the lives of devotees like Dhruva, Prahlāda, Harishchandra, Bali, Sudāma, the Gopis and others. The Mārkandeya Purāna is the smallest of all the Purānas, having 9,000 *shlokas*, and the Skanda Purāna is the largest, having 81,000 *shlokas*. A very important work called the Vāsudeva Māhātmya is a part of the Vishnu *khand* (section) of the Skanda Purāna. It emphasizes *ekantika dharma*, i.e., dharma, *jñāna, vairagya* and bhakti, as well as ahimsa or nonviolence.

The growth of the Purāna literature continued through time. They were accommodated under the title 'Upapurānas'. They were considered to be of lesser importance than the Mahāpurānas. Some of the Upapurānas are, Ādi, Narasimha, Kāpila, Kalikā, Vāruna, Vishnudharmottara and Devibhāgavata. The general content of the Upapurānas is on similar lines to the Mahāpurānas. There are also a large number of Sthalapurānas that deal with holy places.

SUMMARY

1. After the Vedas and Upanishads the next authoritative texts are the Smruti shastras which include the Dharma Shastras, Itihāsas, Purānas, Sutra works and others. Smruti means "that which is remembered".

2. The Dharma Shastras were written by Manu, Yājnavalkya, Shankha-Likhita, Parāshara, Nārada and others. They prescribe a moral code of conduct for individuals, communities and states. They deal with the religious, social, political, economical and legal realms of society. The Smrutis are man-made and they have interpreted Vedic principles to guide human practices in changing contexts. Consequently, their canons have grown and some aspects have been changed. This capacity for

change has been important for combating the rigidity in traditions and practices that might develop through time and human failings.

3. The Itihāsas comprise the two great epics: the Rāmāyana and the Mahābhārata. Sage Vālmiki wrote the original Rāmāyana. It is a poetic narration of Bhagwan Rāma's life and work. The Rāmāyana portrays the character of an ideal man, family, society and state.

4. The Mahābhārata, written by Veda Vyāsa, is regarded as the fifth Veda by the Hindus. It vividly depicts an epic war between good and evil, justice and injustice, and dharma and *adharma*. In the end, dharma prevails.

5. The Bhagavad Gitā, a part of the Mahābhārata, is the divine discourse of Bhagwan Krishna to Arjuna on the battlefield of Kurukshetra. Bhagwan Krishna urges Arjuna to perform his duty as a Kshatriya, that is, to fight and protect the righteous and punish the wicked. He imparts *jnāna* yoga, karma yoga and bhakti yoga to Arjuna. Eventually, Arjuna rises, fights and wins.

6. The 18 Mahāpurānas and Upapurānas were written by Veda Vyāsa. Through stories, that describe the genealogies of devas and kings, and teachings, they sing the glory of God's avatars, convey theism, devotion to God, philosophy, *murti-pujā*, ethics, festivals, rituals and ceremonies. They also include cosmology, law codes, moral life, pilgrimages, sacrifices, etc. They are very important literary sources for history of India up to the Gupta dynasty (320 to 600 CE).

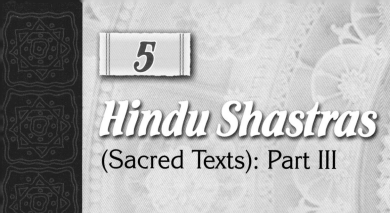

5

Hindu Shastras
(Sacred Texts): Part III

The Āgama sacred texts deal with mode of worship, building of mandirs, etc. (Inset) Items used during worship

Āgamas, Vedic Literature and Sciences
(i.e., Vedāngas, Upavedas and
Sutra literature)

INTRODUCTION

The Āgamas, Vedic literature and sciences, Upavedas and Sutra literature form an important part of the corpus of Hindu shastras.

The Āgamas are a class of Hindu religious literature which practically form the basis of almost all Hindu religious practices of the post Vedic era. The name Āgama means "that which teaches the Truth from all aspects", and so its followers hold the Āgamas in equal importance to the Vedas or any sacred book. In practice, they deal with deities like Shiva, Shakti and Vishnu, and also their respective mandirs and worship rituals. The three groups of Āgamas are Shaiva Āgamas, Shākta Āgamas and Vaishnava Āgamas. They deal mainly with philosophical subjects, yogic practices, mandir architecture, science of *murti* consecration, rituals and code of conduct. The Āgamas are treated by their respective followers as equal in importance to the Vedas.

The Vedic literature and sciences include the Vedāngas or "limbs of the Veda", Upavedas ('lesser' or 'complementary' Vedas) and Sutra literature (short formulaic statements). The Vedāngas are texts of the subsidiary sciences of phonetics, prosody, grammar, etymology, astronomy, geometry and sacrificial rituals that help one understand and study the Vedas in their proper context.

The four Upavedas include Ayurveda (science of medicine), Gāndharvaveda (science of music and dance), Dhanurve (science of archery and warfare) and Sthāpatyaveda (science of architecture). Some scholars also include Arthaveda or Arthashāstra within the Upavedas.

The Sutra literature consists of short formulaic statements or aphorisms, expressing a general truth. They had to be memorized by students and commented upon and explained by teachers. It includes the Kalpasutras, *Bhaktisutras,* Brahmasutras, *Sānkhyasutras.*

We will examine in detail each of these types of literary forms, beginning with the Āgamas.

1. THE ĀGAMAS

The Āgamas or Tantras[1], like the Vedas (also called Nigamas), are another class of very sacred Hindu texts. The Āgamas deal with beliefs and practices related to Vishnu, Shiva and Shakti. It is difficult to fix their time of origin, however it can be stated that some of the Āgamas of the early Vishnu sects were in existence by the time of the Mahābhārata. The development of the Āgamas of the other schools might have continued till 800 CE.

The Āgamas are considered to be revealed *(shruti)* like the Vedas and are thus held in equal importance and authority by their devout followers.[2] They deal with God, sacred living, mode of worship, building of mandirs, consecration of images, yoga, creation and philosophy.

The three main groups of Hindu Āgamas or Tantras are: Vaishnava, Shaiva and Shākta. There are also the Buddhist and Jain Āgamas or Tantras. Of the Hindu Āgamas, there are ⁸8 main Vaishnava Āgamas, 92 main Shaiva Āgamas and 77

antras proper are the Word of Shiva and Shakti." Sir John Woodroffe (1865-1936
ritish Orientalist, *Shakti and Shakta, Essays and Addresses on the Shakta Tantrashastra.*
Luzac & Co., 1918, p. 21.
ly, it [Tantras] got restricted to a particular class of literature, a literature primarily
the cult of Shakti or the Divine Mother." Swami Harshananda. *A Concise Ency-*
Hinduism, Vol. 3, 2008, p. 379.
e the *Agampramānya* by Yāmunāchārya. Baroda: Oriental Research Institute.

main Shākta Āgamas. Though each of the three groups has different doctrines and regards itself as superior, they share common elements in prescribed spiritual practice (sadhana) and ritual practice. The Āgamas consist of four parts called *pādas*, each having many Sanskrit verses in metrical form: (1) the contents of the *charyā pāda* deal with observance of religious injunctions, right conduct, the *guru-shishya* relationship, community life and town planning – with focus on the mandir as its centre, (2) the *kriyā pāda* describes and defines worship rituals and mandir – from site selection for construction of mandir, architectural design, construction methods, iconography (*murti* sculpture), rules for pujaris, festivals and home-shrine rituals; (3) the *yoga pāda* reveals meditation and yogic discipline to purify body and mind and awaken the *kundalini shakti* and (4) the *jnāna pāda* elaborates on philosophical topics like the doctrine and nature of Bhagwan, *jivas, māyā* and the means to attain *moksha*.

A brief description of the three groups of Āgamas follows:

I. Vaishnava Āgamas

The Vaishnava Āgamas, also called Samhitās, consist of the Pāncharātra Āgamas and the Vaikhānasa Āgamas. Both teach that Vishnu is the "Supreme Truth" and the highest deity, and emphasize the various types of worship in mandirs. This worship involves *murtis* of several deities and devotees known as *nitya muktas*.

The Pāncharātra Āgamas were revealed by Bhagwan Nārāyana to five disciples in five nights. They consider Bhagwan Vishnu and Lakshmiji as the principal deities or divine couple (*divya dampati*) and deal extensively with rituals of *murti-pujā*, rules of mandir architecture, and the path of bhakti. The Pāncharātra Āgamas also prescribe a devotional way of life for followers that include five fundamental practices: (1) going to the mandir and concentrating on God with mind, body and

Bhagwan Vishnu and Lakshmiji are the principal deities in the Pāncharātra Āgamas

speech *(abhigama)*; (2) collecting materials for the worship of God *(upādāna)*; (3) actual worshipping God *(ijyā)*; (4) studying shastras *(swādhyāya)* and (5) meditating on the *murti* of God (yoga).

The Vaikhānasa Āgamas claims to have their roots in the Vedas. They deal with daily rituals of making Vedic offerings into fire and the daily worship of Bhagwan Vishnu's *murti* in the inner sanctum of a mandir. The daily worship rituals include welcoming Bhagwan Vishnu as a royal guest and offering him food with the chanting of Vedic mantras. The votaries of Vaikhānasa came to function as chief pujaris in many south Indian mandirs. Even today this is true, particularly at the Tirupati Venkateshwara (Bālāji) Mandir, the most famous Vaishnava pilgrimage centre in Andhra Pradesh, South India.

The Vaikhānasa sect clearly insists upon its purely orthodox or Vedic status.

The *Catalogue of Pāncharātra,*[3] with about 460 Vaishnava Āgamas, was recently researched and compiled by two BAPS Swaminarayan saint-scholars.

II. SHAIVA ĀGAMAS

The Shaiva Āgamas are the sacred texts of the Shaiva Sampradāya in which Bhagwan Shiva is the presiding deity. They contain information on the Shaiva philosophical doctrine, rituals, worship, religious practices, architecture of Shiva mandirs, sculpture of the *murtis* and art in general. The Shaiva Āgamas say that souls are in bondage, and *moksha* is attained through an understanding of the nature of six principles: (1) Lord (Pati); (2) knowledge *(vidyā)*; (3) false knowledge *(avidyā);* (4) individual soul *(pashu)*; (5) noose of impurities *(pāsha)* and (6) worship of Shiva *(moksha-kārana)*. They emphasize on the worship of Shiva *(Pati)* for removing the noose of impurities

Bhagwan Shiva is praised in the Shaiva Āgamas

3. *Catalogue of Pāncharātra.* Researched and compiled by Sadhu Shrutiprakashdas and Sadhu Parampurushdas. Gandhinagar, Gujarat: AARSH (Akshardham), 2002.

(*pāsha*) from the individual soul (*pashu*). Only through Shiva's grace do the souls (*pashus*) attain liberation.

The Shaiva Āgamas principally prescribe *murti-pujā* and rituals, and propagate the realization of Shiva as the ultimate goal.

III. SHĀKTA ĀGAMAS

In the Shaiva Āgamas one finds dialogues between Bhagwan Shiva and Pārvati, in which the former is the master and the latter his disciple. However in the Shākta Āgamas, also known as Tantras, the opposite can be seen, where Pārvati (also known as Sati, Devi, Umā and Kāli) is the guru and Bhagwan Shiva is her disciple. So it is Shiva who asks questions to her and Pārvati answers.

There are two main groups of Shākta Āgamas or Tantras: the Dakshināchāra Tantras or the "right-hand path", also known as Samaya or Sāmāyika *marga* and the Vāmāchāra Tantras or the "left-hand path", also called Kaula. The Dakshināchāra teaches the worship of the deity Dakshina Kālikā according to Vedic modes of worship and sadhana for ultimate realization. And the Vāmāchāra promotes the ritual use of "five Ms" (*panchamakāras*), namely, wine (*madya*), fish (*matsya*), meat (*māmsa*), parched grains and gestures (mudra) and extra-marital sexual union (*maithuna*) for spiritual realization. So, the Dakshināchāra teaches spiritual practices that are decent and morally acceptable, whereas the Vāmāchāra advocate the belief that even aberrations can be raised to the level where they become spiritual practice, resulting in the realization of Truth.

The Shākta Āgamas teach about the worship of Shakti or the Universal Mother – the female principle of Shiva – namely, Pārvati and her other forms, such as, Durgā, Ambā, Kāli and others. The objective is to attain material power, prosperity and finally liberation.

Durgā is one of the devis praised in the Shākta Āgamas

Students of a gurukula recite Vedic mantras on the banks of River Gaṅgā

2. VEDIC LITERATURE AND SCIENCES

There are other shastras which have their origin in the Vedas and were later developed by different rishis. They are known as Vedic literature and sciences and are classified as Smruti shastras. These texts are, (i) Vedāngas (limbs of Vedas), (ii) Upavedas ('lesser' or 'complementary' Vedas), (iii) Sutras (short formulaic statements or aphorisms) which include the Brahmasutras. A brief description of each is as follows:

I. VEDĀNGAS

To make the spiritual and ritual concepts of the Vedas easily understandable, the rishis developed the Vedāngas – "limbs of the Vedas". These are subsidiary works of Vedic knowledge that help one to study, understand and practice the teachings of the Vedas. The six Vedāngas are Shikshā (phonetics), Chandas (prosody), Vyākarana (grammar), Nirukta (etymology), Jyotisha (Astronomy, Astrology, Mathematics, and Geometry) and Kalpa (Science of sacrificial rites and rituals).

Shikshā and Chandas are aids for pronouncing and reciting Vedic mantras correctly, Vyākarana and Nirukta are for understanding their meaning, and Jyotisha and Kalpa provide appropriate times and methods for performing the Vedic sacrificial rites and rituals. The origins of these six auxiliary

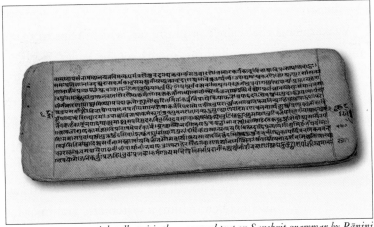

Ashtādhyāyi is the renowned text on Sanskrit grammar by Pānini

'sciences' are found in the Vedas. A brief description of each of them follows.

❖ Shikshā

This branch teaches the science of phonetics or pronunciation and recitation of the Vedic mantras. Any deviation in the pronunciation can change the meaning and thus mar the desired effect or purpose for which the mantras are chanted and applied in sacrifices.

Some outstanding examples of Shikshā texts include the *Pāniniya Shikshā* by the great grammarian Sage Pānini and the writings of Sage Bhāradwāja.

❖ Chandas

Chandas is the science of prosody. It deals with versification, or the rules for the metres in which Vedic mantras and poems were composed. There are eleven major and minor metres like, Gāyatri, Anushtup, Ushnik, Trishtup, Jagati, etc. Pingala is the earliest known author of the Chanda shastra written in *sutra* form, which became popularly known as *Pingala* shastra.

According to tradition, before reciting any Vedic mantra the reciter has to pay respect to the respective rishi, *devatā* and *chandas* of the mantra.

❖ Vyākarana

Vyākarana is the science of grammar, which helps to make language clearer. It is called the 'mouth' of the Vedas. Without it, the Vedas and all other Shruti works would be impossible to understand correctly. The earliest available text on Sanskrit grammar today is the *Ashtādhyāyi* of Pānini (c. 500 BCE). Pānini wrote his work for the understanding of the Vedic and mainly the classical Sanskrit language, and especially for the style of Sanskrit spoken in his day. Though the Vedas were revealed and chanted many millennia before him, a systematic grammar for both Vedic and classical Sanskrit was first given by Pānini. The *Ashtādhyāyi* is considered to be the most basic and standard work in Sanskrit grammar today. It has been recognized as one of the greatest intellectual achievements of all time. Pānini, however, mentions several scholars who were grammarians and lexicographers before him.

It is worth noting that some ancient grammarians like Patanjali (200 BCE) and Bhartruhari (between 450 and 500 CE) developed a spiritual philosophy out of grammar. They identified the eternal aspect of sound with Brahman (*shabda* Brahman) of Vedānta by writing the *Mahābhāshya* and *Vākyapadiya* respectively. Vyākarana also includes dictionaries like *Amarakosha, Halāyudhakosha* and others.

❖ Nirukta

There was a Sanskrit work called *Nighantu,* now extinct, which was a dictionary of difficult Vedic words. The work is attributed to Yāska by some scholars, but it is not certain who the real author was. According to Yāska, the difficult words were collected and classified by the descendants of ancient sages.

The *Nirukta* is the oldest Indian treatise on etymology, philology and semantics, also ascribed to Yāska. The work is available today, and it is a commentary on the *Nighantu.* It thus enables one to understand the Vedas. Sage Yāska was the last of the commentators on *Nighantu*. His work on *Nirukta* is the best known work available. It is considered to be the earliest Vedabhāshya or commentary on the Vedas. It consists of three parts: (1) a list of synonyms called *Naighantuka Kānda,* (2) a list of words used only in the Vedas called *Naigama Kānda,* and (3) a list of words relating to deities and rituals known as *Daivata Kānda.* In the *Daivata Kānda, Yāska* gives the etymological explanation of the names of the deities. Finally, *Nirukta* ends with instructions, teachings and eulogies of the Vedic devas.

❖ Jyotisha

Jyotisha is the Vedic science of astrology that includes astronomy, geometry and mathematics. Movements of the sun, moon, planets and constellations are observed and recorded in order to fix suitable days and auspicious times for the commencement and conclusion of sacred rites and *yajnas* for various purposes. The influence of the movement of celestial bodies on human life was also studied (astrology). References to eclipses are found in the Rig Veda.

Two Jyotisha books available from the early Vedic period are *Archajyotisha* of the Rig Veda with 36 verses and *Yajusjyotisha* of the Yajur Veda with 43 verses, and from the later period we have the *Atharvajyotisha* with 162 verses.

Later, the astronomy section of *jyotisha* science was gradually advanced by the works of Āryabhatta I (476 CE), Varāhamihira (580 CE), Brahmagupta (628 CE), Bhāskarāchārya I (700 CE), Āryabhatta II (c. 950 CE) and Bhāskarāchārya II (1114 CE). These rishi-scientists helped in the development of Hindu astronomy and astrology.

❖ Kalpa

Kalpa is one of the Vedāngas which lays down the rules for the correct performance of rituals, ceremonial and sacrificial acts. Kalpa means *prayoga* or practical method to conduct Vedic sacrifices correctly. We will deal with Kalpa in detail in the Sutra literature section, following the section on Upavedas.

II. UPAVEDAS

In addition to the four Vedas and Upanishads there are four Upavedas or subsidiary Vedas. These deal mainly with 'secular' sciences such as Āyurveda (science of medicine), Gāndharvaveda (science of music and dance), Dhanurveda (science of archery and warfare) and Sthāpatyaveda (science of architecture). Some scholars consider Arthaveda or Arthashāstra instead of Sthāpatyaveda as one of the four Upavedas. The four Upavedas are important because they deal with worldly subjects, namely, man, matter and society. They are considered to be very important for their contribution in the development of Indian civilization and culture.

We shall deal briefly with each of them.

✦ Ayurveda

Ayurveda is a science that deals with 'knowledge of life' and longevity. The main texts of this life science are *Sushruta Samhitā* and *Charaka Samhitā*. Ayurveda deals with medicine and health. A long and healthy physical and mental life is necessary for a prolonged spiritual practice and experience. The source of this science, according to sage Sushruta (600 BCE), lies in the Atharva Veda which is aptly called Bhaishajya Veda (the Veda of medicine and treatment of diseases). Ayurveda includes methods of diagnoses and treatment for physiological and psychological illness. It deals with embryology, hygiene, anatomy, surgery, etc.

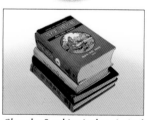

Charaka Samhitā is the principal text of Ayurveda

Dominik Wujastyk, a Senior Research Fellow at the world-famous Wellcome Centre for the History of Medicine at the University College of London and the author of *The Roots of Ayurveda*, writes in his article 'The Science of Medicine', "Indian medicine, as a systematic and scholarly tradition, begins historically with the appearance of the great medical encyclopedias of Charaka, Sushruta and Bhela about two thousand years ago. Just as Pānini's famous linguistic study of Sanskrit leaps into the historical record fully formed, like the Buddha from Queen Maya's side, so the medical encyclopedias too emerge with a learned medical tradition in an almost fully articulated form."[4] Obviously from this one can infer that medical science must have developed fully in ancient India before the emergence of the *Sushruta Samhitā* and *Charaka Samhitā*.

According to Ayurveda, the material bodies of human beings are composed of *kalā* (protective layer), *dhātu* (component matter), *mala* (eliminations), three *doshas* (humours), *agni* (digestive fire) and *kriyā* (movement or activity). Among these six the most important is the principle of three constitutional elements called humours in the human body, namely, *vāta* (air), *pitta* (bile) and *kapha* (phlegm). *Vāta* (air in body) includes all phenomena of motion and its essential components are ether and air. *Kapha* deals with cooling and preservation, and production of various secretions like mucus and cough. Its essential components are earth and ether. *Pitta* (bile) is made of fire and ether. It deals with metabolism, energy production, process of digestion, etc. A person may be constitutionally brisk (with *vāta* dominating) or fiery (with *pitta* in dominance) or phlegmatic (with *kapha* being the prevalent element). But, according to Ayurveda, only when all three elements are in equilibrium in the human body a person is said to be healthy.

Āchārya Charaka, father of Ayurveda

An ayurvedic doctor diagnoses a patient with reference to the relative levels of his or her *vāta, pitta* and *kapha*. The ancient Indian rishis, Charaka and Sushruta, practised ayurveda and surgery respectively. Āchārya Charaka (c.100 CE), who wrote the *Charaka Samhitā,* is known as the 'Father of Indian medicine'. Through his intuitive powers he had realized the medicinal qualities of 100,000 plants and herbs. Since the medications are herbal with least side-effects, they are becoming increasingly

Āchārya Sushruta, the Father of Indian surgery

---

4. *The Blackwell Companion to Hinduism,* edited by Gavin Flood. Oxford: Blackwell Publishing, 2005, p.393.

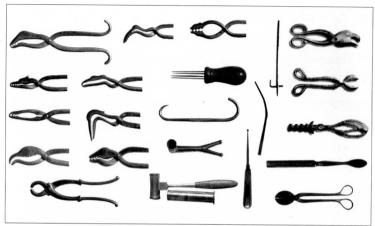

Some of the surgical instruments during Sushruta's time

popular throughout the world.

According to Charaka a long and healthy life is not possible if a person does not live morally. Morality gives rise to *prajñā* or wisdom, which gives peace of mind and leads to longevity and happiness. When this *prajñā* is abused, it causes all types of sickness.

Ācārya Sushruta (600 BCE) is popularly known as the 'Father of Surgery in India'. In the *Sushruta Samhitā*, a unique encyclopaedia of surgery, he details 300 types of operations he performed, along with 125 types of surgical instruments that he used. He is lauded as an early pioneer of plastic surgery and anaesthesia.

Ayurvedic science is divided into eight major topics:

1. Shalya-tantra — surgery and midwifery
2. Shālakya-tantra — study of diseases of head, eyes, nose, throat, etc.
3. Kāyachikitsā — therapeutics
4. Bhutavidyā — mental diseases (psychiatry)
5. Kaumārabhrutya-tantra — paediatrics and obstetrics
6. Agada-tantra toxicology — remedies for venoms
7. Rasāyana-tantra — geriatrics, prevention of disease and improvement of vigour, memory
8. Vājikarana-tantra — prevention of venereal diseases, virilification

Some Indian musical instruments

Tableau depicts ancient Indian weapons, Swaminarayan Akshardham, New Delhi

Ayurveda also deals with the treatment of plants and animals. Texts of Ayurveda prescribe a strict code of conduct for the physician.

❖ Gāndharvaveda

According to tradition *gandharvas* are expert musicians of *swarga* (the abode of the devas). It is believed that there used to be a work called Gāndharvaveda with 30,000 verses on music, which is not available now.

Gāndharvaveda dealt with the science of music and the sacred performing arts. It derived its origin in the Sāma Veda. It included vocal and instrumental music, dance and drama. There are seven *svaras* (notes) from which *rāgas* are produced, corresponding to the appropriate time of day and season. The *rāgas* create astonishingly powerful physical, psychological and spiritual effects. While Western music has only two modes — major and minor scales — Indian music uses dozens of different modes.

Bharatamuni's *Nātyashāstra,* available today, is an extraordinary text on music, dance and drama.

❖ Dhanurveda

Dhanurveda is the science of archery, martial arts and

weaponry. It is a military science, which is mentioned in the Rig Veda and Aitareya Brāhmana. It is also known as *shastravidyā* and it originates from the Yajur Veda. It deals with *shastra* and *astra. Shastra*[5] means weapons which are used with one's hands in war, such as swords and maces, and *astra* means weapons that are shot like arrows. Dhanurveda also deals with the manufacturing of and training with weapons.

Although there is no ancient scientific work by the name of Dhanurveda, a text called Dhanurveda Samhitā, belonging to a later period, is still extant.

❖ Sthāpatyaveda or Vāstushāstra

Some scholars consider Sthāpatyaveda or Vāstushāstra as one of the Upavedas. It deals with the Hindu science of sacred architecture and the *sthapati* or architect. Traditionally, there are 18 teachers of architecture to whom Sthāptyaveda is ascribed. The two most well known among them are Vishvakarmā (the architect of the devas) and Maya (the architect of the asuras). This important science has its origin in the Yajur Veda, wherein the sacrificial altar or *yajna vedi* was constructed with utmost precision and care in different geometrical patterns. Similarly, Hindu mandirs were built in different styles like Nāgara, Drāvida and Vesara with painstaking perfection by the master builders-cum-architects. It is remarkable that thousands of mandirs of ancient India, in locations as varied as mountains, caves and seashores, still stand today as majestic reminders of this ancient science.

The continuing discovery of various sites of the Indus Valley civilization in the 20th and 21st century conclusively proves that India of remote antiquity had great architects and town planners.

Vishvakarmā, the divine architect

5. *Shastra* (means weapons) should not be confused with shastra (not italicized because it appears in Concise Oxford English Dictionary, Eleventh edition, 2004.) which means Hindu sacred text.

Some of the ancient books on architecture include *Abhilashitārthachintāmani, Brihatsamhitā, Mānasāra, Samarānganasutradhāra,* and *Mayamatashilpashāstra.* The *Arthashāstra* of Kautilya and some Purānas, like the Agni Purāna, Matsya Purāna and Padma Purāna, also contain much information about architecture.

❖ Arthaveda or Arthashāstra

In ancient India, Arthaveda meant the book containing knowledge of material wealth and the means of acquiring it. The best available work of Arthaveda is the *Arthashāstra* of Kautilya (c. 372 BCE). Kautilya was also known as Chānakya and Vishnugupta. He was the main adviser to King Chandragupta Maurya (340 BCE). Kautilya's *Arthashāstra* has its roots in the Atharva Veda. Shaunaka rishi, in his work *Charanavyuha,* lists *Arthashāstra* as an Upaveda. This work has 6,000 *shlokas* that deal with 180 different topics like politics, law and economics. It is one of the most ancient and brilliant works in the world. In addition to economics it also covers such subjects as relations with enemy states, preparation of army for all types of combat, espionage system, revenue collection, formation of the judiciary and discharging of justice.

III. SUTRA LITERATURE

The Sutra literature is a part of ancient Sanskrit literature, having a unique style of expressing an idea, concept or view in brief through very short statements, formulas or aphorisms. They were introduced because memorizing the increasingly voluminous Smruti literature became impossible. The *sutras* were required in order to carry on the oral tradition, and there are thus a large number of different Sutra works on nearly every traditional subject. Much as a thread in a garland binds everything together, a *sutra,* which literally means 'thread', binds together all aspects of the topics in each work. The *sutras*

Kautilya,
the author of Arthashāstra

The Shrautasutras prescribe the way to perform Vedic yajnas

succinctly deal with the essential ideas or concepts of subjects like religion, philosophy, grammar, and law.

Nearly all systems of Indian philosophy and all subjects of traditional learning in ancient India have their own *sutra* works. In the realm of religion there are Kalpasutras (which has four sections) like the *Bhaktisutras* of Nārada and Shāndilya. In philosophy there are the Brahmasutras (also known as Vyāsasutras or Vedāntasutras), *Mimānsāsutras, Sānkhyasutras, Yogasutras, Nyāyasutras* and *Vaisheshikasutras*. Pānini wrote the *Ashtādhāyi*, a work of Sanskrit grammar, in the *sutra* style.

❖ Kalpasutras of Kalpa

Kalpasutras deal with social and religious ceremonies and rituals. The Kalpasutras belong to a period later than that of the major ancient thirteen Upanishads. They are divided into four sections:

1. The Shrautasutras are concerned with correct performance of Vedic *yajnas* in public. In them, 'social and spiritual' ceremonies and rituals are described. The authors of the Shrautasutras are Āshwalāyana, Shānkhāyana and others.

2. The Ghruhyasutras give an exposition of domestic ceremonies and rituals related to householders, such as

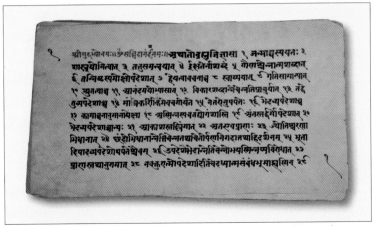

the sixteen samskaras, duties of teachers, pupils, kings and others. They were also employed for home building, cattle breeding and other activities. The Gruhyasutras of Bodhāyana and Āpastamba are well known.

3. The Dharmasutras explain law, religion, customs, usage and duties of varna and ashrama in life. The well known Dharmasutras are of Sage Gautama and Bodhāyana.

4. The Sulvasutras or Sulbasutras are concerned with rules for measuring and building fire altars for *yajnas*. They were concerned with a subject called *lekhā ganita* – the mathematics of measurement. Their preoccupation with this subject yielded extensive knowledge of elementary geometry. Thus the origin of geometry is believed to be in the Sulvasutras.

❖ BRAHMASUTRAS OR VEDĀNTASUTRAS

The Brahmasutras by Bādarāyana or Veda Vyāsa are also known as Vedāntasutras or Vyāsasutras. They are the sacred philosophical book of *sutras* or aphorisms that summarize the teachings of the Upanishads. The Brahmasutras have 550 *sutras* arranged in four parts, dealing with the Ultimate Reality or Brahman, atman, *jagat, māyā* and *mukti* or *moksha*. The *sutras* are very short statements, sometimes consisting of only two or three words. They cannot be understood properly without a profound teacher of a living tradition or a commentary (*bhāshya*) of the great, erudite *āchārya*.

The Brahmasutras are one of the three most important works of Indian philosophy, called the Prasthānatrayi. The Upanishads are called Shrutiprasthāna, the Brahmasutras are Nyāyaprasthāna and the Bhagavad Gitā is Smrutiprasthāna. *Prasthāna* means a treatise.

The Brahmasutras are a work of philosophy based on logic or Nyāya, whereas the other two are based on Shruti and Smruti traditions respectively. It seems that the Brahmasutras were a part of the ancient oral tradition of the Vedānta system. Their *sutras* were memorized by students and the meanings were explained by authorized teachers.

The Brahmasutras begin with the *sutra, "Athāto Brahma jignāsā"*, which means, "Now then [let us have] an enquiry about Brahman," and concludes with the *sutra, Anāvruttihi sabdāt, Anāvruttihi sabdāt*, which means, "Not returning back in samsāra, in the mundane world – which means the attainment of *mukti*."

In the first chapter (or *pāda*) there is a discussion on Brahman as the sole and supreme cause of all things and rejection of other philosophical systems (i.e., Sānkhya, etc.) that do not accept Brahman to be the Supreme Reality.

In the second chapter, arguments for the rejection of Sānkhya continue from the first chapter. The Bhāgavata system is mentioned at the end.

The third chapter deals with *jivātmā*. There is also a discussion on the state of dreams, dreamless sleep, meditation and types of knowledge of Brahman.

The fourth chapter continues discussing the topic of meditation and it ends with the description of conditions of a knower of Brahman after his death.

The Brahmasutras say that Vedic authority is the highest in

matters of *moksha*. The Brahmasutras became so popular that almost all the renowned *āchāryas* wrote their commentaries on them. The first commentary available to us is that of Ādi Shankarāchārya who wrote the *Shānkarabhāshya* to establish his own school of Kevalādvaita Vedānta.

Some of the *āchāryas* who have written commentaries on the Brahmasutras are:

COMMENTATOR	SAMPRADĀYA OR SCHOOL OF VEDĀNTA	NAME OF BHĀSHYA ON THE BRAHMASUTRAS
1. Ādi Shankarāchārya	Kevalādvaita	*Shānkarabhāshya*
2. Bhāskarāchārya	Bhedābheda	*Brahmasutra bhāshya*
3. Rāmānujāchārya	Vishishtādvaita	*Shribhāshya*
4. Nimbārkāchārya	Dvaitādvaita	*Vedāntaparijāta-saurabha*
5. Madhvāchārya	Dvaita	*Brahmasutra bhāshya*
6. Vallabhāchārya	Shuddhādvaita	*Anubhāshya*
7. Baldevāchārya	Achintyabhedābheda	*Govindabhāshya*
8. Shripati	Dvaitādvaita	*Shrikarabhāshya*

The above mentioned eight well-known schools of Vedānta are but a few of the many important ones. Each of the *āchāryas* explained the most diverse philosophical and theological views in their interpretation of the very same aphorisms. They have the liberty to interpret, because the *sutras* are brief, containing mostly two, three or four Sanskrit words which have more than two or three meanings.

Undoubtedly the Brahmasutras have influenced all important aspects of Hindu philosophy, religion and culture, including the modern Hindu movements.

SUMMARY

1. The Āgamas are believed by some to match the Vedic texts in spiritual and religious authority. They prescribe the mode of worship of deities in mandirs and prescribe a way of life in relation to the systems of devotion and worship.

2. The other shastras include the Vedāngas or limbs of the Vedas and the Upavedas or 'complementary' Vedas. The Vedāngas include Shikshā (phonetics), Chandas (prosody), Vyākarana (grammar), Nirukta (etymology), Jyotisha (astronomy, astrology, mathematics and geometry), and Kalpa (science of sacrificial rites and rituals).

3. The Upavedas or subsidiary Vedas, derived from the Vedas, are Āyurveda (science of health), Gāndharvaveda (science of music), Dhanurveda (military science) and Sthāpatyaveda or Vāstuveda (the science of sacred and 'secular' architecture).

4. The Brahmasutras or the Vedāntasutras are a systematization of the teachings of the ancient Upanishads by Bādarāyana Veda Vyāsa. They are one of the three shastras that form the Prasthānatrayi. The other two are the Upanishads and the Bhagavad Gitā. Almost all the great *āchāryas* have written commentaries on them to establish their own independent Vedānta philosophies.

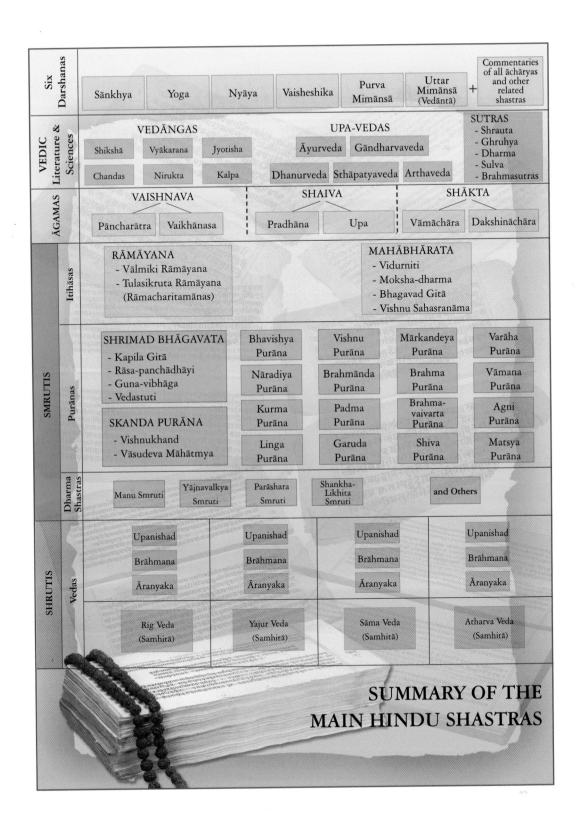

Six Darshanas	Sānkhya	Yoga	Nyāya	Vaisheshika	Purva Mimānsā	Uttar Mimānsā (Vedāntā)	+	Commentaries of all āchāryas and other related shastras

VEDIC Literature & Sciences

VEDĀNGAS			UPA-VEDAS		SUTRAS
Shikshā	Vyākarana	Jyotisha	Āyurveda	Gāndharvaveda	- Shrauta - Ghruhya - Dharma - Sulva - Brahmasutras
Chandas	Nirukta	Kalpa	Dhanurveda	Sthāpatyaveda	Arthaveda

ĀGAMAS

VAISHNAVA		SHAIVA		SHĀKTA	
Pāncharātra	Vaikhānasa	Pradhāna	Upa	Vāmāchāra	Dakshināchāra

SMRUTIS

Itihāsas

RĀMĀYANA	MAHĀBHĀRATA
- Vālmiki Rāmāyana - Tulasikruta Rāmāyana (Rāmacharitamānas)	- Vidurniti - Moksha-dharma - Bhagavad Gitā - Vishnu Sahasranāma

Purānas

SHRIMAD BHĀGAVATA	Bhavishya Purāna	Vishnu Purāna	Mārkandeya Purāna	Varāha Purāna
- Kapila Gitā - Rāsa-panchādhāyi - Guna-vibhāga - Vedastuti	Nāradiya Purāna	Brahmānda Purāna	Brahma Purāna	Vāmana Purāna
SKANDA PURĀNA	Kurma Purāna	Padma Purāna	Brahma-vaivarta Purāna	Agni Purāna
- Vishnukhand - Vāsudeva Māhātmya	Linga Purāna	Garuda Purāna	Shiva Purāna	Matsya Purāna

Dharma Shastras

Manu Smruti	Yājnavalkya Smruti	Parāshara Smruti	Shankha-Likhita Smruti	and Others

SHRUTIS

Vedas

Upanishad	Upanishad	Upanishad	Upanishad
Brāhmana	Brāhmana	Brāhmana	Brāhmana
Āranyaka	Āranyaka	Āranyaka	Āranyaka
Rig Veda (Samhitā)	Yajur Veda (Samhitā)	Sāma Veda (Samhitā)	Atharva Veda (Samhitā)

SUMMARY OF THE MAIN HINDU SHASTRAS

6

Shad Darshanas

Six Orthodox Systems of Indian Philosophy

*Tableau of guru teaching his disciples in Vedic times,
Swaminarayan Akshardham, New Delhi.
(Inset) The four Vedas*

Sānkhya, Yoga, Nyāya, Vaisheshika,
Purva Mimāmsā and Uttara Mimāmsā

INTRODUCTION

The literal meaning of the word *darshana* is 'to view, perceive or look at' from all aspects. It also means a philosophical system. In the devotional context, *darshana* means seeing the divine image or deity with reverence.

Philosophically, *darshana* gives a perspective on all metaphysical and ontological realities, including the highest Reality. In its profoundest sense *darshana* implies direct spiritual perception and realization of the essence of all things. The realization of the highest Reality is the aim of almost all the orthodox systems of Indian philosophy. In other words understanding the true nature of the Ultimate Reality is the aim of Indian philosophy. The rishis, founders and original teachers of the specific *darshanas*, are referred to as *drashtās*, which means the seers of truth.

Indian philosophy is not merely an exercise in intellectual or spiritual speculation, but it is a way of life. It is an essential part of the way religion is practised even today by millions of Hindus all over the world. Philosophy is the theoretical aspect, and religion deals with practices. So, Hinduism is a synthesis of both.

The *darshana* shastras are principally divided into the Orthodox (Āstika) and Heterodox (Nāstika) schools. The former accept the authority of the Vedas, believe in the eternal existence of the Highest Controller or Creator, atman, rebirth, karma principle, and the latter do not accept some or all of these fundamental tenets. The six Orthodox schools are Sānkhya, Yoga, Nyāya, Vaisheshika, Purva Mimāmsā and Uttara Mimāmsā (Vedanta). The three Heterodox schools are Jainism, Buddhism and the hedonistic philosophy of Chārvāka (also known as Lokāyata). Indian philosophy is lauded for its open, non-dogmatic approach, liberalism in embracing many different streams of thought and also for including those that do not subscribe to the sanctity of the Vedas.

The Orthodox schools were traditionally founded by different rishis: Sānkhya was founded by Sage Kapila, Yoga by Sage Patanjali,[1] Nyāya by Sage Gautama, Vaisheshika by Sage Kanāda, Purva Mimāmsā by Sage Jaimini and Uttara Mimāmsā by Sage Bādarāyana, also known as Veda Vyāsa. Each *darshana* was presented by its founder in the form of *sutras* (aphorisms). So we have the *Sānkhyasutras* of Kapila, *Yogasutras* of Patanjali, *Nyāyasutras* of Gautama, *Vaisheshikasutras* of Kanāda, *Mimāmsāsutras* of Jaimini and Vedāntasutras of Bādarāyana. On each of them there are commentaries or *bhāshyas* by the *āchāryas* of different *sampradāyas*.

The common characteristics of the six Orthodox schools or Āstika *darshanas* are:

1. The Vedas are the supreme authority.
2. *Moksha* is the final goal of human life.
3. They explain basic Hindu concepts like atman, Brahman, Purusha, *moksha*, etc. through commentaries in *sutra* form on the primary texts of respective *darshanas*.
4. They speak of the transcendent Reality.
5. They deal with the nature of matter and function of consciousness.

Let us first consider the basic features of each orthodox school before going into detail:

1. Sānkhya is the 'enumeration' school, listing twenty-five ontological realities. It also postulates a fundamental

---

1. Some sources say that Sage Hiranyagarbha is the founder.

dualism between matter (Prakruti), which is inert or without consciousness, and the self (Purusha), which is conscious; both of which are real, separate and independent.

2. Yoga is the school of meditation, and physical and mental control. According to it, *moksha* is concentration on God, which results in the cessation of all mental activities. It accepts the metaphysics of the Sānkhya system and adds God to be the 26th Reality, which is the highest.

3. Nyāya is the school of logic that gives a detailed account of the theory of knowledge, besides dealing with metaphysical matters such as the nature of the self and the means to final liberation.

4. Vaisheshika is the atomist school, associated with Nyāya, that assumes plurality of independent souls and eternity of atoms – the tiniest particles of matter.

5. Purva Mimāmsā is the school that deals with the interpretation of Vedic rites and rituals, their applications in fire rituals and the fruits thereof. Thus, it emphasizes the Karma-*kānda* part of the Vedas. It believes in the reality of many souls.

6. Uttara Mimāmsā or Vedānta is the system of Upanishadic philosophy stressing on the *jnāna-kānda,* i.e., the knowledge of atman, Brahman and *jagat* for final liberation or *moksha* from the cycle of births and deaths. It is the most popular system of philosophy, both in India and abroad.

Manuscript of Sānkhyasutras

1. SĀNKHYA DARSHANA

Sānkhya Darshana is said to be the oldest system of Indian philosophy. Some thinkers believe that its name was derived from *sankhyā,* which means number; and thus from its enumeration of 25 categories or elements in the process of creation Sānkhya gets its name. Others, however, think that

Sage Kapila, founder of Sānkhya

because Sānkhya emphasizes *jnāna* or knowledge for liberation it derives its name from *sānkhya*, which also means *jnāna*.

Sānkhya Darshana greatly influenced all the later systems of philosophy. It is the backdrop of Yoga Darshana, and it had great impact on as diverse systems as Tāntric Shaivism and Shri Vaishnavism. Both Sānkhya and Yoga, in their various forms, have profoundly influenced Hindu religion and culture in all their different aspects.

The founder of Sānkhya Darshana was Sage Kapila. The *Sānkhyasutras* available today are believed to have been written later in his name. Today, however, Ishwarakrishna's *Sānkhyakārikā* (c. 350 to 450 CE) is a very popular text on Sānkhya. It has about 70 *shlokas,* and it is perhaps the oldest and most authentic. Two famous teachers, Gaudapāda (700 CE) have written commentaries on it. The Sānkhya philosophy believes in twenty-five *tattvas* or categories. It is a system of realism because it accepts the reality of the physical world (Prakruti) that is independent of the individual soul (Purusha). There are many Purushas or souls. The Sānkhya philosophy is dualistic because it advocates that matter (Prakruti) and soul (Purusha) are different from each other and are the only two basic realities. It also advocates pluralism, because it recognizes the plurality of souls. Sānkhya Darshana accepts perception *(pratyaksha pramāna)*, inference *(anumāna pramāna)* and verbal testimony *(shabda pramāna)* as valid means of acquiring knowledge.

Its aim is to overcome suffering and attachment to *māyā* or Prakruti through discrimination and understanding of the transient nature of things.

The important principles in Sānkhya Darshana are the Purusha (soul) and Prakruti (matter), and causation and evolution of the world. The Sānkhya school defines Purusha and Prakruti as two independent, eternal realities. The former is sentient and the latter is non-sentient. Purusha is the male principle who, on contact with Prakruti, causes the evolution of the world. The concept and position of Purusha is unique in the Sānkhya system in that it is sentient yet indifferent and inactive. Just as a blind man and a lame man cooperate in order to get out of a forest, so also by the cooperation of the material and unintelligent Prakruti with the sentient and intelligent but inactive and indifferent Purusha, creation takes place. Prakruti, the original material substance, consists of three *gunas* – *sattva, rajas* and *tamas*. When Prakruti is in a state of equilibrium of the three *gunas* there is no creation. The very proximity of Purusha disturbs the balance of *gunas* in Prakruti and then creation begins. Mahattattva, also called *buddhi* (intellect), is the first product of creation. It is the great germ of this vast physical world of objects. In its psychological aspect it is *buddhi*, the cosmic intellect from which the individual *buddhis* are produced in course of time. From Mahatattva comes *ahamkāra* (ego).

From *ahamkāra* emerges the mind (*manas*), the five cognitive senses (*pancha jnāna indriyas*), five organs of action or conative organs (*pancha* karma *indriyas*), five subtle elements (*pancha tanmātras*) and five gross elements (*pancha bhutas*). (See table on next page).

Sānkhya Darshana advocates the principle of Satkāryavāda, i.e., the principle that the effect already exists subtly in its material cause.[2] For example oil (effect) already exists in an unmanifest form within a peanut, sesame seed or cotton seed (cause). So the products of creation have already been existing inside the cause, though in an unmanifest form. Further, Sānkhya Darshana concludes that whatever is there has always existed and whatever is not there has never existed. For example there is no oil in sand, therefore it had never been there and shall never be there.

Purusha (soul) is a sentient principle. It is pure consciousness, which presides over every individual mind. The soul by mistakenly identifying itself with *ahamkāra*, body and mind

---

2. Ishwarakrishna. *Sānkhyakārikā* 9.

experiences misery and bondage. Once the soul realizes that it is not related to Prakruti it attains *kaivalya* – the state of liberation. Sānkhya believes in *jivan-mukti* – liberation can be attained in this life itself.

Sage Kapila's Sānkhya mentioned in the Shrimad Bhāgavata Purāna and Mahābhārata is theistic *(seshvara)*, believing God to be the 25th category. Ishwarakrishna's Sānkhya is atheistic, and within its 25 categories Purusha (soul) comes first and Prakruti second. The later believers and scholars either followed the theistic Sānkhya or the atheistic Sānkhya.

Twenty-Five Categories

The 25 categories in the Sānkhya system (see table below) include the five *bhutas* (gross elements), five *tanmātras* (subtle elements), five karma *indriyas* (organs of action), five *jnāna indriyas* (cognitive senses), *manas* (mind), *ahamkāra* (ego), *mahattattva (buddhi)*, Prakruti (material matrix) and Purusha (individual soul).

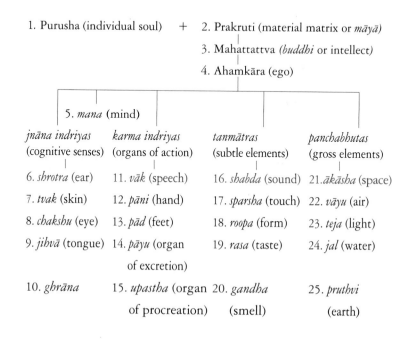

1. Purusha (individual soul)   +   2. Prakruti (material matrix or *māyā*)

3. Mahattattva *(buddhi* or intellect*)*

4. Ahamkāra (ego)

5. *mana* (mind)

jnāna indriyas (cognitive senses)	karma indriyas (organs of action)	tanmātras (subtle elements)	panchabhutas (gross elements)
6. *shrotra* (ear)	11. *vāk* (speech)	16. *shabda* (sound)	21.*ākāsha* (space)
7. *tvak* (skin)	12. *pāni* (hand)	17. *sparsha* (touch)	22. *vāyu* (air)
8. *chakshu* (eye)	13. *pād* (feet)	18. *roopa* (form)	23. *teja* (light)
9. *jihvā* (tongue)	14. *pāyu* (organ of excretion)	19. *rasa* (taste)	24. *jal* (water)
10. *ghrāna*	15. *upastha* (organ of procreation)	20. *gandha* (smell)	25. *pruthvi* (earth)

Liberation or *mukti* according to *Sānkhyakārikā* of Ishwarakrishna is to become free from suffering of the three-fold miseries, namely, *ādhyātamika* – due to mind, *ādhidaivika* – due to natural forces controlled by devas and *ādhibhautika* – due to living beings and humans,[3] and the clear recognition of the self or Purusha as the reality which is pure, eternal and beyond the 24 categories. The Sānkhya *darshana* believes in *jivan-mukti* or liberation during one's lifetime and also in *videha-mukti* or liberation after death.[4]

The most interesting feature of the Sānkhya system is that it has shown creation, comprising of the external physical world and all living beings, in an organized and innovative manner. Many systems of Indian philosophy derive their cosmology from the Sānkhya system.

2. YOGA DARSHANA

Sage Patanjali was the founder of Yoga Darshana.[5] He gave the *Yogasutras* as the basic text, which has 195 *sutras*. Yoga is the pathway to God through self-control of mind *(chitta vrutti nirodhaha)*.[6] This means it begins with partial control and leads to the complete control or cessation of the *chitta vruttis,* i.e., mental inclinations towards sense objects. Later it came to mean union with God. The ultimate goal of Yoga is to attach oneself to God or realize him by retracting the *vruttis* of the mind from the external world and focusing on him. Yoga Darshana also includes the holistic development of the individual, both physical and mental. It prescribes eight steps *(ashtānga)* for development:

Manuscript of Yogasutras

1. *Yama* means restraint. It includes *satya* (truthfulness), *dayā* (compassion), ahimsa, *brahmacharya* (celibacy), *asteya* (non-stealing), and *aparigraha* (non-possession).

Sage Patanjali, founder of Yoga

---

3. *Sānkhyakārikā* 1.

4. *Sānkhyasutras* I.56. and III. 66-75.

5. It is also believed that the Yoga shastra was initially founded by Sage Hiranyagarbha but was made most popular by Sage Patanjali.

6. *Yogasutras* 1.2.

2. *Niyama* means observances. It includes *saucha* (purity), *santosha* (contentment), *tapa* (austerity), *swādhyāya* (self-study) and Ishwarapranidhāna (surrender to God).

   Both *yama* and *niyama* are necessary to lead a pure, moral and spiritual life.

3. Asana refers to postures through which one disciplines the body.

4. Pranayama is the process of controlling one's breath.

5. *Pratyāhāra* involves the withdrawing of senses from worldly objects in order to tame the mind.

   Asana, pranayama and *pratyāhāra* discipline the body, breath (vital force), senses and mind respectively.

6. *Dhāranā* involves the practice of concentrating one's mind on God.

7. Dhyana or meditation is the steady contemplation of God or an object.

8. Samadhi is the final step and the ultimate goal. It is the divine experience of God in which one becomes totally absorbed in the Divine and oblivious to all mundane objects.

A yogi or practitioner of yoga learns to initially steady himself physically by performing yogic postures or asanas. At the same time he cultivates virtues *(yama* and *niyama),* controls his breathing *(pranayama)* and withdraws his senses from the worldly objects of enjoyment *(pratyāhāra)*. Furthermore, he concentrates his mind on God *(dhāranā)* and then meditates upon him *(dhyana)*. As a result the yogi experiences the gradual arresting of his mundane mental inclinations (desires) and the dawning of a new type of wisdom called *prajnā*. Ultimately, the total disintegration of ignorance or *avidyā* and revelation of the true nature of his self *(purusha)* in his transcendent loneliness is *kaivalya* or final liberation.

This systematic technique of body and mind control taught by Patanjali is popularly known as Yoga Darshana. Millions around the world experience the efficacy of its practice and significance in different life situations, remaining healthy, peaceful and calm.

There are 26 categories in the Yoga Darshana, having the same 25 categories as in Sānkhya, with Ishwara or God as the 26th category. The three fundamental realities are Ishwara, Purusha (soul) and Prakruti *(māyā)*. The God or Ishwara of Yoga is the Ultimate Reality. Unlike the Purusha of Sānkhya he never gets entangled with Prakruti *(māyā)*. Ishwara is the focus of meditation in the Yoga system. From Prakruti arise Mahattattva and other evolutes. The Purusha or individual soul, due to desires or *avidyā*, becomes involved in the evolutes of Prakruti and suffers from the cycle of births and deaths. Once it realizes its true nature through sadhanas it becomes free.

Yoga has been modified and applied in the service of different Hindu traditions, most importantly in the Vaishnava and Shaiva traditions.

3. NYĀYA DARSHANA

Nyāya is concerned with logical thinking to understand the Ultimate Reality and world. It traces its beginning to the Vedic times and encompasses the realistic view of the world on logical grounds and critical reflection. Sage Gautama, the author of *Nyāyasutras,* noted that anyone can claim anything, so how do we decide who is right. So he devised a clear and methodical system of logic. It emphasizes the rules of correct thinking through logic, epistemology (theory of knowledge) and methodology. Like all other Indian *darshana* shastras its ultimate aim is liberation.

Nyāya propagates four means of valid knowledge, called *pramānas*: (1) perception *(pratyaksha),* (2) inference *(anumāna),* (3) analogy *(upamāna)* and (4) testimony *(shabda).*[7]

Manuscript of Nyāysutras

Sage Gautama, founder of Nyāya

---

7. *Nyāyasutras* 2.

1. Perception *(Pratyaksha)* means knowledge that is acquired or defined through the physical senses. This is a direct means of acquiring knowledge where the senses and objects are involved.

2. Inference or deduction *(Anumāna)* means knowledge of objects based on correct sense data through some sign or mark that is invariably related to it. For example, we can state that where there is smoke there is fire, because smoke is invariably related to fire.

3. Analogy *(Upamāna)* is the means of knowledge in which a similarity is related to the object concerned from the object previously observed. For example, a tiger is something like a lion with stripes.

4. Verbal Testimony *(Shabda)* means verbal or revealed knowledge. In this case the Vedic words or statements are the sources of knowledge of objects. All verbal knowledge is not valid. *Shabda* is of two kinds – Vedic and *laukika* (secular). The Vedic words or sentences are the statements of God so they are perfect and infallible. Secular words are not perfect because a person may have faulty or biased views and perceptions. They are valid only when they are spoken by God or are in consonance with the Shruti shastras.

The Nyāya system is therefore about the external validity of knowledge. And all knowledge by its very nature points to an object. Only that knowledge is authentic or valid which agrees with all the essential features of an object. Nyāya accepts sixteen *padārthas* or categories, namely, (1) *pramānas* (means of valid knowledge, like perception, inference, etc.), (2) *prameyas* (objects of true knowledge like atman, body, senses, objects, etc.), (3) *samshaya* (doubt), (4) *prayojana* (utility, end in view), (5) *drashtānta* (example), (6) *siddhānta* (doctrine), (7) *avayava* (member of a syllogism), (8) *tarka* (logic), (9) *nirnaya* (conclusion or final decision), (10) *vāda* (argument to find truth), (11) *jalpa* (to argue merely to win), (12) *vitandā* (destructive criticism), (13) *hetvābhāsa* (apparent, but not valid, reason), (14) *chala* (unfair reply), (15) *jāti* (false analogy) and (16) *nigrahasthāna* (a ground of defeat in debate). The sixteen *padārthas* explain the whole universe.

The souls *(jivas)* and God are considered as special substances. The soul is distinct from the body and mind. The mind is particular to each individual soul and is of atomic size. Atman or soul as well as *ākāsha*, *dik* and *kāla* are eternal and omnipresent. The body is made up of matter. The soul is all-pervading and eternal. Nyāya believes that one's worldly desires compel the soul to perform good or bad actions which are responsible for its happiness or misery, merit or sin, and the cycle of births and deaths. Liberation means cessation of all suffering and pain that is achieved through the realization of the Ultimate Reality. Nyāya believes, unlike Sānkhya's Satkāryavāda, that the effect does not exist in its cause before its production. The effect is a new product or new creation altogether. This is known as the principle of Asatkāryavāda.

In the Nyāya system God is the ultimate cause of creation, maintenance and destruction of the world. God is the efficient *(nimitta)* cause of the world.

Sage Gautama's work is called the *Nyāyasutras*. It has 523 *sutras*. Other famous Naiyāyikas who followed include Vātsyāyana, Udyotakāra, Vāchaspati Mishra, Udayana and many more. The modern school of Nyāya or Navya-Nyāya was founded by Gangesha Upādhyāya (1200 CE), who wrote its fundamental text called *Tattvachintāmani*. In this work he has dealt with the four *pramānas*. He did not touch upon *prameya* (object to be known) at all. The *Tarksangraha* of Annambhatta with his own commentary called *Dipikā* is a popular and primary text in the modern school of Nyāya.

Nyāya sharpens intellect and leads to logical and critical thinking. Western philosophers and scholars have realized and praised the subtleties and depth of Indian logic.

Udayana (100 CE), a great Naiyāyika, advocates in his work, *Nyāyakusumāñjali,* that God must exist because:

1. Atoms, which are inert, cannot come together or separate by themselves to form or dissolve the universe that is orderly and exact.

2. The principle of karma, which is accepted by Nyāya, does not run by itself. There is a divine intelligence that dispenses the fruits of the karma of each soul.

Furthermore, Udayana advocates two very important aspects in the *Nyāyakusumāñjali,* devotion to God and Divine grace for the attainment of liberation.

Though Nyāya Darshana is famous for its logical and analytical reasoning with everything, it also substantially deals with suffering, soul and liberation. So, this school of logic, which is a way of truth, is also a means of liberation.

4. VAISHESHIKA DARSHANA

Sage Kanāda was the founder of Vaisheshika Darshana, and his work is called the *Vaisheshikasutras.* This is the second oldest philosophical system in India. But in the words of Prof. S.N. Dasgupta, the *Vaisheshikasutras* is "probably the oldest and pre-Buddhistic."[8] It focuses on metaphysics and ontology (nature of being) while Nyāya elaborates upon logic and epistemology (theory of knowledge).

The Vaisheshika Darshana accepts the existence of three realities: atoms, souls and God. God is the supreme controller of the other two. The *darshana* believes that physical things are real and not illusory as propagated by some philosophers. They are produced by a combination of atoms, and destroyed by separation of atoms. The atoms are eternal and so are the souls. The souls are innumerable, separate and distinct from each other. The Vaisheshika Darshana believes in pluralistic realism, meaning that the atoms and souls are many, independent and

Sage Kanāda, founder of Vaisheshika

8. Dasgupta, S.N. *History of Indian Philosophy, Vol.1*. UK: Cambridge University Press, 1961, p.282.

real. The followers of Kanāda believed that God is the efficient cause, which means that as the creator he brings about atoms in different proportions to make the world.

Kanāda classified all things on earth into seven categories or *padārthas:* (1) *dravya* (substance), (2) *guna* (quality), (3) karma (action), (4) *sāmānya* (universality), (5) *vishesha* (individuality), (6) *samavāya* (inherence), and (7) *abhāva* (negation).

The Vaisheshika system believes in the authority of the Vedas and in the moral law of karma. It also believes that dharma is the means to obtain both worldly prosperity and liberation. Kanāda, the founder, does not refer to God, but his disciples considered God as the efficient cause *(nimitta kārana)* of the world and the eternal atoms as the material cause *(upādāna kārana)*. Atoms, souls and God are eternal. God gives motion to the atoms. The bondage of each soul is due to ignorance, and liberation can be attained through right knowledge.

The doctrine of plurality of atoms and souls and the singularity of God in the Vaisheshika Darshana is accepted by Nyāya Darshana. Because of this commonality both are spoken of together as Nyāya-Vaisheshika. Nyaya accepts the four means of knowledge – perception, reasoning, inference and verbal authority whereas Vaisheshika accepts only two – perception and inference. Out of these, both schools give prominence to sense perception *(pratyaksha pramāna)*, similar to what Jaimini and Veda Vyāsa have given in the Purva and Uttara Mimāmsa (Vedānta) respectively.

In both the Vaisheshika and Nyāya Darshanas the concept of *moksha* is known as *apavarga*. It is a state of freedom from all pain and suffering. It is also a state in which the soul is released from its connections with the body and its senses. To attain *moksha* one should listen to sacred textual instructions, understand them by means of reason and meditate on the self in accordance with the principles of Yoga.[9]

---

9. *Nyāyabhāshya* 1.1.1 & 2.

5. PURVA MIMĀMSĀ

Mimāmsā means critical investigation or enquiry. When the different *darshanas* or systems of Indian philosophy developed, some of the orthodox thinkers tried to maintain the supremacy of strictly orthodox practices and world views of the Vedas. Among them there were two classes. The first was solely concerned with and interested in Vedic rituals (*karma-kānda* of the Vedas) and the second emphasized upon knowledge of the Upanishads (*jnāna-kānda*). The first is called Purva Mimāmsā and the second is known as the Uttara Mimāmsā (Vedānta). The principle goal of the Purva Mimāmsā Darshana, where Purva means earlier school, is to investigate, explain and justify the truth behind Vedic mantras and rituals. It is also called Karma Mimāmsā. It firmly believes in the sanctity and the authority of the Vedas and the rituals prescribed in them.

The Uttara Mimāmsā (later school) deals with Upanishadic doctrines (that are mainly philosophical) and is known as Jnāna Mimāmsā or Vedānta. Both the Purva and Uttara Mimāmsās accepted the exclusive and final authority of the Vedas and also the Varnāshrama system.

The Purva Mimāmsā, established by Jaimini rishi, is a school of rituals derived from the *karma-kānda* section of the Vedas. It focuses on the performance of right ritual sacrificial action prescribed by the Vedas. Further, it is a system of in-depth interpretation of Vedic rituals. The *Mimāmsāsutras* of Jaimini is the primary text. It does not deal with the nature of God or atman but with the importance and performance of Vedic rituals in order to lead virtuous lives on earth and thereby attain *moksha* by going to *swarga*.[10] Subsequently, the great Purva Mimāmsā scholars like Kumārila and Prabhākara believed in atman and *moksha*. According to them *moksha* is described as self-realization and liberation from ultimate misery.

Darshanam

The Mimāmsāsutras deal with Vedic rituals

10. Dr P.V. Kane states, "The *swarga* of the (Purva) Mimāmsakas is different from that of the Vedas and the Purānas." *History of Dharmashastras, Vol.V, pt.II,* Poona: BORI, 1930-1962, p.1,212.

Dharma (religious duties) is the main subject of enquiry of the Mimāmsā. Jaimini Rishi defines dharma as commands of the Vedas that inspire mankind to perform actions. Action or karma basically means performance of sacrificial ritual in accordance with Vedic instruction. This is the message of the Vedas. It commands to do certain acts (*vidhi*) and restrain from doing certain acts (*nishedha*).

The main concepts of the Purva Mimānsā are:

1. It denies the existence of God or an omniscient being, and the creation and dissolution of the world.

2. It asserts: (a) the eternity of the world, (b) the self-validity of knowledge, i.e., eternity of the truth of the Vedic statements, (c) the eternity of words and of relation between words and their meanings, (d) dharma (virtue or duty) is explained as that which is known from the commands or injunctions of the Veda only, (e) the power of every action to produce the fruit long after its performance by a person. This power is called *apurva* which in due course brings about an appropriate effect or result to be experienced by the agent who carried out or executed the action and (f) the fundamental validity of cognition (knowing through one's senses) as valid and reliable means of knowledge both for the world around us and of individual selves as knowers within all living beings.

6. UTTARA MIMĀMSĀ (VEDĀNTA)

The Uttara Mimāmsā Darshana deals with the philosophical doctrines taught in the Upanishads. The Upanishads are the essence of the Vedas, therefore they are also called Vedānta. The exercise of systematizing the philosophical principles of the Upanishads was accomplished by Bādarāyana or Veda Vyāsa. His work is called the Brahmasutras, Vedāntasutras Shāririkasutras or Vyāsasutras.

Sutras are aphorisms that are very short, skilful statements

Bhagwan Veda Vyāsa, author of Brahmasutras

expressing truths. This style of writing is cryptic. Each *sutra* consists of just a few words whose meaning and context are far from self-evident. They invariably require further interpretation from the teacher who is well versed in the subject. The interpretation is called a *bhāshya*. The first available commentary on the Brahmasutras is by Ādi Shankarāchārya (788-820 CE), a brilliant thinker and writer. He also wrote commentaries on the ten ancient Upanishads and the Bhagavad Gita. From his time onwards a tradition was introduced to write commentaries on the Brahmasutras, Upanishads and the Gita, which are collectively known as Prasthānatrayi, in order to establish any Vedānta school of philosophy.

The text of Brahmasutras is interpreted from different philosophical perspectives by various *āchāryas* to produce the Vedantic schools of Advaita, Vishishtādvaita, Dvaita, Dvaitādvaita, Shuddhādvaita, Achintyabhedābheda, Shri Swaminarayan Vedant Darshana and others. They are dealt with in the next chapter.

COMMON THREADS AMONG THE SIX ORTHODOX SYSTEMS OF INDIAN PHILOSOPHY (SHAD-DARSHANAS):

1. They accept Vedic authority because it is divine revelation.
2. The ultimate goal according to all is liberation or *moksha*.
3. They give explanations on the basic Hindu concepts of atman, Brahman, Purusha, *moksha* through their individual commentaries on the primary texts, called *sutras* or *Kārikās* (i.e., *Sānkhyakārikā* and *Sānkhyasutras, Yogasutras, Nyāyasutras, Vaisheshikasutras, Mimāmsāsutras* and Vedāntasutras), of the respective *darshanas*.

SUMMARY

1. The word *darshana* means 'to perceive or to look at from all aspects'. It refers to direct spiritual perception and

realization. In the devotional context, *darshana* means seeing the divine image or deity with reverence. It also means a philosophical system.

2. There are two basic divisions of the Darshana Shastras or Indian Schools of Philosophy, namely, the Orthodox – which accepts the authority of the Vedas, beliefs in Creator, rebirth, etc. – and the Heterodox – that does not accept the authority of the Vedas and the Creator. The ultimate goal of all the six orthodox Darshana Schools, also known as Shad Darshanas, is to attain *moksha*.

3. The Sānkhya school propagates that liberation from suffering and *māyā* is realized through knowledge, discrimination and understanding of the transient nature of things that originate from Prakruti and of the fact that the true self is Purusha.

4. Yoga is a pathway to God through self-control of mind and senses, *ashtānga* yoga, austerities, self-study, repeated practice and total detachment from worldly pleasures.

5. Nyāya is a methodical system of logic that employs four means for acquiring valid knowledge, namely, perception, inference, analogy and testimony.

6. The Vaisheshika school deals with metaphysics and ontology (nature of being). It says that all physical things are produced through a combination of different atoms.

7. Purva Mimāmsā deals basically with Vedic ritualism or *karma-kānda* for the purpose of living righteously on earth and to attain *moksha*, i.e., *swarga*.

8. Uttara Mimāmsā or Vedānta deals with the philosophical truths taught in the Upanishads by explaining the Brahmasutras of Veda Vyāsā. Liberation is attained through correct knowledge of *prakruti* (matter), individual soul and universal soul. There are two main divisions: non-theistic (monism) and theistic (monotheistic) Uttara Mimāmsā. The latter is also known as the Bhakti Vedānta schools.

7

Vedāntic Teachings

The aim of the Vedāntic philosophies is the liberation of soul; an artist's impression (Narayanprasad Swami)

Ādi Shankarāchārya, Rāmānujāchārya,
Nimbārkāchārya, Madhavāchārya...

INTRODUCTION

Hindu tradition has two major parallel currents of thought for achieving the final goal of life, i.e., *moksha:* one advocating the path of *jnāna* (knowledge) and the other of bhakti (devotion). Both paths are based upon the principal Hindu sacred texts, namely, the Upanishads, Brahmasutras and Bhagavad Gitā. The Bhakti schools also accept the Purānas like the Vishnu and Bhāgavata, and the Āgamas. The Jnāna schools emphasize that *mukti* is possible only through correct knowledge of self (*ātmajnāna*) and God. The Bhakti schools, however, say that liberation is possible only through God's grace, which is attained through *prapatti* or total devotion to him. Some *āchāryas* or teachers have reconciled these two viewpoints.

A true *āchārya* is a teacher of Vedic, Āgamic, epic and *purānic* (or *paurānik*) lore. He imparts the principles of the shastras and lives by those teachings. India has had a succession of great *āchāryas* or practising philosophers, many of whom interpreted and wrote commentaries on the Upanishads, Brahmasutras and the Bhagavad Gitā (Prasthānatraya or Prasthāntrayi) to establish their own schools of Vedāntic thought. Each *āchārya* subsequently perpetuated his own philosophy through a *paramparā* or succession of disciples. The main *āchāryas* in Hinduism are Ādi Shankarāchārya, Shri Rāmānujāchārya, Shri Madhvāchārya, Shri Nimbārkāchārya and Shri Vallabhāchārya. The philosophies of Chaitanya Mahāprabhu and Bhagwan Swaminarayan have been included in this chapter because of their novel contributions.

At the end of the 19th century Hindu spirituality was introduced to the West by Swami Vivekananda at the World Parliament of Religions in Chicago in 1893. His modern version of Shankarāchārya's non-dualist Vedānta became well known and people assumed it to be Hinduism in its entirety. When scholars and aspirants started visiting India in large numbers during the 1960s and 1970s they came in touch with gurus and spiritual movements of other Vedāntic schools. They saw and learned about the popularity of devotional, theistic Hinduism based on the theological principles of Rāmānujāchārya, Madhavāchārya, Chaitanya Mahāprabhu and others. Kim Knott writes, "From the traditional Shri Vaishnava Sampradāya developed by Rāmānujāchārya in south India to the modern bhakti movements of the Swaminarayans in Gujarat and the Hare Krishnas (ISKCON) in Bengal and beyond, the devotional theology which had challenged early non-dualist ideas (of Shankarāchārya and others) about ultimate reality and the self was flourishing."[1]

We shall briefly consider the Vedāntic principles and schools established by the *āchāryas*.

1. ĀDI SHANKĀRĀCHĀRYA (788-820 CE)
Kevalādvaita (Absolute or Pure Monism)

Shri Shankarāchārya was born into an orthodox Brahmin family in Kāladi (or Kalady) in the State of Kerala. He is revered as an incarnation of Shiva. He became a sannyasi at a young age and travelled throughout India. He was a great thinker, writer, philosopher, orator and sannyasi. Wherever he travelled he reasserted the authority of the Vedas, which Buddha had earlier rejected due to excessive ritualism. The

---

1. Knott, Kim. *Hinduism, A Very Short Introduction.* Oxford: OUP, 2007, p. 31.

school established by Shankarāchārya is known as Kevalādvaita Vedānta (absolute monism). It is the most famous school of Indian philosophy and is often mistakenly taken to be the only true representative of Vedāntic thought. The term *advaita* means non-dual and refers to the Sampradāya's philosophy of absolute monism that maintains the reality of the one and only one Brahman which is identical with all individual souls. Shankara states that the basic Truth or Reality behind this universe of multiplicity of names and forms is only Brahman. It is one without a second. But it appears to be many due to illusion *(māyā)*, which is indescribable and veils or covers the minds of human beings with ignorance, forcing them to believe that the multiple names and forms are ultimately real. His philosophy states *"Brahma satyam jagan mithyā, jivo brahmaiva nāparaha"* – meaning, "Brahman, the Absolute, alone is real; this world is unreal; and the *jiva* or the individual soul is not different from Brahman."[2] Shankarāchārya did not believe in the plurality of souls. To him Brahman is both *nirguna* or formless and *saguna* or with attributes. He said that for an ordinary aspirant who is on a worldly level Brahman is *saguna*, but for a realized soul on the transcendental plane Brahman is *nirguna* or formless. The renowned Indian scholar S.N. Das Gupta writes, "Shankara did not reject the gods, but taught that they were the primary manifestations of the impersonal Absolute (Brahman). Their worship might help humble souls, but the spiritual athlete strove to pass beyond them, to direct knowledge of final reality, which was to be found in his own self."[3] He said that *moksha* is the realization of one's soul to be identical to Brahman. Becoming one with Brahman is *moksha*. Shankarāchārya opposed the mechanical manner in which Vedic rituals were performed, the dualism of the Sānkhya doctrine, and the Buddhist doctrine of momentariness

2. *Vivekchudāmani* 20.

3. Das Gupta, S.N. Philosophy. In *A Cultural History of India,* edited by Basham A.L. New Delhi: OUP, 2008, p.119.

Ādi Shankarāchārya *Shri Rāmānujāchārya*

and nihilism. His three major philosophical works were commentaries on the ten Upanishads, Brahmasutras and Bhagavad Gitā. His philosophy, based on the Prasthāntrayi (Upanishads, Brahmasutras and Bhagavad Gitā), became the dominant Advaita philosophy. Shankarāchārya established four seats *(mathas)* in India for the propagation and perpetuation of Sanātana Dharma and Advaita Vedānta, namely, at Badarinātha, Jagannātha Puri, Shringeri and Dwārikā. Shankarāchārya passed away at the age of only thirty-two. Thereafter his direct disciples, Totaka, Padmapāda, Sureshvara and Hastāmalaka headed the four *mathas* and continued the tradition of writing extensive literature on Advaita Vedānta. The later *āchāryas* (Rāmānujāchārya, Nimbārkāchārya, Madhvācharya, Vallabhācharya, etc.) or their followers also wrote commentaries on the Prasthāntrayi and established their own views by partially accepting or rejecting Shankara's Advaita philosophy.

A number of works, namely, commentaries, treatises and hymn books, are ascribed to Ādi Shankarācharya. He is fondly remembered for writing erudite works (on Prasthāntrayi) and devotional hymns (like *Bhaja Govindam),* thus restoring the pristine glory of Vedic religion and Hindu monasticism.

2. SHRI RĀMĀNUJĀCHĀRYA (1017-1137 CE)
Vishishtādvaita (Qualified Non-Dualism)

Shri Rāmānujāchārya was a Brahmin, born in Bhootapuri (now called Sriperumbudur) near Chennāi (Madras) in Tamil Nadu. He founded the Vishishtādvaita school of philosophy. He is considered by his followers to be a reincarnation of Lakshmana, the younger brother, (i.e., *anuja*) of Rāma, and hence his name was Rāmānuja. Unlike Shankarāchārya, Rāmānujāchārya believed that Parabrahman is God, who has a divine form, and the *jivas* are neither parts of nor identical with Parabrahman. He propagated the doctrine of three realities: God (Ishwara), *jivas* or souls (that is *chit* or sentient) and *māyā (prakruti)* or matter (that is *achit* or non-sentient). God is independent and the other two are dependent on him. The relationship between God and *jivas* and *māyā* is that of *sharira-shariri* or body-soul. This means that God is the soul or *shariri* and the *jivas* and *māyā* constitute his body or *sharira*. Both the *jivas* and *māyā* are distinct, but not independent from God as they are entirely dependent on him for their very existence. God is qualified *(vishishta)* by *jivas* and *māyā* and is ultimately non-dual *(advaita)*. Just as the soul or *jiva* controls its own body, God controls both the material world and the immaterial *jivas*.

Rāmānujāchārya taught that God, whom he calls Nārāyana or Vishnu, is personal and therefore has a divine human form. Nārāyana is always accompanied by his divine consort, Lakshmi. Together they are called *divya dampati* or the divine couple. He is the supreme moral governor and giver of *moksha*. He incarnates from time to time to liberate *jivas* from the bondage of *māyā* and to destroy evil. He is present in five aspects, namely: (1) *para* – transcendental form of Vishnu in Vaikuntha *dhāma*, (2) *vyuha* – emanations of Vishnu, i.e., Aniruddha (creator), Pradyumna (sustainer), Sankarshana (destroyer) and Vāsudeva (who is superior to the former three), (3) *vibhava* – 10 avatars,

(4) *antaryāmin* – in-dweller and controller in all life forms and (5) *archā* – sacred image.

Rāmānujāchārya says that just like a spider itself spins a web out of its own body God himself creates the world of material objects out of his own body (i.e. matter, which is *achit*). Every soul takes on a material body with relation to its karmas. Rāmānujāchārya believes in three types of *jivas*: (1) the *nitya muktas* who are eternally liberated or have never been bound by *māyā*,[4] (2) the *muktas* who have achieved *moksha* but were originally bound to *māyā* and (3) the bound or *baddha jivas* who are still attached to *māyā*. The means to liberation lie in intense bhakti and self-surrender to God *(prapatti)*. Then through God's grace the *jiva* is liberated from *māyā*, and thereafter it offers devotion to God in his divine abode of Vaikuntha. Rāmānujāchārya believes that the *jiva* does not merge with God as is the belief of Shankarāchārya, but it attains a divine body and remains subservient to God in Vaikuntha *dhāma*. His main philosophical writings include the *Shribhāshya* (commentary on Brahmasutras), *Shri Gitābhāshya* (commentary on Bhagavad Gitā), *Vedārthasangraha* and *Gadyatraya*.

The greatest contribution of Rāmānujāchārya was his preaching and establishment of a religio-philosophical system that gave importance to *jnāna* and bhakti, and to both Sanskrit scriptures and the Tamil bhajans of the Ālvārs. This enabled the socially and economically weak people to practise Vishistādvaita and achieve *moksha*.

A summary of Rāmānujāchārya's philosophy:

- He accepts the Ultimate Reality to be non-dual, and calls him Ishwara, Nārāyana or Vishnu.
- He profoundly disagrees with Shankarāchārya's explanation of the Ultimate Reality, nature of soul *(jiva)*

---

4. *Nitya muktas* are Ādishesha (divine serpent) on whom Vishnu reclines, Garuda (divine bird – his vehicle) and Vishvaksena (commander-in-chief of Vishnu's army).

and world *(māyā)*.

- He believes individual souls are different from one another and from God.
- He says that the experiences of one's senses and feelings are real, and not illusory as advocated by Shankarāchārya.
- He states that the Ultimate Reality or Nārāyana is not impersonal *(nirākāra)*, and is not without qualities *(nirguna)* as asserted by Shankarāchārya. Nārāyana has a divine form and is full of innumerable, divine qualities and devoid of all drawbacks and defects.

Rāmānujāchārya's philosophy is more representative of the beliefs and rituals followed by many Hindus. He was both a towering scholar of the sacred Sanskrit texts and Tamil works called *Divya Prabandham* by the Ālvārs, as well as the defender of the Shri Vaishnava Sampradāya. He travelled throughout India but mainly stayed at and managed the great Shrirangam mandir complex on the banks of Kāveri in Tamil Nadu. After him two great scholars who wrote extensively on Vishishtādvaita were Pillai Lokāchārya (1205-1310 CE) and Vedānta Deshika (1268-1369 CE) (also known as Venkatanātha). Pillai Lokāchārya is believed to be the founder of the Tengalai Shri Vaishnava Sampradāya, and Vedānta Deshika is believed to be the founder of the Vadagalai Shri Vaishnava Sampradāya.

3. SHRI NIMBĀRKĀCHĀRYA (1125-1162 CE):

Dvaitādvaita or Bhedābheda (Dualistic Non-Dualism)

Shri Nimbārkāchārya was a Brahmin, born in Nimbāpura in Bellary district, Karnataka. He migrated to Vrundāvan in the Mathurā district of Uttar Pradesh and lived most of his life there. His followers consider him to be an incarnation of *sudarshana chakra* (disc of Vishnu). He established the philosophy of Dvaitādvaita or Bhedābheda in which there are three realities, namely, Parabrahman (God), *jiva (chit)* and

Shri Nimbārkāchārya　　　　*Shri Madhvāchārya*

māyā (achit). Parabrahman is the controller, the *jiva (chit)* is the experiencer and *māyā (achit)* is the object experienced. He propagated that God is *saguna* (having divine qualities) and *sākāra* (having divine form). He is both the material *(upādāna)* and efficient *(nimitta)* cause of the world, meaning that God transforms himself to form the world and he is also the creator of the universe. For Nimbārka God is Shri Krishna and he is always accompanied by Rādhā.

The material world or *māyā* and the *jivas* are dependent upon God (Parabrahman), whereas God is independent. *Māyā* and *jivas* are different from Parabrahman because they have a dependent and separate existence, i.e., they are dependent on God and yet they have their own individual identity. They are also non-different from Parabrahman because they cannot exist apart from him independently. They are related to God like a part to the whole, i.e., like a wave to the ocean or a ray to the sun. This philosophy is known as Dvaitādvaita or dualistic non-dualism or identity-in-difference. The soul is a part of God, but it does not lose its individuality even in the state of *moksha*. It remains subservient to God even in the state of *mukti* in his abode. Through God's grace the layer of *avidyā* (ignorance) on the *jiva* is dissolved. This grace is attained through *jnāna* (knowledge), *upāsanā (*means meditation in this case), bhakti (worship), *prapatti* (self-surrender), good karmas (deeds), and devotion to the guru. Bhakti to God is based on *mādhuryabhāva* – infinite sweetness. Following Shri Rāmānujāchārya, Nimbārka believes that the soul's bondage to *māyā* is real and its destruction is also real.

His two great works are *Vedāntapārijāta Kaustubha* (a brief commentary on the Brahmasutras) and *Dashashloki* (a work of ten verses). Two of his illustrious disciples were Harivyāsadeva and Keshavakāshmirin.

4. SHRI MADHVĀCHĀRYA (1238-1317 CE):
Dvaita (Pure Dualism)

Shri Madhvāchārya, also known as Ānandatirtha, was a Vaishnava Brahmin from Karnataka. He is considered by his followers to be the incarnation of Vāyu (wind-god). He was an exponent of the Dvaita philosophy (pure dualism). He strongly opposed Shankara's *advaita* and the philosophies of Buddhists and Jains. Madhva believed in three entities – God, *jivas* and the material world. He believed that God is the only independent reality and the other two are distinct yet dependent on him. He said that *māyā* or the material world is real. He advocated *panchabhedas* or five kinds of differences: (1) God and soul are different, (2) souls are also different from each other, (3) soul and matter are different, (4) God and matter are different and (5) matter among matter is also different.

Madhva, like Rāmānuja, says that God is Vishnu (or Nārāyana). He believed that God is personal and has a divine form. Also, like other Vaishnava bhakti philosophers, he believed that God is the creator, preserver and destroyer. His consort is Lakshmiji. He advocated the three categories of *jivas*: the *nitya mukta* (eternally liberated), *mukta* (liberated) and *baddha* (those bound by *māyā*). Furthermore, he stated that certain *jivas* like the asuras (demons) are eternally doomed and never get liberated.

In his work he believes that Shruti includes the Vishnu Purāna and the Vaishnava Āgamas, which according to him reveals the dual reality of Brahman and atman. His teachings about the relationship between Brahman and atman is known as Bimba-Pratibimba, meaning image and reflection. This suggests that the atman is a mirror image of God, meaning it is dependent on God and is also similar to God.

Madhva, like Rāmānuja, believed that through correct knowledge *(jnāna)* of God, true bhakti is born; and through bhakti one is blessed with the grace of God and attains *moksha*. For Madhva, "Liberation is the self's enjoyment of its innate being, consciousness and bliss *(sat, chit* and *ānanda)*, which is a participation in the bliss of the Lord, attained through devotion (bhakti) to an icon and the Lord's grace."[5]

Madhvāchārya wrote commentaries on the Brahmasutras, ten principal Upanishads and the Bhagavad Gitā. He also wrote a commentary on the first 40 *suktas* of the first *mandala* of the Rig Veda. In all, 37 works have been attributed to him. Two of his prominent disciples were Shri Jayatirtha and Shri Vyāsatirtha.

5. SHRI VALLABHĀCHĀRYA (1473-1531 CE)
Shuddhādvaita (Pure Non-Dualism)

Shri Vallabhāchārya was a Telugu Brahmin who was born in Champāranya, (near modern Raipur) in Chattisgarh. He founded the Rudra or Vallabha Sampradāya in which Bhagwan Krishna is the supreme deity to be worshipped. Vallabha states that the Parabrahman of the Upanishads is Bhagwan Krishna of the Bhāgavata Purāna who can be realized only by *pushti* bhakti. *Pushti* literally means 'nourishment' – the spiritual nourishment that a devotee gets when God's grace is showered upon him. He is worshipped as the child-God and the devotee believes himself to be his parent. Therefore in this Sampradāya the bhakti towards Krishna is called *vātsalya* bhakti or parental

---

5. Flood, Gavin. *An Introduction to Hinduism.* p.246.

devotion. The devotee is first initiated through a ritual ceremony called *brahmasambandha* in which he gets the mantra of dedication from a guru. He emphasized the role of God's grace in the process of liberation.

Vallabhāchārya's philosophy is known as Shuddhādvaita – pure non-dualism. He propounds that Paramātmā (or Parabrahman) is the highest independent reality. The universe comes from Parabrahman like sparks that emerge from a great fire. Souls and matter are his own manifestations and his parts. Parabrahman becomes all things through his *māyā-shakti*, but these manifestations are real and not illusory. Parabrahman appears as (1) Antaryāmi (2) Aksharabrahman and (3) as Purushottama Krishna. God dwells in all *jivas* as *antaryāmi* (inner controller). Aksharabrahman is believed to be the feet of God and his abode. It appears as Prakruti and Purusha and becomes the cause of all creation. Aksharabrahman is superior to all *jivas*. Akshara appears in three forms: (1) *Kāla* (Time), (2) Karma (Action) and (3) *Swabhāva* (Inner Nature).

The *jiva* is a part of Parabrahman and is eternal. During creation the *jivas* issue forth from Aksharabrahman as sparks from a fire. They are eternal parts of Brahman and are atomic in size. There are three types of *jivas*: (1) those that wallow in *māyā* are known as *pravāna jivas,* (2) those that abide by the Vedic path of morality are *maryādā jivas*, and (3) those that worship God with pure love after receiving his grace *(pushti)* are *pushti jivas.* Vallabha's Bhakti Sampradāya is called Pushtimārga (the way of nourishment through grace of Bhagwan Krishna). Through profound devotion to Krishna the *jiva* receives his grace and is liberated from its material body to attain Goloka, the divine residence of Bhagwan Krishna. God blesses the *jiva* with his abode, where it eternally enjoys the bliss of playing with God *(rāsalilā)*. Vallabhāchārya teaches that the knower of Brahman is absorbed in Akshara-Brahman and not in Purushottama. It is only through bhakti that Purushottama, Krishna, can be

Shri Vallabhāchārya   *Shri Chaitanya Mahāprabhu*

attained and his company can be enjoyed eternally in Goloka.

Vallabhāchārya's written works include commentaries on the Brahmasutras, called *Anubhāshya,* and on the Shrimad Bhāgavata Purāna, called *Subodhini.* He elevated the Bhāgavata Purāna to the position of the most authoritative sacred text.

Vallabhāchārya has greatly influenced Hindi literature through the devotional songs composed by his eight poets *(ash-tachhāpa).* The foremost among them is Surdās, whose bhajans on Krishna were compiled into a work called *Surasāgara.*

6. SHRI CHAITANYA MAHĀPRABHU (1486-1533 CE): Achintyabhedābheda (Inconceivable Difference and Non-Difference)

The great scholar-saint-devotee who synthesized the different trends of Vaishnavism in Bengal was Vishvambhara Mishra. He was a Brahmin from Navadvipa, known as Gaurānga in his early years and Shri Krishna Chaitanya or Shri Chaitanya Mahāprabhu in his later years. He became a great reformer and founded a *sampradāya* that has had a profound influence on Bengal's religious life. He is believed and revered to be an incarnation of Rādhā and Krishna in one body. Shri Chaitanya propagated the *upāsanā* of Rādhā-

Krishna. He believed that Krishna is the supreme God and not an avatar of Vishnu.

Chaitanya emphasized the offering of profound bhakti to Bhagwan Krishna. In addition to dharma, *artha, kāma* and *moksha* he considered divine love for Krishna as the fifth and the best *purushārtha* or goal of human life. This intense divine love or profound bhakti is developed through chanting Krishna's holy name. Through bhakti the *jiva* earns the grace of God and is thus liberated from *māyā*. The culmination of bhakti is self-surrender to God.

Hindu philosophers are broadly divided into two groups, one holding the view that ultimately there is no difference (*abheda*) between Brahman (God) and the *jivas*; and the other believing there is. Shankarāchārya believed that Brahman is the only Reality. Rāmānujāchārya believed that there are three realities, namely, *jiva, māyā* and God. Madhva believed in the eternal duality of God and *jiva*. Chaitanya's philosophy or his Bengal school of Vaishnavism differs from both views and calls it Achintyabhedābheda or 'inconceivable difference and non-difference'. This means that Brahman and *jiva* are identical (*abheda*) in some aspects and different (*bheda*) in others, and the relationship is beyond our comprehension (*achintya*). Since both are *chit* (consciousness) they are identical in that respect. But Brahman is all-pervading consciousness (*vibhu-chit*) whereas the *jiva* is atomic consciousness (*anu-chit*). Furthermore *jiva* is a part (*amsha*) of Brahman who is the whole (*amshin*). He believed that Parabrahman has a divine form (*sākāra*) and is possessed with three principal powers: (1) *swarupa-shakti*, (2) *māyā-shakti* and (3) *jiva-shakti*. *Swarupa-shakti* is God's internal power, *māyā-shakti* is God's external power responsible for creation of the material universe, and the *jiva-shakti* of God is the essence of all *jivas*. The world is believed to be real and not an illusion. The *jiva* is the conscious power of God. It is related to God like sparks to a fire or as parts to a whole.

Chaitanya's philosophical teachings are found in the *Dashamulashloka* and the *Chaitanyacharitrāmruta* of Krishnadāsa. Chaitanya did not write any work except perhaps the *Shikshāshataka*, a collection of eight verses describing his intense joy of devotion to Krishna. Furthermore, though he did not write a commentary on the Upanishads, Brahmasutras or Bhagavad Gita he nevertheless established Gaudiya Vaishnavism (Gaudiya means 'of Bengal', so it is the Bengal school of Vaishnavism) and determined its unique style and character. It emphasizes the concept of Krishna as *prānanātha* (Lord of one's life) and that separation from him is total misery while spiritual union is divine bliss. Spontaneous and unconditional devotion (*ahaituki* bhakti) to him and constant singing of his name *(samkirtanam)* are the best means of attaining *moksha*. This tradition is alive today and ISKCON is one of its many representations.

7. BHAGWAN SWAMINARAYAN (1781-1830 CE)
Shri Swaminarayan Vedant Darshana

Another very popular and recent Bhakti Vedānta *sampradāya* is the Swaminarayan Sampradaya. Though Bhagwan Swaminarayan, the founder, did not himself write commentaries on the three principal shastras (Upanishads, Brahmasutras and Bhagavad Gita), his disciples did so in his time. Bhagwan Swaminarayan established the Swaminarayan Sampradaya on the principles of the Hindu shastras. We shall first briefly consider his life, work and teachings.

Bhagwan Swaminarayan was born in 1781 into a Brahmin family in the village of Chhapaiya, near Ayodhya in north India. He spent his childhood years in Chhapaiya and Ayodhya and then left home at the age of eleven. For seven years he travelled 12,000 km throughout India to enlighten and liberate aspirants, finally settling in 1799 in Gujarat, in the ashrama of Ramanand Swami, a Vaishnava guru. He was appointed as head by Ramanand Swami at the age of twenty-one. Thereafter he

Bhagwan Swaminarayan

travelled in Gujarat edifying the masses. He had 3,000 sadhu-disciples and a large following of devotees. He established six mandirs to propagate bhakti and *upasana*.

Bhagwan Swaminarayan believed in five eternal realities, namely, *jiva, ishwara, maya,* Brahman and Parabrahman. Parabrahman is supreme and independent. Brahman is independent of *jivas, ishwars* and *maya* but dependent on Parabrahman. Both the *jivas* and *ishwars* are bound by *maya*. The *jivas* realize Parabrahman through the spiritual association of Parabrahman himself or Brahman (also known as Aksharbrahman or the Gunatit guru). Bhagwan Swaminarayan revealed that Gunatitanand Swami was the manifest form of Aksharbrahman, his ideal devotee and his eternal abode called Akshardham. Bhagwan Swaminarayan promised to remain ever-present on earth through the *parampara* (tradition) of Aksharbrahman to help the aspirants attain liberation. Thus, he identified Gunatitanand Swami as his first spiritual successor. Thereafter, the succession of Aksharbrahman gurus has continued through Bhagatji Maharaj, Shastriji Maharaj, Yogiji Maharaj and today through Pramukh Swami Maharaj.

Bhagwan Swaminarayan revealed that *maya* is real and that *jivas, ishwars, maya* and Aksharbrahman are separate and independent entities that never merge into or become a part of Parabrahman. Aksharbrahman is always subservient to God (*Swami-sevaka bhava*) and the *jivas* and *ishwars*, on attaining *moksha*, also worship and remain subservient to Parabrahman. Bhagwan Swaminarayan propagated bhakti coupled with the knowledge of God's glory as the means of attaining the grace of God or guru. He also emphasized that by profoundly associating (*atmabuddhi*) with the Gunatit guru one is blessed with *moksha*. He stressed the importance of imbibing *ekantik* dharma, which is identical to *ekantiki bhakti,* that includes dharma, *jnan, vairagya* and *navadha* bhakti (nine types of worship), in life. Daily satsang and observance of the moral commands of the shastras are necessary for spiritual progress. For his sadhus he prescribed five moral vows, namely, celibacy *(nishkam)*, non-greed *(nirlobh)*, non-taste, *(nisswad)*, non-attachment *(nissneh)* and humility *(nirman)*. For his householder devotees he prescribed abstinence from liquor, meat, stealing and adultery, and the observance of social and personal purity.

Bhagwan Swaminarayan explained that God is not formless but has a perfect and divine human form. He is the all-doer, supreme and always present on earth through the God-realized Gunatit guru (Aksharbrahman). Through the grace of the Satpurush or the God-realized guru, aspirants come to realize that they are atman and thus attain God-realization.

His philosophical and spiritual teachings were compiled into a holy shastra called the Vachanamrut, which contains 262 discourses. He has given a moral code of conduct called the Shikshapatri for the benefit of all people.

Bhagwan Swaminarayan established the Swaminarayan Sampradaya wherein he is revered as the supreme God and is stated to be ever-present on earth through the Gunatit guru.

CONCLUSION

Almost every *āchārya* propagated his own teachings after studying and writing commentaries on the Upanishads, Brahmasutras and Bhagavad Gitā. Their works form the Vedāntic philosophies. Sometimes, instead of the founder *āchārya* their disciples wrote commentaries on the Prasthāntrayi. Some *āchāryas* founded *sampradāyas* or fostered existing ones. Their milestone contributions have provided India and the world with a profound legacy of philosophical and theological works. Through the centuries many scholars of philosophy and theology have been impressed with their depth of investigation and perception. The ultimate aim and message of all the Vedāntic schools is to attain *moksha*.

SUMMARY

1. Ādi Shankarāchārya, a Shaiva, enunciated the philosophy of Kevalādvaita (absolute monism). He believed in a sole Ultimate Reality called Brahman. He said that everything is pervaded by Brahman. The world and its forms are an illusion. Only Brahman is truly real, and essentially an individual soul is the same as Brahman. He said that Brahman is all-knowing (*sarvajna*), all-pervading (*sarva vyāpaka*) and all-powerful (*sarva shaktimān*) and formless (*nirākāra*). *Moksha* to him is the realization, through *jnāna*, that one's soul is Brahman.

2. Shri Rāmānujāchārya was a Vaishnava *āchārya* who gave the philosophy of Vishishtādvaita (qualified non-dualism). He believed in the doctrine of three eternal realities: Ishwara, *jiva* and *māyā*. Ishwara or God is independent and the other two are dependent on him, just like the body is dependent on the soul for its existence and function. He said that God is personal and has a divine form. Through bhakti and *prapatti* (self-surrender) to God the *jiva* earns the grace of God and is blessed with *moksha*. Even in this state the *mukta* remains subservient to Nārāyana or God. He promoted the Shri Vaishnava Sampradāya.

3. Shri Nimbārkāchārya was a Vaishnava who established the philosophy of Dvaitādvaita (dualistic non-dualism). His *sampradāya* is known as Kumāra or Hamsa Sampradāya. He believed in three realities: Parabrahman, *māyā* and *jivas*. He said that *māyā* and *jivas* are dependent on Parabrahman but do not lose their individualities. The *jivas*, through *jnānā, upāsanā,* bhakti, *prapatti* and devotion to God and the God-realized guru, attain God's grace and are blessed with *moksha.*

4. Shri Madhvāchārya was a Vaishnava who propagated the philosophy of Dvaita (pure dualism). His *sampradāya* is known as Brahma Sampradāya. He believed in three

realities: God, *jivas* and *mayā*. He advocated the doctrine of pure dualism in which God and soul are totally different, souls are also different from each other, soul and matter are different, God and matter are different, and matter among matter is different. Shri Madhva preached that God is personal and has a divine form. He believed that bhakti is born out of correct knowledge of God, and because of bhakti one is blessed with God's grace and thus attains *moksha*.

5. Shri Vallabhāchārya was a Vaishnava who advocated the philosophy of Shuddhādvaita (pure monism). His Bhakti *sampradāya* is called Rudra or Vallabha Sampradāya. The means to *moksha* is *pushti* bhakti. Pushtimārga means the path of intense love for Krishna. Vallabhācharya says that Parabrahman is Krishna and he is the highest Reality, and the *jivas* and *mayā* are his manifestations like sparks that fly from the great fire. Through profound devotion to Krishna the *jivas* earn his grace and are blessed with *moksha*.

6. Shri Chaitanya Mahāprabhu was a Vaishnava and is believed to have been Krishna in the form of Rādhā. He enunciated the philosophy of Achintyabhedābheda or 'inconceivable difference and non-difference.' His tradition is known as Gaudiya Vaishnava Sampradāya. He believed, like all *āchāryas* of the Bhakti *sampradāyas,* that God has a divine form. Chaitanya Mahāprabhu stressed on offering profound bhakti or intense love to Krishna. Such bhakti is nurtured through chanting of His holy name.

7. Bhagwan Swaminarayan, also a Vaishnava, established the Swaminarayan Sampradaya. His philosophy is known as Swaminarayan Vedant Darshana. He believed in the doctrine of five eternal realities, viz. *jiva, ishwar, maya,* Brahman and Parabrahman. The first two are bound by *maya* and the latter two are eternally untouched by *maya.* For the *jivas* to secure *moksha* they need to attain the state of *brahmarup*

by profoundly associating with Brahman (the God-realized Sadhu). He believed that God has a personal form *(sakar)* and that the *jivas* remain separate and subservient to God even when they attain *moksha*. Bhagwan Swaminarayan declared that he would remain ever-present on earth through his Gunatit Sadhu in human form for the liberation of countless souls. Bhagwan Swaminarayan was revered as the supreme God by devotees in his own lifetime and even to this day millions worship him as such in the Swaminarayan Sampradaya.

8

Hindu Sampradāyas

Hindu sampradāyas or traditions worship Bhagwan
Vishnu, Shiva, Surya, Devi, Ganesha and other deities.
(Inset) Children offer respects at a holy shrine

Vaishnavism, Shaivism,
Shāktism and Smārtism

INTRODUCTION

In later Vedic times there was an increase in the practice
of *yajna* rituals, *varnāshrama* dharma and the ideology of
renunciation. Then there was a surge in worship of individual
deities, with devotees venerating and claiming their respective
deities to be supreme. This led to a proliferation of traditions
and *sampradāyas*.

This phenomenal variety of deities, beliefs, practices and
ways of worship makes it difficult for non-Hindus to get a clear
idea about Sanātana Dharma. They have a general impression
that Hindus worship many 'Gods'. The truth, however, is that
Hindus generally believe in and worship one supreme God. The
Rig Veda and Yajur Veda say *"Ekam sat viprāhā bahudhā vadanti"*
– "To what is One, wise seers give many names." The four main
traditions of Hinduism are Vaishnavism, Shaivism, Shāktism
and Smārtism. The followers of the first three traditions believe
in and worship Vishnu, Shiva, Shakti (Pārvati) respectively.
While the Smārta offer devotion to the God or Goddess of his/
her choice, namely, Vishnu, Shiva, Shakti, Surya or Ganesha.
Thus, Hindu worshippers have a wide choice, but they focus
their attention in worshipping one as the Supreme deity.

The Purānas contain abundant material to enable one to
understand the birth and growth of the four traditions.

1. Vaishnavism: Its followers, known as Vaishnavas or
   Vaishnavites, worship Vishnu in the forms of Nārāyana,
   Rāma, Krishna and other avatars.

2. Shaivism: Its followers are called Shaivas or Shaivites who worship Shiva in many forms.

3. Shāktism: Its followers worship the goddess Shakti, the consort of Shiva, in the forms of Pārvati, Durgā, Kāli, Ambā, etc.

4. Smārtism: Its followers are called Smārtas. They are mostly traditional south Indian brahmins. They pay respect to all five deities, namely, Vishnu, Shiva, Devi, Surya and Ganesha, but worship only one of them with highest devotion. Their worship is based on Smruti texts.

Each of the traditions, except Smārtism, has their own guru *paramparā*, sacred texts, monastic and lay following, holy places and mandirs. Despite the fact that the main three traditions are different and distinct they are interconnected and share a common heritage of concepts and beliefs, like *avataravāda*, karma, reincarnation, worship in mandirs, sacraments, *guru-shishya* tradition, and acceptance of the Vedas as the highest scriptural authority. The four Hindu traditions are widespread in India and throughout the world. Let us consider the salient aspects of each of the traditions.

1. VAISHNAVISM

Sacred tulsi plant

Shālagrāma, sacred stone worshipped as form of Vishnu

This is the largest of all Hindu traditions that mostly worships Vishnu as the supreme God. Vishnu is also known as Nārāyana, Vāsudeva and Purushottama. His popular avatars are Nrusimha, Rāma and Krishna. Vaishnavism is intimately connected with *murti-pujā* and teaches that through God's grace the soul attains *moksha*. The Vaishnavas also worship the tulsi plant and Shālagrāma (a round petrified ammonite pebble from the Gandaki River in Nepal). Vishnu is believed to be present in both of them.

Vaishnavism is the largest theistic Hindu denomination. Theism is the idea that there is a supreme distinct God (or Goddess in case of Shāktas) who is the originator, governor and destroyer of the entire universe. He or she has the power to save people from the cycle of births and deaths and grant them freedom through his sheer grace. There are clear references to Vishnu and Nārāyana in the Vedic literature. But there were independent faiths of Vāsudeva-Krishna, Krishna-Gopāla, Sātvatas and Bhāgavatas. Vaishnavism has resulted from the merging of all these traditions. As a result Vaishnavas have diverse philosophical and religious concepts but they do have certain fundamental features common to all: (1) Paramātmā or Parmeshwara (Vishnu, Nārāyana, Vāsudeva, Nrusimha, Rāma, Krishna) is the supreme Person (Purushottama). (2) He is *saguna* and *sākāra*. (3) He and only he is the cause of creation, governance and destruction. (4) He reveals himself through incarnations, sacred shastras, divine *murtis* in the mandir and God-realized gurus. These principles are found in the Pāncharātra Samhitās, known as Vaishnava Āgamas, and Tantras in Sanskrit.

Shri Vaishnavism was popularised by the Ālvārs, the God-immersed twelve saint-poets of south India, who lived between the sixth and ninth century CE. They composed and sang heart-stirring Tamil devotional songs in praise of Bhagwan Vishnu or Nārāyana and his consort, Lakshmi, Rāma and Krishna. They travelled from mandir to mandir and helped in establishing pilgrimage sites. They attracted people from all social classes because they themselves were from different strata of society. The most famous of them was Nammālvār. He was from a low caste called Vellala. The seventh Ālvār was a woman of unknown origin adopted by the sixth Ālvār, a Brahmin priest named Vishnuchitta. She was called Āndāl, who wrote soul-stirring devotional bhajans in praise of Bhagwan Krishna. She is considered to be the incarnation of Vishnu's wife, Lakshmi. According to Vaishnava legends, she merged into the *murti* of Vishnu in the Shrirangam mandir. The other Ālvārs are considered to be Vishnu's incarnations or the personifications of

Āndāl, one of the twelve Ālvārs

his holy articles, namely, mace *(gadā)*, disc *(sudarshana chakra)*, jewel *(kaustubha)*, etc. The Tamil songs written by the Ālvārs were collected by Nāthamuni, the teacher of Yāmunāchārya, and are known as *Divya Prabandham* ('divine compositions'). This book of 4,000 verses was set to music, and the verses are sung during worship of the deity in the Shri Vaishnava mandirs. The *Divya Prabandham* became accepted as authoritative as the Shruti texts or Vedas by all the *āchāryas* of Shri Vaishnavism. Vishishtādvaita Vedānta accepts the *Divya Prabandham* as one of its two principal sacred texts.

BHAKTI MOVEMENTS OF VAISHNAVISM

From the sixth century onwards Hinduism initially found inspired champions of the bhakti creed in the Ālvārs of Tamil Nadu. Their powerful bhakti songs started regenerating Hinduism gradually and eliminating the non-Vedic influence of Buddhism and Jainism. The Ālvārs were straightforward, simple *bhaktas* rather than philosophical or theological pundits. They worshipped the supreme God, called Nārāyana, Vishnu, Vāsudeva, Rāma, Mādhava, Krishna or Hari. He was described as a king, master or beloved to be wooed and revered by the *bhaktas* pure at heart. He did not reveal himself to the proud, the argumentative and the devoutless intellectual pundits, but to loving and surrendered *bhaktas*, who felt that without his grace they could not live! This bhakti movement of the Ālvārs started in the southern State of Tamil Nadu. The devotees went about singing their bhajans to their beloved deities (who are manifestations of Vishnu) enshrined in different mandirs during public worship or performance of daily ritual in the Tamil language. It is believed that the bhakti movement spread from Tamil Nadu to the Kannada-speaking regions, giving birth to the Haridāsa movement in Karnataka and other such movements in Maharashtra. Thereafter the Hindi, Bengali, Assamese, Oriya, Gujarati, Marwadi and Punjabi speaking

Bhagwan Vishnu

regions took it up and the whole of India became awash with this resurgent bhakti movement. Thus the real source of the vitality of the Bhakti religion was always the enthusiasm of its saint-poets and mystic poets who travelled the length and breadth of India to sing the glories of God.

A very striking feature of almost all the bhakti poets and mystics is their insistence on the cultivation of high moral virtues such as purity, truthfulness, patience, forbearance, love, renunciation, selflessness, contentment, self-control, pity, freedom from greed and hypocrisy, sincerity and humility. Almost all of them recommended the traditional Vaishnava sadhana as the means to liberation. The sadhanas consisted of satsang, kirtan, *nāma japa*, worshipping of a sacred *murti* and submission to a God-realized guru. Almost all of them emphasized that it is God's grace that saves the *bhaktas*. The spiritual sadhanas only prepares them to receive the divine grace. There were many Vaishnava movements that sustained, strengthened and helped the Vaishnava Sampradāya to flourish. Some of the important movements are outlined briefly:

1. The Ālvārs of Shri Vaishnavism were located in the Tamil country and nearby regions. The Shrirangam Mandir was its main centre. The shrine situated on an island in Kāveri River near Tiruchirapalli. The mandir also helped in the development and growth of the Vishishtādvaita philosophy of Shri Rāmānujachārya.

2. The Haridāsa Movement of Karnataka consisted of two branches, namely, the Vyāsakuta and Dāsakuta. The former was fostered by the sannyasis of the Madhva School, namely, Shripādarāya (15 century CE) and Vyāsarāya (1447-1539 CE). The latter, Dāsakuta Movement, meaning 'an assembly of the servants {of God}', was nourished by Purandaradāsa (1484-1564 CE), Kanakadāsa (15th century CE), Vijayadāsa (1687-1755 CE) and other householder devotees.

The sannyasis of the movement wrote scholarly works in

Sant Jnāneshvar

Sanskrit and composed devotional songs in Kannada, the vernacular of Karnataka. Through the devotional songs they spread Krishna bhakti and the truths of Dvaita Vedānta of Madhvāchārya.

3. The group of Maharashtrian saint-poets, who were mainly ardent devotees of Shri Vitthala or Pānduranga or Vithobā (Krishna) and his wife Rukmini, were large in numbers and profound in devotion. The doyen was Jnānadeva or Sant Jnāneshvar (1275-1296 CE). He was the author of *Jnāneshvari,* a Marāthi commentary on the Bhagavad Gita, as well as a composer of many *abhangas* (bhajans). So he was both a scholar and an ardent devotee. Nāmdev (1270-1320 CE) of Pandharapura and Jānabāi (14th century) were also great devotees and poets of Vithobā. They composed extraordinary *abhangas*. The saint-poets Ekanātha (1533-1606 CE) and Tukārām (1598-1649 CE) are famous even today for their *abhangas*. They helped found the Vārakari Sampradāya whose members regularly sing the *abhangas* of Tukārām and others in fortnightly gatherings even today. Also, during pilgrimage by foot to Pandharpur they sing them continuously.

4. The North Indian Bhakti Sampradāya of Shri Rāmānanda (14th or 15th century), located mainly at Ayodhyā and Janakapuri, is devoted to Rāma and Sita. He accepted disciples from all castes. It is believed that Kabir, a Muslim weaver; Raidās or Rohidāsa (15th century), a shoe-maker; Sena, a barber; and Padmāvati, a woman, were his disciples. In this movement a devotee is a servant and God is the master. Hanumān is considered an ideal devotee worthy of emulation.

5. Gaudiya or Bengal Vaishnavism is located mainly in Bengal, Orissa and Vrindāvan (Uttar Pradesh). It was founded by Shri Chaitanya Mahāprabhu with the focus of devotion on Krishna and Rādhā. This movement represents pure emotionalism

Rashtrotthana Sahithya

Nāmdev, saint-poet of Maharashtra

Rashtrotthana Sahithya

Tukārām, saint-poet of Maharashtra

Raidās or Rohidāsa of Vārānasi

or ecstatic love for Krishna and Rādhā, and *nāma japa* as the easiest means to *mukti*. The 'Hare Krishna Movement' established by the late Swami Bhaktivedānta Prabhupāda, follows this tradition of Gaudiya Vaishnavism.

6. Assamese Vaishnavism is widespread in Assam and northeast India. It was founded by Shri Shankaradeva (1486-1568 CE). He had visited many pilgrim places over a period of 12 years, briefly meeting Shri Chaitanya Mahāprabhu. He was greatly influenced by Jagadisha Mitra who taught him the Shrimad Bhāgavata Purāna. Shri Shankaradeva translated the *dashama skandha* (tenth chapter) of the Shrimad Bhāgavata Purāna into Assamese, which is very popular in Assam today.

Shri Chaitanya Mahāprabhu

Shankaradeva worshipped Krishna as Madanagopāla in a special prayer hall called *nāmaghara*. He initiated aspirants. The initiation ritual was called *sharana*. In the prayer halls built under his guidance he installed the sacred text of the Bhāgavata Purāna instead of Shri Krishna's *murti* to avert the prevailing need of formal worship, which only a Brahmin priest could perform. Thus the Bhāgavata Purāna was not only revered as a scripture but also as a sacred object of worship. He believed Krishna to be supreme, and the *jivas* and *māyā* to be his parts. He considered total surrender to Krishna with *dāsya* bhakti (devotion as a servant) as the best means to attain *moksha*.

Shankaradeva of Assam

7. In addition to the movements mentioned above, there were two individual devotees who were institutions by themselves. They were Shri Tulasidāsa (1496-1622 CE), author of the Hindi Rāmāyana called *Rāmcharitamānas* and Surdās (1479-1584 CE), the author of *Surasāgara*. They are two of the greatest saint-poets of the Bhakti Movement and Hindi literature. The former was a great devotee of Shri Rāma and the latter of Shri Krishna. Their life and work empowered Hindu society with devotional pride.

Tulasidāsa

Thus the Vaishnava Bhakti movement that started somewhere in 600 CE developed into an exuberant and emotional form or path of devotion. It originated in the south due to the great efforts of Ālvār saints, and developed and united with the Bhakti traditions of the north, north-east and west. Its association with people of lower social strata, simple rituals, emphasis on easy to perform rituals like *nāma japa*, dance and music helped Hinduism to survive even in the most challenging times.

PHILOSOPHICAL BASIS OF BHAKTI IN VAISHNAVISM

The philosophical branches of Vaishnavism were established in the Middle Ages by the great *āchāryas,* namely, Rāmānujāchārya (1017-1137 CE), Nimbārkāchārya (1125-1162 CE), Madhvāchārya (1238-1317 CE), Rāmānanda (1400-1470 CE), Vallabhāchārya (1473-1531 CE) and Chaitanya Mahāprabhu (1486-1533 CE). From the fifteenth century onwards prominent Vaishnava poet-devotees like Narsinh Mehtā, Surdās, Tulasidāsa, Mirābāi, Tukārām and Tyāgarāja spread and gave an impetus to the Vaishnava tradition in the whole of India.

All the Vaishnava traditions or *sampradāyas* generally worship Bhagwan Vishnu and his various forms as they believe in his *sākāra swarupa.* The principal means of associating with God and attaining liberation are profound bhakti or devotion and *prapatti* or total surrender. *Murti* worship in mandirs and celebrations of holy days are elaborately observed. Worshipping the *murti* of God by bathing, clothing, decorating, offering food, performing *ārati* and singing bhajans describing the glory of his divine form are some of the daily acts of devotion performed by the devotees at home and in mandirs. Vaishnava devotees traditionally apply an *urdhvapundra tilaka* (U- or Y-shaped mark) of sandalwood paste with a round red mark or a red vertical line of *kumkum* at its centre on their forehead and wear a *kanthi* or necklace made of tulsi beads around their neck.

Surdās

The main shastras of the Vaishnavas include the Vedas, Vaishnava Āgamas, Rāmāyana, Mahābhārata, Bhagavad Gitā, Vishnu Purāna, Bhāgavata Purāna, and bhajans of the Ālvārs and other saint-poets. The important pilgrim places for Vaishnavas include Badarinātha, Jagannātha Puri, Ayodhyā, Chhapaiya, Dwārakā, Vrundāvan, Mathurā, Kānchipuram, Guruvāyur, Shrirangam, Tirupati, Nāthadwārā, Pandharapura, Māyāpura and many others.

The great *āchāryas* (philosophers) revitalized the bhakti movement through immense efforts by writing Sanskrit commentaries on the Prasthāntraya. Their philosophies are dealt with in detail in Part 1, Chapter 7. We shall now briefly consider the philosophical basis of bhakti taught by the *āchāryas*.

1. Shri Rāmānujāchārya (1017-1137 CE)

Shri Rāmānujāchārya was born in a Brahmin family in 1017CE at Shriperumbudur (ancient name was Bhootpuri) near Chennāi. He rejuvenated the path of bhakti, and propagated bhakti and *prapatti* (absolute surrender) to God as a means to liberation for all. Prior to him Ādi Shankarāchārya had propagated the *jnāna-mārga* and declared that the soul is identical to Parabrahman (God).

Rāmānuja's philosophy of Vishishtādvaita (qualified monism) has three realities: *jiva* (*chit* or soul), *jagat* (*achit* or world) and Ishwara (Parabrahman). He believed God is Shri Vishnu, also called Shri Nārāyana, and Shri Vāsudeva. The abode of Nārāyana is Vaikuntha and Lakshmi is his consort. They are described to be a divine couple, i.e., *divya dampati*. Lakshmi-Nārāyana is worshipped for *moksha*. He said that *jagat* is real, and when the *jiva* attains *moksha* it never merges with God but forever remains subservient and offers bhakti to him in a divine form in Vaikuntha *dhāma*. He did not believe in *jivan-mukti*.

The recumbent figure of Shri Ranganātha (Bhagwan Vishnu) at Shrirangam Mandir, Tamil Nadu, worshipped by Rāmānujāchārya. In the foreground are Utsava murti of Vishnu with his consorts, Bhudevi and Nilādevi

2. Shri Nimbārkāchārya (1125 to 1162 CE)

Shri Nimbārkāchārya was born to a Telugu Brahmin couple in the Bellary district of Karnataka. He was a devotee of Krishna and later settled with his parents in Vrundāvan (near Mathurā in Uttar Pradesh). He emphasized upon *mādhurya* bhakti (loving devotion) towards Krishna as the means of liberation. The devotee has to attain the divine attributes of Rādhā to become eligible for offering profound devotion to Krishna. Nimbārka believed that God has two aspects – the majestic and the sweet. He is all-powerful and also all-merciful, transcendent and also immanent, all-pervading *(sarva-vyāpaka)* and also residing in the hearts of all *(antaryāmin)*. He prescribed five sadhanas that enable the devotee to attain *moksha*: (1) *nishkāma* karma – selfless action in accordance with the shastras, (2) *jnāna* – knowledge of Parabrahman and self, (3) *upāsanā* – meditation on Rādhā-Krishna, (4) *prapatti* – self-surrender to God and (5) *gurupāsati* – strict obedience to guru or master.

Shri Rādhā-Krishna

Bhagwan Vishnu and Lakshmiji

Nimbārka's philosophy is known as Dvaitādvait (identity-in-difference). Like Rāmānujāchārya he accepts three realities, Ishwara (Paramātmā), *jivas (chit)* and matter *(achit* or *prakruti)*. Paramātmā is supreme and independent, whereas the *jivas* and matter are dependent upon him. In this sense there is non-duality between Ishwara and *jivas* and matter. But they are different from Paramātmā, hence the principle of duality. He compares this relation of identity-in-difference to that of the sun and its rays. The rays are part of the sun and yet they are not the sun itself. Likewise, the *jivas* and *jagat* are part of God, yet they are not God. Nimbārka's identity-in-difference is the first philosophical expression of the Rādhā-Krishna faith which became extremely popular in India.

3. Shri Madhvāchārya (1238-1317 CE)

Shri Madhvāchārya was born in a Brahmin family in 1238 CE

in the village of Pājaka, near Udipi in south Karnataka. He is the founder of the Dvaita School of philosophy which is contrary to the Advaita philosophy of Shankarāchārya. Madhva maintained that Parabrahman and *jivas* are eternally distinct, and that the *jivas* are superior to and distinct from matter. The *jivas* are dependent on Paramātmā. He further expounded that there are differences between Paramātmā and *jivas*, Paramātmā and matter, individual *jivas, jiva* and matter and matter and matter.

Madhva propagated bhakti towards God based on the knowledge and glory of His form (*jnāna*). He propagated the worship of Vishnu or Nārāyana and Lakshmi who reside in Vaikuntha *dhāma*. Through profound bhakti Vishnu is pleased and grants the devotee *moksha*. The relationship between Parabrahman and *jiva* is that of a master and servant.

4. Shri Rāmānanda

Shri Rāmānanda was a renowned sannyasi who lived during the 14th or 15th century. He was born at Prayāga (Allahabad). His parents were Puyāsadana and Sushilā. He was an erudite scholar in Sanskrit and the Hindu shastras. He was initiated as a sannyasi by his guru, Rāghavānanda, of the Shri Vaishnava tradition of Rāmānujāchārya in south India.

It is believed that Rāmānanda travelled from south India to live mostly in Kāshi. Thereafter he spread Rāma bhakti in north India. He believed Rāma to be the God or Brahman of the Upanishads. He advocated chanting of Rāma mantra and devotion to Rāma and Sita as the best means of liberation. The main feature of bhakti in this tradition is that of servant-master relationship. The devotee offers *dāsya* (humble) bhakti to Rāma. Hanumānji's humble devotion and servitude to Rāma is held to be ideal in this *sampradāya*.

There are no writings of Rāmānanda available at present, but the theology of the Rāmānanda *sampradāya* seems to be based on Tulasidāsa's *Ramacharitmānas*.

Shri Rāma, Sitā and Hanumān

Rāmalilā is enacted in New Delhi and other cities every year: Rāma, Sitā and Lakshmana during their 14 year exile in the forest

The Rāmānandi Sampradāya is mainly ascetic. He accepted disciples regardless of caste and social status. Among them were Kabir (a Muslim), Raidās (a shoemaker), Sena (a barber), and Padmāvati (a woman).

Their most popular festival, besides Rāma Navami, is Rāmalilā. It is celebrated in most places in north India for nine days in September-October, and especially on a grand scale at Rāmanagar near Vāranāsi. In it the story of Rāma and Sitā is dramatized, covering the main events of Rāma's life – his marriage, exile, forest travels, war against Rāvana, his victorious return to Ayodhyā and the establishment of Rāma *rājya*.

5. Shri Vallabhāchārya (1473-1531 CE)

Vallabhāchārya was born to Telugu Brahmin parents in 1473 CE in Champāranya near Raipur in Chattisgarh. He was the founder of the Pushti Mārga in the Vaishnava tradition. Pushti means to nourish or support. For offering bhakti to God he accepted *dāsa bhāva* (feeling of servitude), *sakhā bhāva* (feeling of friendship), *madhura bhāva* (sentiment of intense love) and *vātsalya bhāva* (sentiment of parental love). Among these, *vātsalya bhava* is predominant in Pushti Mārgā. The devotee regards himself as a parent of the child-form of Shri Krishna (Bālamukunda) – the presiding deity worshipped in

Shri Krishna as Bālamukunda

the Vallabha Sampradāya. The devotee offers his devotion and love and care for the *murti* of child Krishna.

Vallabhāchārya fostered the path of devotionally serving (*sevā*) the *murti* of child Krishna from morning till night and in accordance with the six seasons. It included performing five-time *āratis*, adorning and decorating the *murti*, offering *thālas* (food and drinks), doing darshan and celebrating festivals. He also introduced singing of bhajans before the deity. He inspired eight great poet-devotees (*ashtachhāpa*), out of which he initiated Kumbhanadāsa, Surdās, Paramānandadāsa and Krishnadāsa; and his son, Vitthaladāsa, initiated Govinda Swami, Chhita Swami, Chaturbhujadāsa and Nandadāsa. Among them all, Surdās is known as the sun of devotional Hindi poems. Vallabhāchārya believed that only by God's grace does the *jiva* attain *moksha*.

His son Vitthalanāthaji laid down rituals and conditions for serving and offering bhakti to the deity.

Vallabhāchārya founded the Shuddh-Advaita (pure non-dualist) philosophy. The relation between Parabrahman and the world is one of pure non-difference, i.e., they are one. Vallabhāchārya propounds that the *jivas* and *māyā* are parts (*amsha*) of God, like sparks that spring forth from a great fire. And both the *jivas* and *māyā* are eternal.

6. Shri Chaitanya Mahāprabhu (1486-1533 CE)

Shri Chaitanya Mahāprabhu or Krishna Chaitanya was born into a Brahmin family in 1486 CE in Navadvipa (Nadiā), Bengal. His guru, Ishwara Puri, belonged to the Madhva *paramparā*. His disciples believed Chaitanya Mahāprabhu to be an incarnation of Krishna and Rādhā in one body. He was a great scholar and teacher of Sanskrit and philosophy. He believed and propagated *nāma samkirtanam* (chanting God's name) as the easiest and the most effective way of bhakti that leads to *moksha*. He spread the tradition of Rādhā-Krishna bhakti which is flourishing throughout India today. Unlike Vallabha he took the formal

Beautifully adorned murtis of Shri Rādhā-Krishna, ISKCON Mandir

ISKCON, Ahmedabad

vow of renunciation and established his own ascetic order.

The chanting of the names of Radhā and Krishna is necessary because according to Chaitanya Radhā is Krishna, in the sense that she is his *shakti* and he is *shaktimān* or the holder of power. Through Radhā the cosmos becomes manifest.

Chaitanya's philosophy of Achintyabhedābheda explains that God and the *jivas* are 'inconceivably one and different'. Chaitanya did not formally establish a *sampradāya* by writing a commentary on the Prasthānatrayi, but he introduced Gaudiya Vaishnavism, which became a popular bhakti tradition. He propounded that Paramātmā or Krishna has three principle powers: *swarupa-shakti* – his internal power, *māyā-shakti* – external power from which the material world emerges, *jiva-shakti* – which forms the essence of finite *jivas*.

Chaitanya propagated intense love (bhakti) for Shri Krishna which results in constant divine joy. Liberation according to Gaudiya Vaishnavism is the constant ecstatic experience of the divine love or *rāsalila* between Radhā and Krishna in a spiritual body.[1] This he believed to be *moksha*.

7. Bhagwan Swaminarayan (1781-1830 CE)

Bhagwan Swaminarayan was born in a Brahmin family in

Murti of Bhagwan Swaminarayan

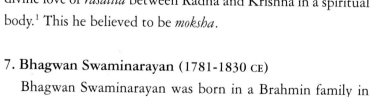

1. Flood.G. *An Introduction to Hinduism.* p.139.

1781 in Chhapaiya, near Ayodhya. He mastered the Hindu shastras by the age of ten, and at eleven he left home on a seven-year pilgrimage to liberate souls throughout India. After arriving in Gujarat he was initiated by guru Ramanand Swami. Two years later the guru appointed him as his spiritual successor. Thereafter he was popularly known as Bhagwan Swaminarayan.

He campaigned against the social evils of addictions, sati custom, dowry, animal sacrifices and superstitions. Philosophically, he believed in five eternal realities: *jiva, ishwar, maya,* Brahman and Parabrahman. He preached that by becoming *brahmarup,* through the association of a God-realized guru, one attains the state of liberation. He consecrated six traditional *shikharabaddh* mandirs in Gujarat for the propagation of bhakti and *upasana.* He stated that one should offer bhakti to God coupled with dharma and intense glory for God. He promoted art and music among his *paramhansas* as a means to offering bhakti. Muktanand Swami, Brahmanand Swami, Premanand Swami and Devanand Swami were some of his saint-poets who wrote and sang bhajans that were profuse with bhakti towards God. He celebrated Hindu festivals with great fervour and devotion. He discoursed daily on the Hindu shastras, which were compiled into a sacred text called the Vachanamrut.

Even today, after more than 200 years since its birth in Gujarat, the Swaminarayan Vaishnava tradition is vibrant in its thousands of mandirs and millions of homes in India and abroad. The devotees worship the *murtis* of Bhagwan Swaminarayan and other deities.

2. SHAIVISM

Shaivism is the tradition and philosophy of those who believe Shiva to be Parameshwara, the highest God and Supreme Being. After Vaishnavism, Shaivism is the second largest tradition. Bhagwan Shiva combines in himself the characteristics of

Bhagwan Shiva

Rudra deva, who is ferocious and terrible, and also of Shiva or Shambhu, who is benevolent. The Rig Vedic Rudra deva becomes the highest God in the *Shatarudriya* of the Yajur Veda and the Shvetāshvatara Upanishad (1.10; 3.2). Shaivism might have started as a simple faith with a prayer to Rudra (Rig Veda 7.46.2) to be propitious to children, cattle and property (Rig Veda.1.114.8). And later it grew over the centuries into various faiths and traditions.

Bhagwan Shiva is also respected as a yogi, as can be seen from the seals found in excavations of the prehistoric cities of Mohenjo-daro and Harappa. He has been depicted as the Lord of animals and thus named Pashupati or Bhutanātha. Bhagwan Shiva is described as an exemplary ascetic and simultaneously as a great householder always accompanied by his wife. He is further shown to be meditating in the severe cold of the Himalayas and in the eerie calm of a cemetery remaining totally indifferent to the surroundings and the world. He is portrayed as a master teacher of yoga and also a king of dancers (Natarāja). He is worshipped both in *murti* form and in symbolic form, i.e., as a *linga* in mandirs and homes.

On the whole it seems that Shaivism gives more importance to detached asceticism, yoga and contemplation rather than to bhakti or devotion. But there is also a strong tradition of profound devotion within Shavism, especially in South India.

In Shaiva theology there is a monistic *(advaitic)* school, known as Kashmir Shaivism, that believes the soul to be identical with Shiva. There is also a dualistic school, namely Shaiva Siddhānta, that believes the soul and Shiva to be eternally different, and in its liberated state the soul attains the qualities of Shiva but never merges in him. The dualistic school, which has a very strong bhakti component, was propagated and enriched by the saint-poets of south India known as Nāyanārs (also written as

Tirumular (Nāyanār saint) writing Tirumurāi – hymns on Shiva

Some Shiva saint-poets or Nāyanārs who composed the Tirumurāi

Nāyanmārs), who composed Shiva hymns, collectively known as *Tirumurāi*,[2] between 700 and 1000 CE. Even today they are sung daily by devotees. This Shiva bhakti school was opposed to the rigid *varnāshrama* system. The Nāyanārs, like the Ālvārs of Shri Vaishnavism, disregarded distinctions of gender, caste, creed, etc. Among them were Brahmins, oil sellers, toddy tappers, kings and princes. All devotees of Shiva, according to them, are the slaves of Shiva and each has a personal relation with him outside any institutionalized form. The Shaiva Siddhānta School in south India is mainly based upon the *Tirumurāi*.

Shaivism has five main traditions: (1) Purānic Shaivism, (2) Pāshupata Shaivism (Nepal), (3) Shaiva Siddhānta (mainly in Tamil Nadu), (4) Kashmir Shaivism or Shiva Advaita (formerly in Kashmir) and (5) Vira Shaivism or Lingāyata (mainly in Karnataka). An outline about each is as follows:

1. Purānic Shaivism

Purānic Shaivism started before the advent of the Gupta Dynasty (320-500 CE) and reached its zenith during the Gupta

---

2. The *Tirumurāi* is a collection of Tamil poems and songs compiled into twelve books. They contain fervent invocations of Shiva. A German scholar, K. Zvelebil, states, "The hymns [of *Tirumurāi*] have played, since the very days they have been composed until the present time, an immense and often decisive role in the religious, cultural and social life of the entire Tamil people." Zvelebil, Kamil. The Smile of Murugan. In *Tamil Literature of South India*. Leiden: Brill, 1973.

period. Stories of Bhagwan Shiva's glory, from the six Shaiva Purānas, were spread rapidly throughout the subcontinent by devotees who were writers, poets, singers and reciters. The six Shaiva Purānas are Matsya, Kurma, Linga, Shiva, Skanda and Agni. The most popular stories are from the Linga and Shiva Purānas. They contain *purānic* topics as well as Shaiva topics like installing *linga*, building Shaiva mandirs, forms of Shiva, asceticism, yoga, etc. The followers of the Purānic Shaivism are called 'Māheshwaras' by Ādi Shankarāchārya in his commentary on the Brahmasutra (2.2.37). They believe that the devoted among them will be liberated and reach Shiva-*loka* which is at the top of our *brahmānda* (universe).

2. Pāshupata Shaivism

Lord Shiva is also known as Pashupati – the Lord *(pati)* of all beings *(pashu)*. The sect is believed to have been founded by Lord Shiva who is regarded as omniscient, omnipresent and omnipotent. Pāshupata Shaivism is the oldest Shaiva sect. It is mentioned in the Nārāyaniya section of the Mahābhārata. The most important text of the faith is the *Pāshupata Sutra* of Sage Lakulish. He is considered to be the last incarnation of Shiva. It was initially an ascetic's path, in which the ascetics had to be male Brahmins. As per the sect the individual soul *(pashu)* fails to recognize Shiva *(pati)* owing to material desires *(pāsha* or fetters). The spiritual sadhana of the disciples or Pāshupatas involved overcoming of the ego in order to elicit Shiva's compassionate grace. The sadhana included a strict code of ethics, stressing on *brahmacharya* (celibacy), ahimsa (non-violence) and *tapas* (asceticism). The ascetics practised Shiva-intoxicated laughing, singing and dancing. Then they would act strangely in society by uttering to themselves, making snorting sounds, walking as if crippled and engaging in senseless gesturing to purposefully invite public censure. This was a sadhana to uproot their ego and overcome the dual feelings of like and dislike, praise and

Lakulish Mahādeva in Pāshupata Shaivism, Kāyāvarohan, Gujarat

Lakulish Mahādeva Mandir of Pāshupata Shaivism, Kāyāvarohan, Gujarat

insult and happiness and misery. The main focus of their sadhana was to break away from all types of mundane bondage and consolidate their bonds of love with Shiva. They also performed austerities, meditation and yoga to awaken the *kundalini shakti* and experience a rapport with Shiva. When this was achieved they acquired supernatural powers of omniscience, etc. which were similar to that of Shiva's. The Pāshupatas believe that the path of asceticism is realized when a person is steadfast in virtue and able to equally accept with equanimity all abuse and insult hurled at him. Liberation from karma and rebirth occurred at death, although ultimately this liberation was through the grace of Shiva.

Gavin Flood writes, "The Pāshupatas seem to have been very much on the edges of orthodox householder society, going beyond the four stages (ashramas) to a fifth 'perfected stage' or 'Siddha Ashrama' and spurning Vedic householder injunctions on purity and family life. Yet unlike many other Shaiva groups, the Pāshupata never completely abandoned or explicitly rejected Vedic values wishing to see his tradition as in some sense the culmination and fulfilment of Vedic life rather than its rejection."[3]

The five main topics discussed at length in the philosophical

3. Flood.G. *An Introduction to Hinduism.* p.156.

works of this sect are called Pancha-arthas – five subjects or categories. They are: (1) *Kārana*, (2) *Kārya*, (3) *Yoga*, (4) *Vidhi* and (5) *Dukhānta*. A brief explanation of each is as follows:

1. *Kārana* means primeval cause. Shiva is believed to be the *kārana*, i.e., the creator, maintainer and destroyer of the universe. He is without beginning and indestructible, transcendent, immanent, with limitless compassion. Om is his best symbol.

2. *Kārya* or effect is defined here to mean the world, which is dependent upon Shiva who is the *kārana* or independent cause. At the same time the *jivas* or individual souls are also *kārya* because they are dependent on Shiva. However even *jivas* and *prakruti* (world) are responsible for further evolution of the world. So they are also *kārana*, or cause. Thus they are both *kārya* (from Shiva's point of view) and *kārana* (being responsible for further creation). So *jiva* and *prakruti* are called *kārya-kārana*.

3. *Yoga* is called *samyoga* or union of *jiva* or atman (*pashu*) with Shiva, i.e., Ishwara. This union is possible through the grace of Shiva.

4. *Vidhi* means regulation and action that lead to yoga and the end of miseries. It consists of activities like covering one's body with holy ash, deliberately acting in such a way that people will shun the company of the *sādhaka* and isolate him, repeating the holy names of Shiva and circumambulating the Shivalinga. In short, *vidhi* means dos and don'ts for aspirants.

5. *Dukhānta* means end of all types of suffering and attaining the final bliss by withdrawing the mind and senses from worldly objects and directing them and surrendering them to Shiva. In Pāshupata *mukti* there is neither *kaivalya* (living alone) nor total merging or *aikya*. The released soul (*pashu*) will be in the eternal company of Ishwara or Shiva.

The venerable Lakulisha is believed to be the 28th or last

Shiva shown as creator, preserver and destroyer (Hinduism Today)

Abhisheka of crystal Shivalinga, Kauai's Hindu Monastery, Hawaii

Pashupatinātha Mandir, Kathmandu, Nepal

human incarnation of Shiva. He was a popular guru of the Pāshupata Sampradāya, born in Kāyāvarohan or Kārvan, near Vadodarā, Gujarat, around 200 BCE. The Sampradāya was very prominent in Gujarat and Rajasthan.

The householder path arose out of the former ascetic order. Somanāth (or Somnath) Mandir and the Pashupatinātha Mandir in Nepal are its prime centres of pilgrimage. It is believed that the Kālamukha and Lingāyata Shaivite sects originated from the Pāshupata Sampradāya.

3. Shaiva Siddhānta

The Shaiva Siddhānta is the most important, normative form of Shaivism in South India. It uses Tamil sacred texts yet it is interesting to note that it originated in Kashmir. The term means the doctrine of Shaivism in general. It is more of a religious devotional mysticism than a systematic philosophy.

The Shaiva Siddhānta school has a four-fold path that leads to enlightenment and liberation through bhakti of Shiva. They are: (1) *Vidyā*, which refers to knowledge of Pati (Shiva), Pashu (soul) and Pāsha (fetters, i.e., karma and *māyā*), (2) *Charyā*, which means virtuous and moral living, (3) *Kriyā*, which involves the worship of the deity in the mandir and performing of rituals and (4) Yoga, which refers to austerities and internalized worship.

Somanāth Mandir, Gujarat

This four-fold path results in union with Lord Shiva, through the blessings and grace of the living Satguru.

The final goal of the Shaiva Siddhānta, like that of other Hindu *sampradāyas,* is to attain liberation from the cycle of births and deaths. Here *mukti* is to become equal to or like Shiva. A devout Shaiva follower at death becomes omniscient and omnipresent like Shiva, but never Shiva himself. The Shaiva Siddhānta is a dualistic system of thought placing great emphasis on profound devotion. It maintains that there is an eternal distinction between God (Isha, i.e., Shiva) and the soul *(jiva)*, which is in total contrast to the monistic Kashmir Shaivism which believes Shiva and soul to be one.

The Shaiva Siddhānta School flourished in south India. The *Tirumurāi* is a compendium of lyrics in praise of Shiva by 63 Tamil saint-poets (Nāyanārs) who lived between 700 and 1000 CE. Along with the Vedas and Shaiva Āgamas it forms the basis of the shastras of Shaiva Siddhānta.

Shaiva Siddhānta has its own mandir tradition, festivals, sadhus and *guru-shishya paramparā.* The Shaiva Siddhānta School is the most prominent among the 60 million Tamil Shaivites who live mostly in south India and Sri Lanka.

Ranvireshwara Mandir of Kashmir Shaivism, Jammu

4. Kashmir Shaivism or Shiva Advaita

Kashmir Shaivism developed in northern India, with its earliest written texts in the eighth or ninth centuries CE, but the roots of the sect may be several centuries older. It is monistic and accepts the identity of the Lord (*pati* – Shiva), the individual soul (*pashu*) and the world (*pāsha*) or bond. *Pati, pashu* and *pāsha* are essentially one reality. *(Pati)* Shiva is immanent and transcendent, and performs through his *shakti* the five actions of creation, preservation, destruction, revealing and concealing. Kashmir Shaivism or Shiva Advaita includes both knowledge and devotion as sadhana for the realization that the soul is Shiva. There are three stages in attaining

Pancha Bakhtar Mahādeva (five-faced Shiva), Kashmir Shaivism, Jammu

realization: (1) worship rituals, yogic effort and purification through breath control, (2) constant awareness of Shiva in one's thoughts and (3) attainment of Shiva-consciousness. Finally, the guru endorses that the disciple has become Shiva. Realization depends upon the guru's grace. The basic philosophy of this school is given in the *Shivasutra* text of Vasugupta (900 CE). The Shiva Advaita philosophy is known as the Pratyabhijnā Darshana or 'Recognition School' – the recognition that the Lord (*Pati* – Shiva) is one Reality. Its main advocates were Utpala and Abhinavgupta. Kshemrāja wrote the *Pratyabhijnā-hrudayam* which is the heart or main text of the Recognition School.

Kashmiri Shaivites are few in numbers and reside mainly in Jammu and northern India.

5. Vira Shaivism or Lingāyatas

Vira Shaivism was made popular by Shri Basavanna or Basava (1105-1167 CE), of Karnataka, South India, a Brahmin who lived in the 12th century. He rejected the caste system, respected women to be equal to men and entitled for *diksha,* and promoted honest labour. Vira Shaivism is also called Lingāyata Sampradāya because its followers wear a small *linga,* symbol of Shiva, around the neck. They believe it always keeps them in touch with Shiva and reminds them of their innate Shiva nature. The Lingāyata School considers the Shivalinga to be the chief support or basis for final release or *mukti.*

Basavanna popularized Vira Shaivism

The Lingāyatas believe Shiva is both the efficient (*nimitta*) and material (*upādāna*) cause (*kārana*) of creation. The soul is a part (*amsha*) of Shiva. Through the six-stage path of devotion and surrender, namely, bhakti, selfless service, Shiva's grace, experience of everything as Shiva, refuge in Shiva and oneness with Shiva, the soul merges in Shiva. The soul in its liberated state becomes one with Shiva as water merges into the ocean.

The holy text of Vira Shaivism is called the *Vachanas* in the

Siddheswara Mahādeva, Siddhaganga Math (Lingāyat Mandir), Tumkur, Bangalore

Kannada language. The *Vachanas* are little pieces of rhythmic prose sermons meant for common people. They inspire bhakti towards Shiva.

The 28 Shiva Āgamas and the teachings of 63 Nāyanārs are the main sacred texts for the Vira Shaivas. The *Vedānta sutra* or *Shrikarabhāshya* of Shripati is their main philosophical work. Their philosophy is known as 'Shakti-Vishishta-Advaita'.

3. SHĀKTA

The Shākta tradition or Shāktism became an organized sect in India in the fifth century CE. Shāktism believes the Supreme Being to be the female form. This means that Sati or Pārvati, the consort of Lord Shiva, is revered as the Supreme Being. She is believed to be the creator, sustainer and destroyer of the infinite universes. Pārvati is worshipped as goddess Ambā in her benign form and as Chandi, Kāli, Chāmundā, etc. in her fierce form. The worship of Lakshmi, Sitā and Rādha is not part of Shāktism. The shastras that deal with the ritualistic worship of Shakti of Shiva (Pārvati, Durgā, Kāli, etc.) are known as Shākta Tantras. The sacred texts are in dialogue form between Shiva and Pārvati. In the Shaiva Tantras, Shiva, as the teacher, answers Pārvati's questions, and in the Shākta Tantras the goddess answers Shiva's questions. They are generally called Tantras, though the term Āgamas is also used. There are 64 Tantra shastras.

Pārvati Devi

Chandi and Chāmundā Mātā, Chotilā, Gujarat

The Shāktas or followers of Shāktism look upon the Devi as the Goddess. The name Devi is often interchangeable with Durgā, though it has a wider connotation. She is both a metaphysical principle and has a concrete divine female form that plays an active part in creation. Devi is also all-pervading and the means to liberation. Like a child the devotee surrenders himself or herself to the affectionate love of the Divine Mother. What the *jnāna* yogi tries to attain through the contemplation of God, the Shākta follower tries to realize through chanting of mantras, meditation and rituals involving the Goddess. There are three types of Shākta followers, namely, the lowest (*pashu-adhikāri*), the intermediary (*vira-adhikāri*) and the highest (*divya-adhikāri*). The *pashu-adhikāris* are bound by base instincts, *vira-adhikāris* are battling against their base instincts to overcome them, and the *divya-adhikāris* have already overcome their base instincts.

There are three different traditions in the Shākta Sampradāya, namely, the Vāma or Kaula *mārga* (left path), Dakshina or Sāmāyika *mārga* (right path) and Mishra *mārga* (combined school).

The Vāma Mārgi in Shāktism uses magic, trance, fire walking and animal sacrifice for healing, fertility and power. Some of the Vāma or Kaula Mārgi rituals are characterized by the use of the 'pancha-makāras' (five M's), namely, *madya* (intoxicating drinks), *māmsa* (meat), *matsya* (fish), *mudrā* (parched grains or certain hand postures) and *maithuna* (extramarital sexual intercourse) for transcending all the social norms. In this practice the *sādhaka* is required to face attractive objects of physical enjoyment and overcome them and fix his mind on the Goddess. The drinking of wine and contact of women are not meant for gratification, but to resist the pull of these enticements and concentrate on the Devi. The principle being that once the mind is focused on an attractive sense object, then instead of getting overwhelmed by it the Tantras direct him to turn his focused mind towards the Goddess. Some of the Tantra rites require the *sādhaka* to meditate on the Goddess after awakening the sexual impulse through contact with women. This is a very risky endeavour because the *sādhaka* is most susceptible to yield to his or her passions and become immoral. Another rite requires the *sādhaka* to fix his mind on the Devi in the most dreadful surroundings. He has to sit on a corpse in a crematorium on the darkest night of the month.

The Dakshina or Sāmāyika School worships the Devi as

Durgā Devi

the supreme Goddess with Vedic rites and rituals. It prescribes Kundalini yoga wherein the Kundalini *shakti* is made to rise in the spinal cord through the various *chakras* by performing mudras (touching fingertips on different parts of fingers) and yogic practices. The aim of this practice is to gain union with the Goddess and attain *moksha*.

The Mishra school worships and meditates upon the Goddess in the *murti* form or in the form of a geometrical diagram (*yantra*) engraved or drawn on metal, paper or palm leaf or through chanting of certain mantras (*hrim, krim,* etc.). The Shākta devotionalists perform puja rites on the *yantra* to establish a spiritual unity with the Goddess.

The Shākta doctrine propagates that matter and spirit are not different. It is *advaitic,* prescribing that the soul's merging with Devi is *moksha*. So, the Shāktas worship Devi for both material gains and liberation of the soul. Shāktism accepts the concept of *jivan-mukti* according to the Devi Bhāgavata Purāna (9.1.44).

4. SMĀRTAS

The fourth prominent living Hindu tradition is the Smārta tradition. It predominantly believes in and is based upon the Smruti shastras – Rāmāyana, Mahābhārata, Bhagavad Gitā, Purānas and Dharma Shastras. The Smārta devotees follow the Purānas and also revere the Vedas.

Bhagwan Vishnu

With the popularity and propagation of the Purānas, a powerful Sampradāya developed and grew in the Medieval Ages. With the blessings and encouragement of several Shankarāchāryas it has continued to flourish even today, mainly in South India. It is essentially a Brahmanical religion that has immense faith in the Smriti shastras and the Vedas. So the followers are called Smārtas. Sometimes they are known as *paurāniks* as they follow the ideals of the Purānas. They have an eclectic approach to the Supreme, and believe in worship of any one or all the five Purānic deities known as *panchāyatana* puja.

Bhagwan Shiva

The five deities are Vishnu, Shiva, Devi, Surya and Ganesha. Therefore they are called Hindu Universalists. The Smārtas de-emphasize the exclusivity of sectarian worship. They also oppose those Shrautas who have faith only in the performance of Vedic sacrifices and the Tāntrikas who follow non-Vedic Āgamas only. Smārtas follow both the Vedic and Purānic rules of purity and moral values.

SUMMARY

Surya Deva (sun-god)

1. There are four main Hindu traditions, namely, Vaishnavism, Shaivism, Shāktism and Smārtism. They all accept the authority of the Vedas, sacred texts, holy places, mandirs and rituals, and some have their own guru *paramparā*. The four traditions share common beliefs and practices like *avatāravāda*, karma, reincarnation, mandir worship and sacraments.

2. The Vaishnavas mostly worship Vishnu or Nārāyana and his manifestations, such as Nrusimha, Rāma, Krishna, etc. Bhakti and total surrender to God are their core principles for liberation. The great Vaishnava *āchāryas*, devotees and poet-mystics nourished and gave a fillip to the Bhakti Sampradāyas.

Shri Ganesha

3. The Shaivas worship Shiva as the Supreme Reality. They too have a tradition of rituals, *murti-pujā*, festivals, guru *paramparā*, saint-poets and canons to abide by.

4. The Shākta tradition worships the forms of Devi, Sati or Pārvati, the consort of Lord Shiva. The Goddess is worshipped in her benign and fierce forms as Pārvati and Ambikā, and, as Chandi, Kāli and Chāmundā.

Pārvati Devi

5. The Smārtas espouse the universality of Hinduism through the worship of Vishnu, Surya, Shiva, Devi and Ganesha. The tradition was nourished by Ādi Shankarāchārya and his successors in the ninth century and thereafter. The Smārta devotees may give equal respect or prominence to any one or all the five deities.

9

One God or Many "Gods"?

Bhagwan Vishnu and his ten principal avatars.
(Inset) Replica of the holy feet of God that symbolize his
advent on earth

Avatars of Bhagwan Vishnu,
Brahma, Shiva, Partial Manifestations...

INTRODUCTION

While the dominant impression of Hindus is that they worship many "Gods", the reality is that for many Hindus, their experience of Hinduism is through devotion to a single God. Hindus believe in one supreme Paramātmā or God. Some Hindus believe in one supreme deity and consider the other deities to be distinct and lower, while others believe that they are manifestations of the one supreme God. The focus of supremacy in different Hindu traditions and *sampradāyas* is on the deity or *ishtadevatā* that is worshipped. Among the Vaishnavas some believe Bhagwan Vishnu to be supreme, while others believe Bhagwan Rāma, Krishna or Swaminarayan as the *ishtadevatā* of their respective *sampradāyas* and so consider them to be the supreme God. The Shaivites believe Bhagwan Shiva to be supreme and the Shāktas believe goddess Pārvati or her manifestations to be supreme. The Smārtas either worship Vishnu, Shiva, Shakti, Surya or Ganesha as the supreme deity or they believe in all five of them. Hinduism allows this freedom of worship and belief of supremacy by devotees of various deities in different traditions. Therefore in each Hindu *sampradāya* there prevails the principle of one supreme Paramātmā without denying the existence of the other deities. This does not mean that there are many supreme Gods or deities in Hinduism, but that the one supreme Paramātmā is believed by various followers to be the respective deity they worship in their tradition and *sampradāya.* The Rig Veda states *"Ekam sat viprāhā bahudhā vadanti."* – "To what is One, wise seers give many names." Furthermore, any devotee, through his or her sadhana of genuine devotion, prayer, meditation, service, etc. to his own deity, will eventually be blessed with the realization of the supreme Paramātmā.

What is important is that the different deities, as *murtis* or sacred images, in mandirs help the devotee in realizing the divine Reality. Before we briefly describe the avatars and deities of the Hindu pantheon a special note for the readers is that this chapter conveys a predominantly Vaishnava perspective on Hinduism.

VISHNU

Bhagwan Vishnu, also known as Mahāvishnu, is responsible for sustaining and protecting all creation. Vishnu means "one who pervades" within all souls and all of creation and beyond. So he is both a transcendent and an immanent reality.

Another name of Vishnu is Nārāyana. Vishnu is described as reclining on the coils of the giant serpent Shesha or Ananta in an ocean of milk (Kshira-Sāgara). Shesha is believed to have one thousand heads that support the worlds. Lakshmiji, Vishnu's consort, massages his feet while he sleeps between the period of destruction of one *yuga* (cycle) and the creation of the next. In his *yoga nidrā* (contemplative light sleep), when he thinks about creating the next *yuga* (era), Brahmā emerges from his naval sitting on a lotus. When Vishnu wakes up, he instructs Brahmā to commence the process of creation.

Vishnu is commonly described as having a sky blue skin, because like the blue sky he is vast, infinite and all-pervading. Iconographically, he is shown to be standing alone or reclining on Shesha with Lakshmi pressing his feet. He has one face and four arms holding a *shankha* (conch), *chakra* (disc), *gadā* (mace) and *padma* (lotus); he wears the jewel called Kaustubha, has a curl of hair on his chest called Shrivatsa and wears a garland called Vaijayanti. His four arms represent the four directions, thus it is believed that he has absolute power in all directions. The sound of his *shankha* frightens the demons and they run away. With his *chakra* and *gada* he destroys the enemies of humanity. And the *padma* symbolizes purity and transcendence.

Bhagwan Vishnu is generally accompanied by Lakshmiji (or Shri), his consort. He also has a second consort called Bhumi. His mount is the Garuda (divine eagle). According to the Vishnu Purāna, Vishnu dwells in his divine abode called Vaikuntha. Through his grace his devotees attain Vaikuntha after death. The Vaishnava tradition maintain that Bhagwan manifests himself in the world in mainly four ways:

1. Through his avatars *(vibhava)* upon earth in times of darkness.
2. Through the consecrated *murti (archā)* in mandirs.
3. In the hearts of all beings as their inner controller *(antaryāmin)*.
4. Through the God-realized guru.

AVATARS (INCARNATIONS) OF BHAGWAN VISHNU

Bhagwan comes on earth in a human or other form to destroy evil and restore dharma and thus preserves the socio-ethical order.[1] His major avatars or incarnations are ten, however the Purānas and other shastras mention that there are twenty-four and more.[2] With respect to the magnitude of his task he either takes an *amshāvatāra*, *āveshāvatāra* or *purnāvatāra*.[3] Given below is a brief account of Vishnu's ten principal avatars.

---

1. B.G. 4.7.
2. The basis for the differing numbers of avatars rests on different *sampradāyas'* individual understandings and theological beliefs.
3. The avatars are mainly classified into three types. In the *amshāvatāra* there is a partial manifestation of the Divine, as in Sage Vyāsa. In the *āveshāvatāra* there is a temporary entry of the Divine, as in Bhagwan Nrusimha. And in the *Purnāvatāra* the manifestation of the Divine is complete or full, as believed in the case of Bhagwan Rāma, Krishna and Swaminarayan.

Matsya avatar, Vishnu's incarnation as fish *Kurma avatar, incarnation as giant tortoise*

1. MATSYA

Matsya avatar is the incarnation of Bhagwan Vishnu in the form of a fish *(matsya)*. It is associated with the rescue and liberation of Manu and the seven rishis (Saptarshis) with their wives from the great flood.[4]

The Purānic shastras state that a fish came into the hands of Prince Satyavrata while he was performing ablutions and prayers in a river. The prince was the son of King Vivasvān, who later became known as Vaivasvata Manu. The fish prayed to the prince to take care of it. So he put it in his waterpot, but by the time he reached his palace the fish had grown so big that it could not be contained in the waterpot. So, Satyavrata placed it in a tank but still it continued to grow, so he released it into a lake. Even the lake could not hold the fish. So, finally the prince released the fish into the ocean. The way the fish kept on growing compelled Satyavrata to believe that the fish was no ordinary creature but must instead be divine.

The fish, Bhagwan Matsya, told Satyavrata that there was going to be a terrible deluge after seven days and everything would be drowned. He would send a boat and save him. Then Satyavrata, as instructed by Matsya, filled the boat

---

4. *Shatapatha Brāhmana* 1.8.1. 1-6. and Matsya Purāna 1.11-35.

The Kurma avatar supports Mt. Mandarāchala to aid the devas and dānavas in successfully churning the ocean to get amruta, the immortalizing nectar

with varieties of seeds, pairs of animals of both genders and took the seven rishis and their wives on board. On the seventh day the devastating flood drowned the entire earth. Not a single dry spot could be found. The boat was saved by the giant golden fish or Matsya avatar, which had a horn. The boat had been tied to the horn of the fish with Vāsuki, the serpent-king, used as the rope. The deluge subsided and the world was repopulated by Prince Satyavrata, the seven rishis and their wives, and the animals and seeds they had with them.

2. KURMA

Bhagwan Vishnu appeared as a giant tortoise known as Kurma avatar. He incarnated to aid the churning of the ocean of milk by the devas (gods) and *dānavas* (demons).

The reason for churning the ocean was that the abode of Indra, king of the devas, was invaded and defeated by Bali, king of the *dānavas*. The devas prayed to Bhagwan Vishnu to protect them and to help them to regain their kingdom. Vishnu told them to churn the ocean to get *amruta*, the immortalizing nectar. The nectar would make them both victorious and immortal. The devas convinced the *dānavas* to be partners in this project. So, the devas and *dānavas* brought Mount Mandarāchala to use as

One God or Many "Gods"?

the churning rod and Vāsuki, the serpent, as a rope. However, upon placing the mountain in the ocean, the mountain sank. So they prayed again and Vishnu appeared as a giant tortoise. Mount Mandarāchala was placed on the tortoise's rock-hard back for support and then the churning began. In all, fourteen[5] unique items emerged from the ocean, namely, a deadly poison (*halāhala*), wish-fulfilling cow (Kāmadhenu), divine horse (Uchchaishravā), divine elephant (Airāvata), priceless jewel (Kaustubhamani), divine wish-fulfilling tree (Kalpavruksha), celestial dancer (Apsarā), goddess Lakshmiji, liquor (Surā), physician of the devas with a pot of *amruta* (Dhanvantari), moon (Chandra), divine conch (Pānchajanya Shankha), and finally a divine bow (Sāranga Dhanushya). When the immortalizing nectar emerged it was exclusively allotted to the devas only, who became immortal and invincible. The devas then defeated the *dānavas* and reclaimed their own kingdom.

3. VARĀHA

Varāha avatar is the boar-incarnation of Bhagwan Vishnu. It lifted the earth out of the great floodwaters into which it was submerged.

Varāha was born when Bhagwan Brahmā sneezed. Then the thumb-sized white boar grew into a giant. It dived into the ocean and brought the earth out on its tusks. Hiranyāksha, a demon, and brother of Hiranyakashipu, challenged Bhagwan Varāha to a fight. During the combat, Varāha killed Hiranyāksha and freed the earth from his oppression.

4. NRUSIMHA

Bhagwan Vishnu incarnated as Nrusimha (man-lion), whose head was that of a lion and the rest was that of a human. He came to protect his devotee Prahlāda, son of the demon Hiranyakashipu.

---

5. Skanda Purāna 5.1.44.

Varāha avatar, incarnation as boar   *Nrusimha avatar, incarnation as man-lion*

After the death of his brother, Hiranyāksha, Hiranyakashipu performed austerities and received the boon of apparent invincibility from Bhagwan Brahmā. Then, he terrorized the three worlds – *pruthivi* (earth), *swarga* (heaven) and *pātāla* (realms below earth).

Prahlāda, a pious soul, was born to Hiranyakashipu. Despite being schooled by Hiranyakashipu in his evil ways, Prahlāda remained firm in his faith in and devotion to Bhagwan Vishnu or Nārāyana (God). This angered Hiranyakashipu, and he thus told his men to kill his son. But time after time, they failed in their attempts. Finally, one day, he asked Prahlāda where his Vishnu was. Prahlāda replied that he was everywhere. Then Hiranyakashipu asked him whether his God was present in the red hot pillar that he had prepared. Prahlāda replied unequivocally, "Yes." The enraged Hiranyakashipu asked Prahlāda to embrace it. When again Prahlāda was unhurt, Hiranyakashipu angrily struck the pillar, and to his surprise Bhagwan Nrusimha emerged from it. A fierce combat ensued between them. Finally, Nrusimha took Hiranyakashipu in his lap and killed him with his claws.

Bhagwan Nrusimha manifested solely to protect his devotee Prahlāda.

It is said that once the purpose of Nrusimha's avatar was

One God or Many "Gods"?

accomplished he split himself into two. The lion part became Sage Nārāyana and the human part Sage Nara. Then both the sages retired to Badarikāshram to perform austerities. They were reborn later as Bhagwan Shri Krishna and Arjuna, respectively.

5. VĀMANA

Bhagwan Vishnu assumed the form of a dwarf called Vāmana to restore the lost glory and kingdom of the devas. The demon-king Bali, the grandson of Prahlāda, was a just ruler. He defeated the devas and conquered the three worlds. The devas appealed to Bhagwan Vishnu, who promised to save them. Then, he took birth as Vāmana, a dwarf, in a Brahmin family. He came to the 100th Ashwamedha Yajna[6] that Bali was performing at Dashāshvamedha Ghat in Bharuch, Gujarat. The king asked the radiant Brahmin boy to ask whatever he wished for. Bhagwan Vāmana asked for a gift of land that could be covered by his three steps. King Bali's guru, Shukrāchārya, told him not to grant it to him because the boy was God and that he had come to take away his entire kingdom. But Bali agreed to Vāmana's wish. Then to everyone's surprise Vāmana grew in size to assume a gigantic form. In his first step he covered the earth. In his second, he covered the regions of *swarga*. Then the question arose as to where to place his third step. Immediately, King Bali offered his head. Vāmana placed his foot on it and pushed him to *sutala*, the nether world. Bhagwan Vāmana was pleased by Bali's sacrifice and pledged to remain at his doorstep to give darshan for four months (Chāturmāsa)

---

6. Ashwamedha Yajna is one of the most ancient sacrifices mentioned in the Rig Veda 1.162-163. Only very powerful kings who wished to gain total sovereignty could afford to perform it. A white horse was allowed to wander for a year, guarded by four hundred armed men. The kings of the kingdoms where the horse entered either accepted the sovereignty of the patron of the Yajna and paid contributions, or, tied the horse and faced an armed conflict. When the horse returned, it was ritually immolated in a Yajna. The king performed the Yajna to achieve more sovereignty. The last king to have performed it was Jaya Simha II of Jaipur in the 18th century.

Vāmana avatar, incarnation as dwarf *Parashurāma*

every year. It is said that Bhagwan Vāmana (Vishnu) gave the nether world to Bali.

6. PARASHURĀMA

Parashurāma was the son of Maharshi Jamadagni and Renukā. He was the sixth incarnation of Bhagwan Vishnu, and he rid the earth of the arrogant Kshatriya rulers.

Once, King Kārtavirya Sahasrārjuna visited the ashram of Rishi Jamadagni, a Brahmin sage. The rishi entertained and feasted the king and his huge army using a divine, wish-fulfilling cow called Kāmadhenu (also called Kapilā) to provide all that was required. Tempted by her extraordinary abilities, the king wished to possess the divine cow and thus asked for her. The rishi refused in spite of his generous offer of riches. The king then assaulted Jamadagni, set fire to the ashram and forcibly took away the divine cow and her calf. When Parashurāma returned to the ashram after completing his austerities, what he saw filled him with rage and vengeance. He went to the king, killed him and his entire army, and brought Kāmadhenu back to his father's ashram. When Jamadagni came to know of what his son had done, he told Parashurāma to perform twelve years of penance in atonement for his sins. During Parashurāma's absence the late king's sons raided the ashram and killed Jamadagni. When Parashurāma came to know of it, he killed all the sons of Sahasrārjuna and then every adult Kshatriya on earth, not once but 21 times. Even then somehow eight Kshatriya kings remained incognito as potters, goldsmiths, etc. During his encounter with Rāma, Parashurāma lost all his powers and thus went away to perform penance in the Mahendra mountain range. Later, Parashurāma atoned for his sins. He is regarded as one of the seven immortal beings in Indian culture.

7. Rāma

Bhagwan Rāma is known as 'Maryādā Purushottama'. He possessed sterling qualities as a son, brother, husband and ruler. He adhered to and fostered dharma or righteousness. His father was King Dasharatha of Ayodhyā and his mother was Kaushalyā. The other queens of Dasharatha were Kaikeyi and Sumitrā. Kaikeyi, whom Dasharatha loved the most, was given two boons by the king when once she had saved his life. On the day before Rāma's coronation Kaikeyi asked Dasharatha to fulfil her two boons by banishing Rāma to the forest for fourteen years and crowning her son, Bharata, as the king of Ayodhyā. Dasharatha was shocked by her demand. Rāma willingly accepted to go to the forest. Sitā and Lakshmana voluntarily decided to go with him. Thereafter, Rāma, Sitā and Lakshmana left Ayodhyā and travelled to the forests of Chitrakuta and Dandakāranya. During the concluding part of their exile, the demon, Rāvana, became enamoured of Sitā, abducted her deceptively and took her to his kingdom called Lankā.

To rescue her, Rāma found an ally in Sugriva and his army of monkeys, including Hanumānji. With Rāma's blessings, Hanumānji reached Lankā by flying over the ocean. He found Sitā confined in the garden called Ashoka Vātikā. Then, at the command of Rāma, the army of monkeys and bears

Bhagwan Rāma *Bhagwan Krishna*

built the Rāma *setu (*bridge) under the supervision of architects
Nala and Nila. On landing in Lankā, a fierce war ensued.
The ultimate Rāma-Rāvana battle went on for a long period.
Whenever Bhagwan Rāma severed the head of Rāvana with his
arrows another one of his ten heads would spring up. Finally,
when Vibhishana told Rāma about his brother Rāvana's special
powers, Rāma shot an arrow at his navel and killed him.

On Rāma's return to Ayodhyā with Sitā and Lakshmana, he
was given a hero's welcome. He was crowned as the King of
Ayodhyā. Rāma ruled for many years, and his reign is known
as Rāma-*rājya.* It was a period of peace, progress, prosperity,
good conduct and happiness. Rāma's life is often summarized
as "one word, one wife and one arrow." This means that Rāma
was faithful to his word or promise, faithful to Sitā, and his
valour (Kshatriya dharma) was such that a single arrow would
suffice to destroy his enemy.

Sage Vālmiki wrote the Rāmāyana describing Rāma's
qualities and glory as an ideal person, and Goswāmi Tulasidāsa
wrote the *Rāmacharitamānas* describing him as the supreme
God. For centuries the Rāmāyana has been sung, enacted and
studied, inspiring generation after generation about Rāma's
divine life.

One God or Many "Gods"?

8. KRISHNA

Bhagwan Krishna is one of the most revered and celebrated avatars in Hinduism, and especially so for the Vaishnavas. He was born in a jail in Mathurā to Vasudeva and Devaki, who were imprisoned by Krishna's evil maternal uncle, King Kansa. Then, through a series of miraculous events Vasudeva took him out of the jail, crossed the River Yamunā and handed him to the care of Nanda and Yashodā in Gokula. Many demons like Putnā, Bakāsura, Dhenukāsura and others tried to kill the divine child but Krishna destroyed all of them. He subdued Kāliya, the serpent king, who was poisoning the waters of Yamunā. Once, Krishna lifted Mt. Govardhana to provide shelter and safety to the people of Gokula from the torrential rain and flood. At the age of eight, Krishna charmed the *gopis* (milkmaids) of Vrundāvan and played the divine *rāsa* (dance) with them on the night of Sharad Purnimā. Rādhā became enamoured of Krishna and she is adored as his ideal devotee and consort. When he was twelve he studied with his brother, Balarāma, in the ashram of Sāndipani Rishi.

When challenged to a fight by King Kansa, Krishna killed him. Later, he also destroyed the evil Shishupāla and Dantavakra.

The next most important part of his life was the Mahābhārata War. Krishna could not avert the war despite his best efforts. Duryodhana, the eldest of all Kauravas and the King of Hastinapura, refused all offers of peace. Bhagwan Krishna became Arjuna's charioteer. He preached the Bhagavad Gita to Arjuna on the battlefield when he became despondent and refused to fight his *āchārya* and relatives. Krishna instructed Arjuna to fulfil his duty as a Kshatriya, and for Arjuna to believe himself to be an instrument of God and to have faith in God as the all-doer. Krishna also preached to Arjuna about the temporariness of the physical body, the immortality and eternal joy of atman and that no sin would be incurred by following his dharma, which was to destroy *adharma*. Finally, Arjuna realized his duty and fought against the Kauravas. After eighteen days, the Pāndavas won the war due to Bhagwan Krishna's strategy and divine powers. Yudhishthira, the eldest of the Pāndavas, was crowned king. Shri Krishna then returned to Dwārikā and ruled his kingdom. Later, the Yādava clan of Krishna indulged in vices and addictions, which finally led to their destruction. Shri Krishna passed away when a hunter mistakenly shot an arrow. Before returning to his abode, Krishna enlightened his disciple, Uddhavji, with bhakti yoga, karma yoga and *jnāna* yoga. It is believed by Hindus that Kaliyuga set in with Krishna's departure from earth.

From his birth to his departure, Shri Krishna displayed monumental bravery, love for his devotees, skills of diplomacy and oratory, war strategies and divine powers. Rādhā and Arjuna were his dearest disciples, hence for thousands of years people have been worshipping them as Rādhā-Krishna and Nara-Nārāyana (Arjuna with Shri Krishna) respectively. Some Vaishnavas believe Bhagwan Krishna to be the incarnation of Vishnu or Nārāyana, while others believe him to be the supreme God, *avatāri,* or source of all avatars.

9. Buddha

Siddhārtha was born in the sixth century BCE to King Suddhodhana and Queen Māyādevi of Kapilavāstu, India (now in Nepal). He was raised in a luxurious and protected life, unaware of its sufferings and pains. He married Princess Yashodharā and had a son called Rāhula. One day he went out of his palace to see his city. The sight of an old man, a sick man, a corpse and an ascetic changed his view of life. He realized that life was temporary and full of suffering. To discover the path of ultimate freedom from suffering and to attain liberation (nirvana), Siddhārtha renounced his royal comforts and family. Initially he performed severe austerities in the forest, and then he sat in meditation under a banyan tree in Bodh-Gayā (located

Bhagwan Buddha   *Bhagwan Kalki*

in the modern state of Bihar). He attained enlightenment and became known as the 'Buddha', the 'enlightened one'. He was 35 years old at that time. He travelled for 45 years teaching spiritual wisdom and rejecting excessive ritualism and killing of animals in sacrifices propagated by the Brahmins. He delivered his first sermon at Sārnātha (near Vāranāsi).

Buddha adopted a middle path of sadhana and taught the four noble truths:

1. *Dukha* (existence of suffering in this world).
2. *Dukha-samudāya* (there is a cause of suffering).
3. *Dukhnirodha* (it is possible to stop this suffering).
4. *Dukhnirodha-mārga* (a way to stop the suffering).

Then Buddha prescribed an eight-fold noble path to overcome suffering:

1. Right view *(samyag drishti)*.
2. Right resolve *(samyag sankalpa)*.
3. Right speech *(samyag vāk)*.
4. Right conduct *(samyag karmānta)*.
5. Right livelihood *(samyag jivana)*.
6. Right effort *(samyag vyāyāma)*.
7. Right mindfulness *(samyag smruti)*.
8. Right concentration *(samyag* samadhi*)*.

Buddha calls nirvana the state of enlightenment. It is the

state of extinction of sorrow and suffering.

Buddha established a Sangha or religious order of monks and nuns to spread his teachings. The great emperor Ashoka of India became a Buddhist and thereafter Buddhism spread from India to Tibet, Central Asia, China, Japan, Korea, Indonesia, Laos, Cambodia, Siam, Burma, Sri Lanka and other countries. Even today Buddhism prevails in many countries of the Asian continent and others.

Buddha lived till he was 80 years old.

10. KALKI

Among the *dashāvatāras* Bhagwan Kalki is the last and is yet to appear at the end of Kaliyuga. In the Kalki Purāna, one of the Upapurānas, there is a description of Bhagwan Kalki. It is believed that he will be born as the son of Vishnu Sharmā and Sumati in the town of Shambhalā. He will be educated by Parashurāma. Bhagwan Shiva will gift him a white horse and a divine sword. Kalki will ride the horse and cleanse the world of wickedness. And with the reinstatement of dharma there will be righteousness and happiness everywhere. Thereafter the age of Satyuga will dawn.

BRAHMĀ

Of the three main devas, Brahmā creates, Vishnu sustains and Shiva destroys the world. Paurānik literature describes Brahmā to have emerged out of a lotus that originated from the navel of Vishnu. He is also known as Prajāpati, the Lord of progeny; Vidhi, the decider of one's destiny; and as Vishvakarmā, the architect of the world. His consort is Sarasvati.

Brahmā, the creator

Brahmā represents the Vedas, while Sarasvati reflects their spirit and meaning. All sacred and secular knowledge came from them. The great sages Maricha, Atri and Angiras are Brahmā's 'mind-born' children *(mānas putras)*. Manu is the first man created by Brahmā.

Brahmā, like Shiva, is easily pleased with austerities and grants boons to those who appease him, be they devas, *dānavas* or humans. He possesses five heads, four facing the four main directions and the fifth one facing upwards. The loss of the fifth head is explained variously in different Purānas and Upapurānas. The remaining four represent the four Vedas, the four *yugas* and the four varnas. He has four arms holding different objects in various combinations as described in different Purānas: *akshamālā* (rosary), *kurcha* (sceptre of *kusha* grass), *sruk* (ladle), *sruva* (spoon), *kamandalu* (waterpot) and *grantha* (book). The rosary symbolizes time and the waterpot, the causal waters from which all creation came forth. The *kusha* grass, the ladle and the spoon are instruments used in *yajnas*. These items symbolize the spirit of sacrifice for sustenance. Brahmā is the giver of knowledge – arts, sciences and wisdom. He is credited with giving music, dance and stagecraft to the world.

The *hasta* mudras or hand gestures of Brahmā are *abhaya* (promising protection) and *varada* (granting boons). The *murti* of Brahmā is either standing on a lotus or seated on his vehicle (*vāhana*) – a *hansa* or swan. The swan symbolizes discrimination and wisdom.

There are two main mandirs dedicated to Brahmā in India: one at Pushkara, near Ajmera in Rajasthan, and the other is in a town called Kheda Brahmā in Sābarakānthā district, North Gujarat. In both the mandirs, he is shown as Vishvakarmā – the architect of the universe. Daily, the *murti* of Brahmā is offered worship.

Traditionally, every mandir of Shiva or Vishnu has a niche in the northern wall for Brahmā.

SHIVA

The eternal law is that all that is born must die and anything that is produced disintegrates and gets destroyed. The deity responsible for this phenomenon of dissolution is Bhagwan

Shiva, the destroyer

Shiva. He is described by Shaivities as equally responsible for creation and existence. Shiva means the auspicious one.

Shiva is worshipped both in *murti* (iconic) and *linga* (aniconic) forms. There are also *lingas* with Shiva's faces. The twelve famous *jyotirlingas* or Shiva '*lingas* of light' are said to have come into existence without human agency and manifest special potency. They are spread all over India: Kedāranātha in the Himalayas, Uttarakhand State, Vishvanātha or Vishveshvara in Vārānasi, Uttar Pradesh, Rāmeshvaram in Tamil Nadu, Somanātha and Nāgeshavara in western Gujarat, Omkāreshvara on an island in the River Narmadā in Gujarat, Mahākāla in Ujjayini city in Madhya Pradesh, Bhimeshvara, Tryambakeshvara and Ghrushnesha in Maharashtra, Mallikārjuna in Andhra Pradesh and Vaidyanātha in Bihar. A pilgrimage to these twelve *jyotirlingas* is considered to be very meritorious by Shaivas. The Shiva Purāna *(Kotirudra Samhitā)* narrates the legends connected with these *jyotirlingas*.

There are two main aspects of Shiva's iconographic forms. He is shown as benign or *saumya murti* and angry or *ugra murti*. The former is known as *anugraha murti* (in a blessing form), the latter is *samhāra murti* (in a destructive form). He is commonly portrayed in his benign form where he is smeared with ash and has long matted hair from which the River Ganga flows. He has three eyes and four arms – two holding the *trishula* (trident) and *damaru* (small hand-held drum) and the other two in *abhaya* and *varadamudrās*. He wears the crescent moon as a diadem and tiger and elephant skins on his body. There are snakes around his neck and body to form a necklace, girdle, *yajnopavita* (sacred thread) and armlets.

Shiva's consort is Pārvati. They have two sons, Ganesha and Kārtikeya (also known as Kumara, Skanda and Subrahmanya). Shiva's vehicle is Nandi (bull). His abode, located in the Himalayas, is called Kailāsa. Shiva travels everywhere and resides especially in burial grounds and cremation sites. Shiva was the only one who dared to drink the deadly poison, called *halāhala*, that came out during the churning of the ocean by the devas and *dānavas*. Because he survived he is known as 'the conqueror of death' or 'Mrutyunjaya'.

Shiva is the lord of yoga and yogis. He is often shown sitting in deep meditation, immersed in the bliss of his own self. In this form he is depicted to have two, three, four, eight, ten or even thirty-two hands. Some of the objects in his hands are: *trishula, chakra, parashu* (battle axe), *damaru* (hand-held drum), *akshamālā* (rosary), *mruga* (deer), *pāsha* (noose), *danda* (staff), *pināka* or *ajagava* (bow), *khatvānga* (magic wand), *pāshupata* (arrow), *padma* (lotus), *kapāla* (skull-cup), *darpana* (mirror), *khadaga* (sword) and others.

When Shiva performed the cosmic dance he played the *damaru* fourteen times producing fourteen sounds or basic formulae containing all the Sanskrit alphabet. The formulae are called the *Shivasutras* or *Māheshvarasutras*. So the *damaru* produced the original sound of the alphabet and grammar. It is believed that from this sound the entire creation, including its various arts, sciences and Sanskrit grammar sprang forth. As the master of dance, Shiva is called Natarāja. All the 108 modes of dancing have come from him. The Natarāja image shows Shiva with four hands and two legs. He holds the *damaru* in his upper right hand and fire in his left. The lower right hand is in *abhayamudrā* and the left points towards his uplifted left foot. His right foot crushes the demon Apasmārapurusha, the symbol of ignorance. The whole image is circled by a blazing fire. Shiva's dance pose symbolizes a cyclical process of creation, preservation and destruction. The *damaru* represents the principle of *shabda* (sound) and thus *ākāsha* (ether), which is responsible for further creation or evolution. Fire symbolizes the process of destruction *(pralaya agni)*. Thus the *damaru* and fire symbolize the unending cycle of creation, preservation and dissolution. The other two hands indicate that one who

Natarāja, the master of dance

Hinduism

takes refuge at his feet will be granted protection and will have nothing to fear. He puts his right leg on Apasmāra, the embodiment of ignorance. Ignorance is thus trampled upon by Bhagwan Shiva for the good of his devotees.

The Ardhanārishwara (Lord who is half-woman) is one of many forms that Shiva manifested himself. In this form, Pārvati is the left half of Shiva's body, and symbolizes the identity of Shiva and Shakti. On the worldly plane, the form signifies that man and woman are mutually complementary. In a general sense, the form reflects the bipolar nature of our universe. Some scholars believe that the form may have evolved to compromise the differences between the Shaiva and Shākta *sampradāyas.*

PARTIAL MANIFESTATIONS (AMSHA AVATARS)

1. Dattātreya

Dattātreya was born to the great sage Atri and his wife, Anasuyā (which means one without jealousy). Anasuyā is renowned in Hinduism for her fidelity and chastity. Dattātreya introduced some magical rites and created the *soma*[7] plant.

Ardhanārishwara, form of Lord Shiva as half-man and woman

Dattātreya revered twenty-four gurus, learning something unique from each. His learning and enlightenment endowed him with inner purity.

Later he came to be regarded as the incarnation of Brahmā, Vishnu and Shiva. He is portrayed as having three heads, six hands and accompanied by four dogs of different colours that represent the four Vedas.

His name appears in the Mahābhārata and several other Purānas. He is believed to have played a harmonizing role between the followers of Brahmā, Vishnu and Shiva and even non-Vedic sects. He is also considered to be a great sage, and is ranked among the seven great sages. The fellowship bearing his name, Datta Sampradāya, is predominantly in Maharashtra and

Dattātreya

7. *Soma* was a creeper whose leaves, stalks or branches were crushed to produce *soma* juice. The juice gave immense energy.

Andhra Pradesh. His temples are called Datta mandirs where his wooden slippers or *pādukās* are installed and worshipped. The famous Advaita Vedānta work called *Avadhutagītā* is attributed to him.

2. DHANVANTARI

Dhanvantari is a partial manifestation of Bhagwan Vishnu. He is the divine father of Ayurveda, the life science of health and longevity. Nineteen ayurvedic books are attributed to him. The most important is the *Dhanvantari Nighantu.* Over a period of time Dhanvantari became the title for the best medical expert. Among the different types of his iconic forms *(murtis)* the most prominent is the two-armed divine being emerging from the ocean of milk or *kshirasāgara* holding a pot full of *amruta* or nectar to make the devas immortal. Dhanvantari is known as the physician of the devas, teacher of medicine and an author of books on Ayurveda. He is mentioned in the Rāmayana, Harivamsa, Bhāgavata Purāna and other sacred Hindu texts. Reborn as Divodāsa, the King of Kāshi, he established the science of medicine.

Dhanvantari

3. HAYAGRIVA

Hayagriva, also known as Hayashirsh, is the deity of learning, similar to the goddess Sarasvati. He is known to have a human form with a horse's head and neck *(grivā)*, having four or eight arms carrying the various weapons of Bhagwan Vishnu. There are several stories about the Hayagriva avatar in the Purānic texts.

Sage Yājnavalkya lost his knowledge of Yajur Veda because of his guru Vaishampāyana's curse. Then, pleased with his severe austerities, the sun-god, also called Vājasanihi, appeared before Yājnavalkya as a deity with a horse's head and taught him the Yajur Veda in another form. This new form is known as Vājasaneya Samhitā.

Hayagriva, avatar of Vishnu with human form having a horse's head and neck

There are several stories about Hayagriva in the Vedic and Purānic literature. Once, two demons, Madhu and Kaitabha, ran away with the Vedas and hid them in the ocean. Bhagwan Vishnu took the form of Hayagriva, dived to the bottom of the ocean and brought them up after killing the demons. Hayagriva is considered to be the 18th avatar out of the 24 partial manifestations.

There is an Upanishad in his name called Hayagriva Upanishad, with only twenty mantras, and a Pāncharātra Vaishnava Āgama known as *Hayagriva Samhitā* with 149 chapters.

4. KAPILA

Kapila was a great sage. He was the only son of Kardama rishi and Devahuti, and the brother of Arundhati. Later, Arundhati married the famous sage Vasishtha and she is remembered as a paragon of wifely virtues. Kapila is considered to be the fifth partial incarnation of Vishnu. He founded the Sānkhya philosophy and taught it to his mother, Devahuti, and liberated her soul. This part of the Bhāgavata Purāna is known as the Kapila Gitā.[8] Bhagwan Krishna extols his own greatness in the Gitā by stating that he is Kapila among the sages.[9]

Sage Kapila

5. MOHINI

The story in the Bhāgavata Purāna describes how the *dānavas* (demons) snatched away the pot of *amruta* (nectar) from Dhanvantari's hands when he emerged from the *samudra manthana* (churning of the ocean of milk). On seeing the devas being deprived of *amruta*, Bhagwan Vishnu appeared as a beautiful damsel called Mohini. Her enchanting beauty stunned the demons, who on her word gave the pot of *amruta* to her. Then, Mohini tricked them by distributing the *amruta* only to the devas.

Bhagwan Vishnu takes the beautiful the form of Mohini to distribute amruta to the devas

8. Shrimad Bhāgavata 3.25-33.
9. B.G. 10.26.

Even Shiva was bewitched by Mohini's beauty according to the Bhāgavata Purāna (8.12). It is said that the son of Shiva and Mohini is Lord Ayyappan. He is also known as Hariharaputra, where Hari means Vishnu in the form of Mohini, Hara means Shiva and *putra* means son. Ayyappan, also known as Shāstā (one who commands), was born to kill the female demon Mahishi, the wife of demon Mahishāsura. Mahishi had received a boon from Brahmā that she could not be killed by Vishnu or Shiva. So Vishnu assumed the form of Mohini, and Shiva got a son from her to kill Mahishi. Ayyappan killed her when he was only 12 years old. A grand mandir was built in honour of Ayyappan by King Rājashekhara at Shabarimalai in Kerala State. It is believed the architect of the mandir was Vishvakarmā and the *murti* was made by Parashurāma. Even today the Shabarimalai mandir attracts hundreds of thousands of pilgrims.

6. NARA-NĀRAYĀNA

It is said that after Bhagwan Narasimha destroyed the evil Hiranyakashipu, he split into two. The lion part became Sage Nārāyana, and the human part Sage Nara. Later, Nara and Nārāyana incarnated as Arjuna and Krishna. They are worshipped as Nara-Nārāyana rishis. Both the deities perform austerities in Badarikāshram, believed to be in the Himalayas. To please them thousands of devotees perform austerities. According to another version, Nara and Nārāyana are the sons of Dharma and Ahimsa and they perform intense austerities.

Once, Lord Indra tried to seduce Nara-Nārāyana by sending celestial nymphs. In response Nārāyana produced the nymph Urvashi from his thigh *(uru)*. She was more beautiful than all the nymphs.

Nara is depicted in a human form, and Nārāyana is also shown in a human form, with two or four arms holding the *shankha*, *chakra*, *padma* and *japamālā*.

Nara-Nārāyana

7. VEDA VYĀSA

Krishna-Dvaipāyana, the son of Parāshara Rishi and Satyavati, is popularly known as Veda Vyāsa. Being of dark complexion (Krishna) and since he was born on an island *(dvipa)* he is also known as Krishna Dvaipāyana Vyāsa. He had codified the Vedas, wrote the Mahābhārata and the 17 Mahāpurānas, yet it is said that he remained unhappy and restless. As a solution, Sage Nārada asked him to compose a Purāna describing the enchanting deeds, acts and exploits of the living God, Shri Krishna. He wrote the Bhāgavata Purāna, the eighteenth Purāna, and subsequently experienced immense inner peace. Guru *purnimā* is celebrated as Vyāsa *purnimā* because he is believed to be the first guru.

Veda Vyāsa is believed to be born in every *yuga* to propagate the Hindu shastras.

OTHERS

We shall consider three more popular deities worshipped by Hindus. They are Ganapati, Hanumān and Kārtikeya. The three have thousands of shrines and mandirs dedicated to them, in which countless devotees worship and sing their glory.

Sage Veda Vyāsa

1. GANAPATI

Ganapati or Ganesha is one of the popular Hindu deities worshipped by all sections of society, including the Buddhists and Jains. He is also known as Vināyaka and Vighneshwara (remover of obstacles). Many Hindus begin any new work or undertaking, whether sacred or secular, by first worshipping or honouring Ganapati for success. He has a human body with an elephant's head. He is also revered as a god of knowledge, wisdom, literature and fine arts.

According to the Purānas the story of Ganapati's birth is that Pārvati, prior to her bath, removed the perfumed oil and scurf on her skin and prepared an image of a child. Then she

Ganapati

infused it with life and called him Vināyaka. Pārvati instructed Vināyaka to stand guard while she took her bath and not to allow anyone inside. Bhagwan Shiva, her husband, returned after meditating in the caves of Mt. Kailāsa. The boy, not knowing Shiva, barred his way. Shiva became angry and cut off the boy's head. When Pārvati learnt what had happened she was upset with Shiva. The boy's head could not be found so Shiva fixed an elephant's head on the boy's body and revived him. Since then, Vināyaka is also known as Gajānana (one with an elephant's head). Shiva blessed him and said that whoever wants to perform any auspicious deed has to first worship him to ensure success. Shiva appointed him as the head of his army and so he is also known as Ganapati, where *gana* means 'a group of servants' and *pati* means chief. In Tamil Nadu, Ganapati is known as Pulliyar.

Once, in a fight with Parshurāma, half of one of Ganapati's tusks broke. Later, he used the broken part as a quill to write the epic poem, Mahābhārata, that was dictated by Veda Vyāsa. On another occasion Shiva and Pārvati declared to Ganapati and their other son Kārtikeya (or Skanda) that the one who returned first after circumambulating the earth would be married first. Ganapati was stout and had the slow-moving mouse for his vehicle, while Kārtikeya was slim and had the swift peacock as his vehicle. Kārtikeya sped off whereas Ganapati circumambulated Shiva and Pārvati and declared that it was equivalent to having circled the earth. He thus won the hands of Riddhi and Siddhi (his consorts who are personifications of prosperity and success).

Ganapati's body is often symbolically interpreted in terms of his virtues. Ganapati's bent trunk is believed to be an embodiment of Aum, the most auspicious of all sounds that symbolizes God. He has large ears to listen to all the prayers of everyone, and like winnowing baskets they are capable of sifting what is good for the devotee from what is not. Out of his two tusks, the whole tusk symbolizes Truth and the broken one represents the world which is imperfect. His large belly indicates that he can contain the misery and suffering of others. The noose or *pasha* stands for *rāga* or attachment, and the goad or *ankusha* for anger. Like the noose, attachment binds and like the goad, anger hurts. It is better to surrender our attachment and anger to him.

Ganapati's birthday is celebrated annually on Ganesha Chaturthi, the fourth day of the Bhādrapada month, which falls during August or September.

It is celebrated in homes and in public places. A clay or painted *murti* of Ganesha is ritually installed and worshipped for up to ten days before its ceremonial immersion in a lake, river or ocean. The festival is mainly celebrated in Maharashtra, Andhra Pradesh, Karnataka, Tamil Nadu and Gujarat. It was introduced as a public festival on a grand scale by the Indian freedom fighter, Bal Gangadhar Tilak, in Poona (Pune) to unite people for India's independence movement.

2. KĀRTIKEYA OR SKANDA

Kārtikeya is also the son of Shiva and Pārvati, and the brother of Ganapati. He was born in a forest of arrow-like grass and reared by six divine mothers – who were the presiding goddesses of Krttika constellation. From them he gets the name Kārtikeya. He assumed six faces to suckle the milk of six mothers, and so he got the name Shanmukha (six-faced). He is said to have been born to destroy the demon Tārakāsura. So he was given potent weapons by the devas to destroy him. When he was only six days old he destroyed Tārakāsura with his lance. Since he was an aggressive attacker in war he became known as Skanda. The name also means one who has acquired the power of chastity. He is also known as Subrahmanya which means one who nourishes aspirants for spiritual growth. He liked Brahmins and holy people. His other names in Tamil are

Kārtikeya (Lord Murugan)

Murugan and Guhan (Guha).

In *murti* form he is shown to have either one head and two arms or six heads and twelve arms, riding on a peacock, holding a bow in one hand and an arrow in the other. His six heads symbolize the five senses and the mind. When a person's senses and mind are restrained and sublimated he or she becomes divine. Kārtikeya married Valli and Kaumāri or Devasenā. Thus, he is called Senāpati.

Kārtikeya is worshipped mainly in South India, where there are hundreds of mandirs dedicated to him.

3. HANUMĀN

Hanumān is a great devotee and servant of Bhagwan Rāma. He is one of the prominent and celebrated characters in the Sanskrit epic, Rāmāyana. His physical strength and valour were peerless. He was extremely intelligent and had a profound knowledge of the shastras. He is praised to be the best among all intelligent people *(matimatām varishthaha)*. His speech was extraordinary and yet he was very humble. But above all, his allegiance and devotion to Rāma was unparalleled.

He was the son of Anjanā devi and Vāyu deva or the wind-god (also known as Marut). He was thus known as Ānjaneya and Māruti. As a child he thought the sun was a crimson fruit and so he advanced to eat it. Indra checked him by striking him with his weapon. Consequently, his chin *(hanu)* became swollen and ever since he has been known as Hanumān ('one with a swollen chin'). Indra blessed him that he would remain immortal. He was also blessed with various weapons given to him by several devas.

Once, when his childhood pranks were too much for the sages to bear, they cursed him that he would not remember his strength until someone reminded him. Thereafter, he became quiet and docile.

Hanumān stayed with Sugriva after the latter was exiled by

Hanumān

his brother Vāli. When Sugriva deputed Hanumān to assess Rāma and Lakshmana, Hanumān's courteous manner and speech impressed Rāma. This first meeting and impression of Rāma became the basis for a lifelong bond between Rāma and Hanumān. Satisfied by their nature, Hanumān carried them to Sugriva. When he went to Sri Lanka in search of Sitā, the wife of Rāma, Hanumān remained unenticed by the women he saw in Rāvana's palace and inner rooms. Hanumān is reverently described as a *yati* (celibate). On finding Sitā, he used tact and wisdom in winning her confidence that he was a messenger of Rāma. He then met Rāvana and told him to return Sitā to Rāma or face death at his hands. Rāvana was furious and ordered that Hanumān's tail be set on fire. However, Hanumān destroyed Rāvana's city, setting it on fire with his burning tail, before returning to Rāma. During the war between Rāma and Rāvana, Hanumān fought valiantly and saved the lives of Rāma and Lakshmana. He revived them by bringing the rejuvenating herb called Sanjivani and Vishalyakarani all the way from the Himalayas.

After the victory, Sitā gifted Hanumān with a priceless pearl necklace in appreciation for his valour and devotion to Rāma. Hanumān broke each bead to see whether Rāma was in it, and in not finding him he threw the beads away. He told Sitā that since Rāma was not in the beads he was not interested in the necklace.

When Rāma was about to conclude his stay on earth Hanumān got ready to leave with him. But Rāma told him to stay and listen to the story of his life wherever it was read or recited. It is believed that wherever the Rāmāyana *kathā* (story) is sung or narrated, Hanumān comes in a divine form to listen. A special seat is reserved for him.

Every year, the birthday of Hanumān is celebrated on the full moon day of Chaitra, which falls in the month of March or April. Especially on Saturdays, hundreds of thousands worship him, and offer *abhisheka* of vegetable oil and split a coconut before his *murti*. In the thousands of mandirs and shrines dedicated to Hanumānji many pray to him to ward off evil spirits and to ask for his blessings.

CONCLUSION

The Hindu pantheon comprises innumerable avatars and deities who are worshipped and revered in various ways and to various degrees. Each Hindu *sampradāya* or religious tradition prays to and worships its own deity or *ishtadevatā* with the faith that he or she is supreme.

Among the Vaishnavas, the Shri Vaishnava Sampradāya of Rāmānujāchārya believes Nārāyana to be the supreme God; the Brahma Sampradāyā of Madhvāchārya believes Vishnu to be supreme; the Sanak Sampradāya of Nimbārkāchārya, Rudra Sampradāya of Vallabhāchārya and the Gaudiya Sampradāya of Chaitanya Mahāprabhu believe Krishna to be the supreme God; and the Swaminarayan Sampradaya believes Swaminarayan to be the supreme God.

All the Shaiva Sampradāyas believe Shiva to be supreme, and the Shāktas believe Pārvati to be supreme. The devotees of the Smārta Sampradāya believe in the supremacy of either one or all of the five deities, namely, Vishnu, Shiva, Surya, Ganesh, or Pārvatiji. Hinduism has allowed this freedom of single worship to the deity of one's choice and respect for all the other Hindu deities. It practices genuine religious pluralism in day-to-day life.

SUMMARY

1. Hindu shastras teach that there is one supreme God with many manifestations.

2. Vishnu is responsible for sustaining and protecting our world. The Vaishnavas believe that Vishnu assumes many different avatars for the destruction of evil and

reestablishment of dharma.

3. Ten of his main avatars are Matsya (fish), Kurma (tortoise), Varāha (boar), Nrusimha (man-lion), Vāmana (dwarf), Parashurāma, Rāma, Krishna, Buddha and Kalki, which is yet to manifest.

4. Brahmā is the deity responsible for creation. He creates the world and all living beings and things by the will and power of the supreme God.

5. Shiva is known and revered as the deva of dissolution. Shiva means auspiciousness and he is easily pleased by devotees, so he is called Āshutosha.

6. *Amshāvatāras* include Dattātreya, Dhanvantari, Hayagriva, Kapila, Mohini, Nara-Nārāyana, Vyāsa.

7. Other popularly worshipped deities are Ganapati, Kārtikeya and Hanumān.

Goddesses of India

(L to R) Sarasvati, Pārvati and Lakshmi Devi.
(Inset) Rādhā

Sarasvati, Lakshmi, Pārvati,
Sitā, Rādhā

INTRODUCTION

For millennia the focus of the devotional or bhakti tradition in Hinduism has been Bhagwan Vishnu, Bhagwan Shiva and their avatars. Yet, there is a crucial tradition of goddesses or devis and consorts of avatars and deities being worshipped by a large population of Hindus. The goddesses are either held to be the supreme divinity or the power (*shakti*) of God. She is also considered to be the Mother of the Universe or the source of life. There are two beliefs and practices associated with the goddesses. The majority of goddesses are considered to be benign and auspicious: blessing the devout with wealth, fertility, protection and promise of liberation. While others are worshipped in their terrible forms, which were taken to destroy asuras who harassed or killed the pious.

There is ample evidence that the worship of devis dates to and some also say that it predates the Indus Valley Civilization (2800 BCE).

'Devi' means 'goddess' in Sanskrit. The concept and worship of God as the Mother of Creation is an ancient tradition in Hinduism. The Rig Veda (2.1.11; 8.10.2) mentions many female deities as the consorts of male deities, or as separate goddesses like Aditi, Ushas, Pruthivi, Rātri and others. The holy rivers of India are also worshipped as goddesses, namely, Sarasvati, Gangā, Yamunā and others.

In the Purānic period, the belief in the goddesses or devis came to prominence as consorts of the three main deities (*trimurtis*): Brahmā, Vishnu and Shiva. The three major devis are Sarasvati (consort of Brahmā), Lakshmi (consort of Vishnu) and Pārvati (consort of Shiva). Thereafter, a great number of aspects of the three devis came to be worshipped by the devout. Besides them, Sitā (consort of Rāma) and Rādhā (ideal devotee of Krishna) are also popularly known and worshipped.

Generally, the majority of goddesses are different aspects of goddess Pārvati. In fact, even the word 'Devi' has been specially associated with her. The *Devi Bhagavat* and *Devi Māhātmya* are sacred texts that describe the exploits and glory of the Devi or Divine Mother. We shall deal briefly with the popular goddesses of India.

1. SARASVATI

Sarasvati is the wife of Brahmā, the creator. Sarasvati means the 'flowing one'. She is a deity and also a river. Sarasvati is known as Shāradā (giver of essence), Vāgishwari (mistress of speech), Brāhmi (wife of Brahmā) and Mahāvidyā (deity of knowledge).

Sarasvati personifies all secular knowledge like arts, sciences, crafts and skills and is therefore referred to as the goddess of learning. She is also popularly referred to as the goddess of speech. One who is an orator is believed to have the power of Sarasvati on his tongue. She is very beautiful and dons a white apparel. She is depicted as sitting on a lotus, playing the *vina*, holding an *akshamālā* (rosary), wearing a garland of jasmine (*kund hār dhavalā*) and holding a book. She has four arms that symbolize her power of pervasiveness in all the four directions. Her carrier is the swan or peacock.

In almost all schools of India prayers to Sarasvati are offered daily. On the day of Vijayā Dashami or Dashaharā (Dasherā) which usually falls in October) she is specially worshipped by students and artists of the performing arts.

Sarasvati Devi	*Lakshmi Devi*

2. LAKSHMI

Lakshmi or Shri is the consort of Nārāyana or Vishnu. She is popularly known as the goddess of fortune or wealth. She emerged during the churning of the ocean by the devas and asuras. She appeared with a garland and was stunningly beautiful. The devas and asuras desired her but she pledged herself to Nārāyana who was virtuous and handsome. Since she is the spouse of Bhagwan Nārāyana or Vishnu she is born to be his wife wherever he incarnates. When Vishnu incarnated as Vāmana she appeared as Padmā, with Parashurāma she came as Dharani, with Rāma she became Sitā and with Krishna she appeared as Rukmini.

Lakshmi is the ideal wife and devotee of Vishnu. She is inseparable from Vishnu, like speech from meaning, knowledge from intellect or good deeds from righteousness. She is very beautiful and is shown as sitting or standing on a lotus, wearing a lotus garland and holding lotuses in her two hands. Often, elephants stand on either side, showering water over her. She has four hands, one holding a lotus, another a conch shell, the third a pot of *amruta* and the fourth a *bilva* or citron (*mātulinga*) or pomegranate fruit. Her four hands symbolize her power to grant fulfilment of the four *purushārthas* viz: dharma, *artha*, *kāma* and *moksha*. When she is depicted with eight hands one also finds her additionally holding a bow, arrow, mace and disc. Lakshmi is also worshipped alone in mandirs built exclusively for her. Being the ideal devotee (*bhakta*) of Nārāyana she is also worshipped along with him (Bhakta-Bhagwan). In innumerable Hindu mandirs one finds the *murtis* of Lakshmi-Nārāyana where the devout pray and worship them together.

In the Shri Vaishnava Sampradāya of Rāmānujāchārya Shri means Lakshmi. In his commentary on the Brahmasutra called *Shribhāshya*, Shri again refers to Lakshmiji. Rāmānujāchārya writes in his important philosophical work, *Vedārthasangraha*, "This Shri, the mother of the universe, is eternal and knows no separation from Vishnu. Even as Vishnu is all-pervading, she is all-pervading" (7.70).

3. PĀRVATI

Pārvati is the wife and *shakti* of Bhagwan Shiva, the god of destruction. The majority of devis or goddesses of Shāktism in India are forms of Pārvati. In her first incarnation she was known as Sati (the chaste one), the daughter of Daksha and Prasuti. She was also called Dākshāyani – daughter of Daksha. She married Shiva.

Once Daksha did not invite his son-in-law, Shiva, to a *yajna* organized by him. Dākshāyani went to the *yajna* uninvited. When her father Daksha spoke insultingly of Shiva she ended her life in the sacrificial hall itself by burning herself to ashes with her yogic powers. According to some Purānas, she is said to have jumped into the sacrificial fire and died.

In her next birth she came as Pārvati, the daughter of Himavān (Himalaya) and Mena. After she performed rigorous austerities Shiva was pleased with her and accepted her as his wife. During her intense austerities to please Shiva she had refused to eat even leaves to sustain herself, hence she came to be known as Aparnā. Her mother, Mena, tried to prevent her from pursuing such extreme austerity by uttering the words 'Umā' (my dear,

Pārvati Devi *Sitā Devi*

don't do this), which later became her other name, Umā. Being the daughter of Himalaya she also became known as Gauri (the white one). As the mother of the universe she is known as Ambā and Ambikā, both the names mean mother.

Though all the female deities are called *shakti* of their male counterparts, the words 'Shakti' and 'Devi' are mostly used to denote the consort of Shiva.

Like Shiva, Pārvati has two aspects, benign and terrible. Her benign forms are Pārvati, Ambā and Umā. When she is shown with Shiva she has two hands, holding lotuses. When she is shown independently she has four hands — two holding blue and red lotuses while the others are in the *varada* (blessing) and *abhaya* (protection) mudras.

In her fierce forms, known as Chāmundā, Chandi — the terrible one, and Mahākāli, she destroyed many demons. Once a demon called Durgam stole the four Vedas. The Brahmins prayed to her and she killed Durgam and retrieved the Vedas, and from then on she came to be known as Durgā. She had also killed Mahishāsura, the buffalo-demon. The event is annually celebrated with great joy and enthusiasm on Vijayā Dashmi in India and especially in Bengal. On another occasion, two asuras, Chanda and Munda, came to kill her. She destroyed them and thereafter became popular as Chāmundā. Once, in order to kill a demon named Dāruk she took a terrible dark form called Kālika.

Pārvati's two sons, Ganesha and Kārtikeya (or Skanda), are also worshipped together and independently.

4. SITĀ

Sita is the consort of Bhagwan Rāma. She is the paragon of Indian womanhood and devotion to God and husband. She was the daughter of King Siradhvaja Janaka of Mithilā. Sita was found when the king was ploughing the field to perform a *yajna*. A ploughed field in Sanskrit is known as 'sita', hence her name. Sita grew into a beautiful princess and was endowed with character, radiance, intelligence and other virtues.

When Rāma broke the bow of Shiva in the court of King Janaka, the latter offered his daughter, Sita, in marriage. She lived happily with Rāma till a cruel turn of fate forced Rāma to go into exile for fourteen years. Sita and Lakshmana voluntarily followed him to the forest. During the concluding year of their exile Sita was abducted by Rāvana, who was dressed in the garb of a sadhu. Rāvana took her to his kingdom in Sri Lanka and held her captive in his garden called the Ashoka-vātikā. He desired to have her as his wife and tried to entice her in all ways, but she spurned him and remained resolute and chaste. She spent all her time remembering Rāma. Eventually, Rāma destroyed Rāvana and his army in battle. Then at the word of Rāma, Sita underwent an ordeal of fire to prove her chastity because she had lived in Rāvana's house. Before entering the fire, Sita prayed to the fire-god, Agni deva, that if only Rāma had always been in her thoughts then he should save her. She indeed remained unscathed. Rāma accepted her. After returning to his kingdom Rāma was crowned king of Ayodhyā. They lived happily for many years. But, one day, on learning about an accusation by a washerman who, in a quarrel with his wife, said that Rāma would accept Sita but he would never accept her after having lived in the house of another man. Rāma became distressed, because as a king he had to have an unstained and exemplary image. So, he decided to renounce her even though he knew well that she was innocent and pregnant. He called Lakshmana to take Sita away and place her in the ashram of Sage Vālmiki.

Later, Sita gave birth to twins, Lava and Kusha. They grew up in the natural surroundings of the ashram. One day, the princes tied the ceremonial horse of Rāma that had been let loose by him as a part of the Rājasuya Yajna. Subsequently, a battle followed between Lava and Kusha on one side and Rāma's army on the other. The two young brothers defeated the mighty army of Rāma. Then Vālmiki revealed to Rāma that the boys were his sons, and thus reunited him with them and Sita. Vālmiki requested Rāma to accept Sita, but Rāma asked Sita to prove her chastity before all his citizens. She was shocked and dumbfounded at Rāma's words. Sita prayed to her mother Earth and said, "If by mind, deed and speech I have not cherished anyone except my husband Rāma, then O Mother Earth take me in your lap." At once the earth opened up and received Sita. Rāma was left regretting at what he had done. Even in her final moments Sita's thoughts were centred only on Rāma. She is celebrated for her purity, love and allegiance to Rāma.

5. RĀDHĀ

Rādhā was a *gopi* (milkmaid) of Vrundāvan. She was the daughter of Vrushabhānu and Kalāvati. She was closely associated with Krishna, and her devotion and love for him are legendary.

Rādhā is not mentioned in popular sacred texts like the Mahābhārata, Harivansha and Vishnu Purāna. There is however a reference in the Bhāgavata to Krishna going away with a *gopi* after the divine *rāsa*. She is speculated to be Rādhā.

The life of Rādhā is found in the Brahmavaivarta Purāna. She is described as the *shakti* or power of Krishna. Rādhā, as the beloved of Krishna, is probably first mentioned prominently

Rādhā

by the poet Jayadeva (1200 CE), who was the royal poet of king Lakshmanasena of Bengal. Jayadeva immortalized her in his poem, the *Gitagovinda*. He described the deep love of Rādhā for Krishna. The theme of the poem is union, separation and reunion. Rādhā rushed to Krishna whenever he played the flute. He identifies Rādhā with Lakshmi. The Gaudiya Vaishnavas consider this poem as the literary sequel to the Bhāgavata Purāna.

In common with the other *gopis* Rādhā, too, was absorbed in thoughts of Krishna while engaged in her household chores.

Gaudiya Vaishnavism made Rādhā the most important figure with Krishna worship. Shri Chaitanya Mahāprabhu is believed to be an incarnation of Krishna and Rādhā in one body.

Rādhā is worshipped as Bhagwan Krishna's perfect devotee (Bhakta-Bhagwan principle) and an ideal worthy of spiritual emulation. In Vrundāvan, such is the glory of God's *bhakta* that the name Rādhe, representing Rādhā, is hailed seven times before saying the name of Krishna. Mirā, Vidyāpati, Chandidāsa, Surdās, Bihārilāla and others are poets who wrote and sang Krishna's love for Rādhā. The last great poet who described Krishna-Rādhā's love was Guru Gobind Singh. He wrote *Krishna Avatāra* in Brijbhāshā (a Hindi dialect).

SUMMARY

1. The major devis or goddesses worshipped in Hinduism are Sarasvati, Lakshmi, Pārvati, Sitā and Rādhā.

2. Sarasvati devi is the wife of Brahmā. She is popularly known as the goddess of speech and learning. Sarasvati personifies secular knowledge like arts, sciences, crafts and skills.

3. Lakshmi devi is the consort of Nārāyana or Vishnu. She is popularly known as the goddess of wealth.

4. Pārvati devi is the wife and *shakti* of Shiva. The goddesses of Shāktism are the forms of Pārvati. She has both benign and terrible forms.

5. Sitā is the consort of Rāma. She is an epitome of Indian womanhod because of her deep devotion and love for Rāma.

6. Rādhā is the consort of Krishna. Her devotion to him is exemplary.

11

Mandir, Shastra and Sant
Three Pillars of Hinduism

Mandir (temple), shastra (sacred text) and sant (God-realized guru) have sustained and enriched Hinduism through the ages. (Inset) Rushikumars of 'Darshanam' studying a sacred text

Mandir: Origin, Symbolism, Architecture, Murtis; Shastras: Shruti and Smruti, Benefit; Sant: Guru's Glory and Grace

INTRODUCTION

Of the many profound features of Hinduism, the mandir (temple), shastra (sacred texts) and *sant* (God-realized guru) are considered to be the pillars. For millennia Hinduism has been sustained and enriched by them. Despite the ravages of time and foreign rule, the Hindus have kept alive their spiritual practices by worshipping in the mandir and the home, through regular reading and listening of sacred texts and associating with God-realized gurus. In this way these ancient traditions enabled the practitioners to remain connected to God and spirituality. Given below is an account of these three pillars of Hinduism.

1. MANDIR

ORIGIN

For several millennia the Hindus have been worshipping the deities of nature through prayers. They venerated the forces of nature like Varunadeva (the water-god), Agnideva (fire-god), Indradeva (rain-god), Suryadeva (sun-god) and others by offering prayers and sacrifices (*yajnas*) to them. The prayers and *yajnas* became a daily feature in the lives of Hindus in the early Vedic period. To keep the *yajna* fires from being snuffed out by wind and rain, they built shelters to cover the *vedis* (sacrificial platforms). Over time these developed into shrines, and a precise science of mandir building was born. The altar of the sacrificial fire developed into the *garbha-gruha* or sanctum

Kailāsanātha Mandir carved out of rock, Ellorā

sanctorum. By the end of the Vedic period artists and sculptors began to make visual representations of the deities in the form of pictures and sculptures. The *murtis* or images were made of wood, stone or metal. They were installed in the *garbha-gruha*. One finds mention of mandirs in the Atharva Veda. They were generally built with materials like timber and clay that were not long-lasting. Cave mandirs or mandirs carved out of rocks and ones built with bricks came much later. The heavy stone mandirs with intricate carvings and designs belong to a still later period.

The mandir is the home of God. It is a sacred place where man worships him. The term *devālaya* is used to denote a mandir. It means "the house of God." Another word that is used when it is huge is *prāsāda*, which means a 'king's palace'. The text dealing with the science of mandir building is called the Shilpa Shastra or Vāstu Shastra.

SYMBOLIZES THE DIVINE AND OTHER ASPECTS

The mandir is a link between humans and God, between the earthly plane and the divine realm and between the idea of God and the Reality. The seers of ancient India conceived mandirs as sacred representations of God. Miss Stella Kramrisch, the Austrian curator of the Museum of Indian Art in Philadelphia, describes so in her book *The Hindu Temple*, "The temple is the concrete shape of the Essence; as such it is the residence and vesture (clothing) of God. The masonry is the sheath *(kosha)* and body. The temple is the monument of manifestation. The devotee who comes to the temple, to look at it, does so as a 'seer', not as a spectator."[1]

The *kurma shilā* (stone in the mandir foundation) symbolizes God's feet, *jagati* (side wall) his thighs, *sthambhas* (pillars) his knees, *garbha-gruha* (inner sanctum) his stomach, *pithikā* (base of *mandovar)* his heart, *sinhāsana* (throne) his seat, *murti* (image) his soul, *deepa* (lamp) his prana (life-breath), *deepa-prakāsha* (flames of lamps) his eyes, *ghanta* (bell) his tongue, *shikharas* (pinnacles) his shoulders, *shukanāsa* (projection on the main *shikhara* in form of lion statue) his nose, *gavākshas* (windows) his ears, *āmalsāro* or *āmalaka* (stone ring) his neck, *kalasha* (golden pot) his head, *dhvaja* (flag) his tuft of hair and the outer layer of plaster or stone cladding on mandir his skin.[2] The *murti* is the focal point of the mandir. Once the God-realized guru or pious person invokes the presence of the Divine in the *murti*, the mandir becomes spiritually vibrant. It becomes a centre of worship, prayer and peace. The rituals of *pranāma, ārati,* dhyana, chanting mantras, and offering flowers engage the devotees' body, senses, mind and heart with the Divine, thus cleansing him or her of bad karma and imbuing divinity. A restless and wavering mind becomes calm and stable in the mandir.

The mandir also symbolizes God as the cosmos. The different realms are located on different parts of his body. The *bhuloka* (earth) forms his feet, *satyaloka* forms his *shikhā* (tuft of hair) and the other worlds *(bhuvarloka, swargaloka, maharloka, janaloka* and *tapaloka)* form other parts of his body.

The mandir also symbolizes Meru *parvata*, the golden

---

1. Kramrisch, Stella. *The Hindu Temple, Vol.1.* Delhi: Motilal Banarsidass, 1991, p.165.

2. Somapura, Narmadashankar. *Shilparatnākara*, 2nd ed. Dhrangadhra, Gujarat: Somapura Dinkararaya Narmadashankar, 1990, pp.5-6, *shloka* 30-36.

A MANDIR SYMBOLIZES GOD'S BODY
BAPS Swaminarayan Mandir, Junāgadh, of Nāgara Style

Amrut Kalashas or Golden pots: Head

Dhvajā or Flag: Tuft of hair

Āmalsāro or Stone ring: Neck

Ghummat or Dome: Sky

Shukanāsa or Lion statue: Nose

Shikhar or Pinnacle: Shoulder

Sthambha or Pillars: Knees

Garbha-gruha or Inner sanctum: Stomach. The *simhāsana* inside symbolizes the throne. And the *murti* or image represents God's soul

Gavāksha or Window: Ear

Mandovara or Ornate outside wall: Torso

Kanapitha or Base of Mandovara: Heart

Jagati or Bottom side wall: Thighs

mountain described in the Purānas, around which are spread the various worlds.

The mandir also represents the subtle body with the seven *chakras* or subtle centres of consciousness or divine power. The *garbha-gruha* represents the *anāhata chakra* (fourth *chakra* located in the heart) and the tip of the *kalasha* refers to the *sahasrāra chakra* (situated at the top of the head).

The rishis of India prescribed specific rules for the construction of a mandir, with each step having a meaning and every component a function. Its shapes and sizes have been so prescribed that they are in harmony with nature and the universe.

ARCHITECTURAL STYLES

The three dominant styles of mandir architecture in India are determined by the shape of the *shikharas* or pinnacles. If the shape of the *shikhara* is curvilinear, the mandir belongs to the Nāgara class, and if it is pyramidal then to the Drāvida class. The third style, though not as prominent, is a mixture of both. It is called Vesara, which came to prevail mostly in west Deccan and south Karnataka. The Nāgara style predominates in North and West India, and the Drāvida style is a feature of South India with its distinct *gopurams* — the elegant and elaborately carved towering structures that form the entrance gates. Hindu mandirs enshrine the *murtis* of Bhagwan Vishnu, Rāma, Krishna, Shiva, and their different forms, along with their consorts Lakshmi, Sita, Rādhā and Pārvati. There are also mandirs dedicated to goddesses or Shakti and other deities. Each mandir has its presiding deity in the central shrine.

The last 1,500 years of Indian history have witnessed the golden age of mandir building. Kings and rich patrons inspired the construction of huge mandirs in India. The Surya Ratha Mandir of Konārka (Orissa), ancient mandirs like Kedāranātha and Badarinātha (both in Uttarakhand), the famous mandir

Nāgara style of mandir architecture

Drāvida style

Vesara style

Badarinātha Mandir (900 CE)

Kedāranātha Mandir (very ancient)

Jagannātha Mandir (1174 CE)

Surya Ratha Mandir of Konārka (1300 CE)

Rāmanātha Mandir, Rāmeshvaram (c. 1200 CE)

Meenakshi Sundareshvara Mandir (1600 CE)

Venkateshvara Mandir, Tirupati (c. 300 CE)

Somnātha Mandir (1951 CE)

Dwārakādhish Mandir (1600 CE)

Swaminarayan Akshardham, New Delhi (2005)

Tilak Bisht

Hinduism

of Lord Jagannātha in Jagannātha Puri (Orissa), the rock mandir of Kailāsa in Ellorā (Aurangabad, Maharashtra), the stupendous *parikramā* of Rāmeshvaram (Tamil Nadu), intricate and impressive multi-storey gateways of the mandirs of Madurāi and Minākshi (Tamil Nadu), Tirupati Bālāji (Andhra Pradesh), Somnātha and Dwārakā (Gujarat), and Swaminarayan Akshardham in Gandhinagar (Gujarat) and New Delhi – the latter one being the largest comprehensive mandir built in modern times – and many others in India and abroad reflect the rich mandir tradition of India.

Mandirs Abroad

For many years Hindus have travelled throughout the world and continued the Hindu tradition by building mandirs. The Angkor Wat in Kampuchea (formerly Cambodia) is one of the largest Hindu mandirs. The British took indentured Indian labourers to the West Indies, Mauritius, Fiji, Guyana, South Africa and other countries. Despite being thousands of miles away from their religious centres and culture they constructed mandirs for worship and thus passed on the Hindu tradition to their children. Today, though many may not be able to speak their native Indian languages fluently, they have remained Hindus mainly because of their worship practices in mandirs and homes, consisting of singing, dancing, performing different types of rituals and celebrating Hindu festivals.

Murtis

The *murtis* in mandirs belong to the three traditions of Vaishnavism, Shaivism and Shāktism. They are either fixed (*achala*), moveable (*chala*) or sometimes both moveable and fixed (*chalāchala*). The *achala murti* is usually made of stone and it remains fixed in the *garbha-gruha*. The *chala* is made of five metals (*panchadhātu*: gold, silver, copper, lead and iron) or other materials, and it is taken out in procession on festive occasions,

Shayana (reclining): Murti of Bhagwan Vishnu (Budha Nilkanth) sleeping on the great serpent Ananta, Kathmandu, Nepal

A Hindu deity is generally found in one of three poses: Shayana (above), Sthānaka and Āsana (below)

Sthānaka (standing): Murti of Bhagwan Shiva, Haridwāra

Āsana (sitting): Murti of Bhagwan Swaminarayan, Akshardham, Delhi

for bathing, ritualistic worship and sanctification of homes. The chalāchala, which is moveable but fixed, is worshipped in the garbha-gruha and taken out in a procession on special occasions, as in the case of Lord Jagannātha in Jagannātha Puri mandir once a year.

The murtis are generally in one of three postures: sthānaka (standing), āsana (sitting) and shayana (reclining). Only in Vaishnavism one finds murtis in the shayana pose.

Among the mudras (position of hands and fingers) one finds the abhayamudrā (symbolizing protection) and varadamudrā (granting boons). The murtis in Vaishnava mandirs have shankha (conch), chakra, (divine disc), gadā (mace) and padma (lotus) in their hands and the Shaiva and Shākta murtis have damaru (drum), trishula (trident), pāsha (noose), ankusha (goad), bāna (arrow) and khadaga (sword).

WORSHIP IN MANDIRS

Many Hindus, after their daily bath and prayer at home, regularly visit a mandir for darshan and satsang. The mandir darshan visit begins by removing one's shoes before entering the worship area of the mandir. One is also expected to leave one's worldly thoughts there. Since the mandir is a holy place where all come for spiritual elevation everyone is expected to

Devotees revere deities by offering namaskar, prayer and prostration

dress modestly.

On reaching the main worship area devotees touch the floor with their fingers, out of humility and respect, and then place them on their head and heart to feel blessed. Thereafter the devotee goes towards the main shrines for darshan of the deities. Generally, he or she first makes the customary offering of fruits or flowers before the deities. The deities are generally adorned in attractive clothes, ornaments and garlands. During *ārati,* the pujari waves lighted wicks before the deity while the congregation sings a prayer in praise of God. Thereafter the lighted wicks are carried in a tray to devotees who pass their hands over it and then touch them on their head, eyes and heart to sanctify themselves. The *āratis* in many mandirs are a five-time or two-time daily ritual from early morning to evening. Vaishnava mandirs are generally open for darshan from 6.00 a.m. till noon and 4.00 p.m. till 8.30 p.m. Shaiva mandirs generally remain open for darshan throughout the day. After darshan one offers prostrations to the deities. In most mandirs the pujari or his assistant gives a little holy water *(charanāmruta* or *tirthodaka)* in one's right palm. Drinking it and running one's right hand on one's head transfers its sacredness to the entire body. Sometimes the pujari or his attendant will mark one's forehead with kumkum, *chandana* or holy ash that has

A female devotee offers panchānga pranāma to a deity

Children worshipping in their home mandir

been already offered to the deity, as a mark of divine blessings. Finally, the pujari may give *prasāda* either in the form of fruit, flower or food that has been offered to the deities. Then the devotee circumambulates the deities (*pradakshinā*) as a mark of respect, and to consolidate that God plays a central role in his or her life. In some mandirs devotees listen to morning or evening spiritual discourses. Throughout the year, festivals are celebrated on holy days with devotion and joy. Thousands come to have darshan and pray to the deities.

Devout Hindus also have small mandirs in their homes to conduct daily worship and *ārati*. This enables them to remain connected to God and imbued with mental peace and spiritual joy.

2. SHASTRAS

INTRODUCTION

Hindu shastras that teach philosophy accept certain basic sources or means of valid knowledge. They vary from a minimum of three to a maximum of six. They are called *pramānas*: (1) *pratyaksha* (perception), (2) *anumāna* (inference), (3) *upamāna* (analogy), (4) *shabda* (testimony), (5) *anupalabdhi* (non-perception) and (6) *arthāpatti* (postulation). *Shabda* or verbal testimony is of two types, namely, the Vedas and the

Discourse by an enlightened guru contains the essence of Hindu shastras

words of a spiritually enlightened person which are called *āptavākyas*. The former, i.e., the words of the Vedas, are impersonal because they had not been created by any human agency. And the latter, i.e., *āptavākyas*, are personal, yet they have spiritual authority. Among the six, *shabda* or verbal testimony is the most important of all means and source of knowledge. It is rational to believe in the shastras like it is for students to believe in standard textbooks.

Shruti and Smruti Shastras

In Hinduism the Vedas are the ancient shastras revealed by the supreme Paramātmā or Bhagwan to enlightened rishis thousands of years ago. They are called the Shruti Shastras, where 'Shruti' means "that which is heard" or revealed. They contain hymns in praise of and prayers to the deities of nature. They were passed on through an oral tradition from master to disciple for thousands of years and later Veda Vyāsa classified them into the four Vedas.

The Vedic literature, especially the Āranyakas and Upanishads, contain the highest spiritual wisdom about the nature of and relationship between *ātmā* and *Paramātmā*. The secondary source of authentic knowledge is the Smruti Shastras which means "that which is remembered". They include the

Manuscript of the Riga Veda

Itihāsas (Rāmāyana and Mahābhārata), Dharma shastras and eighteen Purānas. They also include the Vedāngas and Upavedas – shastras that elaborate upon Vedic arts and sciences: Ayurveda (science of medicine), Gāndharvaveda (science of music and dance), Dhanurveda (science of warfare) and Sthāpatyaveda (science of architecture). The Dharma shastras, such as, Manu Smruti, Yājnavalkya Smruti and others, prescribe the moral dos and don'ts for happy living. In addition, through the centuries, enlightened gurus, sadhus, devout philosophers and poets have revealed and nourished Hinduism through their writings, preachings and pure lives. The development and spread of Hindu wisdom continues to this day as contemporary gurus speak of and live by the ancient Hindu shastras.

BENEFITS OF SCRIPTURAL STUDY

A shastra is given due honour and respect by placing it on a decorated platform

Ancient India had a *gurukula* system of education in which the student lived and learned in the guru's ashram, usually from the age of eight to twenty-five. On graduating, the student was advised to continue his daily worship rituals and scriptural study at home. The daily reading and study of shastras imbued him with spiritual consciousness and provided moral strength and steadfastness amidst the trappings of *māyā* and mundane desires. Daily reading and study of the shastras also revealed new depths of spiritual truths, thus enhancing his spiritual faith and joy. It also empowered him with *viveka,* i.e., discrimination of right and wrong, enabling him to follow what is right. The Shrimad Bhagavad Gitā says, "The man who rejects the words of the shastras and follows the impulse of desire attains neither perfection, nor joy, nor the path supreme. Let the shastras, therefore, be your authority to what is right and what is not right."[3]

Daily study of or listening to and contemplation on the shastras fosters faith in God, resolves doubts, miseries and

A speaker discourses on a Hindu shastra

3. B.G. 16.23-24.

Shukdevji, an enlightened spiritual master, narrating the Shrimad Bhāgavata to King Parikshit

tensions of daily living and helps pacify the mind. The shastras show an ideal pathway of life. To listen to and understand them from a bona fide spiritual master is imperative because only a God-realized master can reveal the true meaning of the shastras and help one to follow them.

3. SANT

INTRODUCTION

Sant means a sadhu, *satpurusha* or spiritual guru.

From ancient times Hindu society has been focused towards an inward journey, fascinated and attracted by the deeper realities of life. Hindus strive to understand and control the mind, realize the ultimate truth and attain transcendental happiness that is eternal and ultimate. It is for this reason that rishis, gurus and *sants* are venerated and sought after for spiritual inspiration, guidance and blessings.

GLORY OF GURU

Hinduism has a unique *guru-shishya* tradition in which the disciple learns and realizes spiritual knowledge by associating with a guru who is *brahmanishtha* (God-realized) and *shrotriya* (one who understands the true meanings of the shastras and has realized them).

The Shrimad Bhāgavata describes thirty virtues of a bona fide *sant* or *satpurusha*. Bhagwan Shri Krishna states the glory and bond he has with a true *sant*, "*Sādhavo hradayam mahyam, sādhunām hradayam tvaham.*" – "The Sadhu is my heart, and I am the heart of the Sadhu."[4]

Sant Tulasidāsa writes in the *Rāmacharitmānas*, "One who is awake in the darkness of anger, and is not bound by the shackles of greed is equal to you, O Rāma."[5]

The great *āchārya* and pioneer of Advaita Vedānta, Shri Ādi Shankarāchārya, states, "*Gurorangripadme manaschena lagnam tatah kim...*" – "If one has not attached one's mind at the feet of a guru, then of what use is it?"[6]

Bhagwan Swaminarayan has described the qualities of a *sant* or *satpurusha* to be one who is wedded to dharma, *jnāna, vairāgya* and bhakti.[7] He adds, "When one has darshan of such a *sant*, one should realize 'I have had darshan of God himself'."[8]

In India, primary and secondary schools students recite the glory of guru, "*Gurur Brahmā, gurur Vishnuh, gurur devo Maheshvarah, Gurur sākshāt Parambrahma tasmai Shri gurave namah.*"[9] The *shloka* explains that the guru is the creator, sustainer and destroyer. He is God himself therefore one should bow to him.

The renowned English writer, Somerset Maugham, on meeting Ramana Maharshi in India, opines, "It is a mistake to think that those holy men of India lead useless lives. They are a shining light in the darkness. When a man becomes pure and perfect the influence of his character spreads so that those who seek truth are naturally drawn to him."[10]

---

4. Shrimad Bhāgavata 9.4.68.

5. "*Ghora krodha tama nishi jo jāgā, Lobhapāsha jehi gara na bandhāyā, So nara tumha samān Raghurāyā.*" Kishkindhā Kānda. 20.2-3.

6. Ādi Shankarāchārya. *Guru Ashtakam.*

7. Vachanāmrut (Gadhada I.54.)

8. Vachanāmrut (Sarangpur 10.)

9. *Guru Gītā*, shloka 45, in Skanda Purāna.

10. Maugham, William Somerset. *The Razar's Edge.* Michigan: Vanguard Library, 1957, p.254.

A guru imparts Vedic knowledge to his student disciples

Dr S. Radhakrishnan, the former president of India, averred, "Today we live in society not because of scientific inventions, but because of the saints who live in society."

The living guru or *sant* is held in the highest esteem because he guides, pacifies and liberates souls from the vortex of *māyā* and worldly desires – which are the roots of all misery and suffering.

GURU'S GRACE

The disciple cannot fully realize his own atman or God through personal efforts alone. Moreover, since spiritual knowledge is beyond the purview of the senses and mind it cannot be fully realized through them. Also, due to *dehabhāva* (attachment to one's body and its needs) one can never attain spiritual knowledge. Furthermore, the senses themselves are not perfect so they cannot perceive or give one perfect knowledge. And that is why having faith in the testimony of a God-enlightened guru is the best and easiest way to realize spiritual knowledge. If a child wants to know who is his father, then he has to ask his mother – the natural authority. Similarly, accepting the authority of testimony *(shabda)* of enlightened masters is imperative because they are the natural divine authorities. Through verbal testimony of the bona fide guru one comes to know the unknowable. This is not blind faith or dogma but simply accepting what one hears from one who is enlightened. When an aspirant learns and internalizes knowledge from someone who has perfect knowledge, he can be liberated from ignorance and the misery of the cycle of births and deaths. The disciple earns the guru's grace through humility, service and spiritual enquiry.

The Upanishadic gurus imparted spiritual knowledge to their disciples and blessed them finally with spiritual realization. The Shrimad Bhāgavata speaks of Shukadevaji as a God-realized *satpurusha*. When King Parikshita faithfully listened to the Shrimad Bhāgavata from Shukadevaji he became enlightened, attaining *ātmabhāva* and God-realization and thus overcame the fear of death.

Through the ages the spiritually enlightened *sants* of India have protected, sustained and nourished Hinduism. The *sant* tradition in Hinduism is pivotal, because the God-realized *sant* consecrates the *murtis* of God in mandirs, rejuvenates the sanctity of holy places, explains the true meaning of the shastras, and initiates a spiritual aspirant *(diksha)* and helps him attain *moksha*.

SUMMARY

1. Mandirs, shastras and *sant* form the three pillars of Hinduism.
2. In Vedic times Hindus worshipped the deities governing the forces of nature by chanting mantras and singing hymns extolling their glory.
3. Later, they performed *yajnas* to appease and appreciate them. Over time, shrines were made to protect the *yajna* fire which later became transformed into the sanctum sanctorum of mandirs.
4. The mandir symbolizes God, cosmos, Meru *parvata* and the seven *chakras*. Its three styles are Nāgara (curvilinear

A disciple attains spiritual realization through the guru's grace

shikharas), Drāvida (pyramidal *shikharas*) and Vesara (a mixture of both styles).

5. Various rituals of darshan, *ārati*, prostration, circumambulation, prayer, etc. are performed in mandirs by devotees. They spiritually purify and charge the devotees.

6. The Vedas or Shruti shastras were revealed by God to the enlightened rishis. Shruti means "that which is heard" or revealed by God. They include the Vedas, i.e., Samhitā, Brāhmana, Āranyaka and Upanishad texts.

7. The secondary shastras are known as the Smruti texts. Smruti means "that which is remembered". They include the Itihāsas (Rāmāyana and Mahābhārata), Dharma shastras and eighteen Purānas.

8. The third tradition is the *Sant* tradition. Hinduism has the *guru-shishya* tradition in which the spiritual guru or *sant* guides and enlightens the disciple.

9. Through the centuries the traditions of Mandir, Shastra and Sant have protected and nourished Hinduism and the cultural traditions of India.

12

Sacred Places of India

Amar Ujala

Pilgrims bathe in the holy Gangā during the Kumbha Mela (2010) at Harki Paidi ghat in Haridwāra. (Inset) Ārati of River Gangā at Vāranāsi

Amar Ujala

Seven Ancient Holy Cities,
Four Sacred Dhāmas, Kumbh Mela Sites

INTRODUCTION

Among the many Hindu practices *tirtha yātrā* or pilgrimage to a holy place is performed with the sentiments of cleansing oneself of sins, other impurities and consolidating one's spirituality. *Tirthas* are referred to as 'fords' or places for 'crossing over'. A *tirtha* is a place where the divine meets the temporal, where the higher realms meet the lower, the sacred meets the mundane. So, a *tirtha* is a holy place where one 'crosses over' or elevates oneself to a higher spiritual plane by having darshan of the deity, chanting God's holy name, performing circumambulations, listening to discourses, bathing in the holy waters of the lakes, rivers or oceans, performing austerities, giving charity, celebrating a festival, and by engaging in meditation and self-reflection.

Many spiritual seekers perform *tirtha yātrā* to dissolve their sins and acquire *punya* (merit) through divine grace. Specific religious rites like sprinkling the ashes of a deceased relative in a holy river or ocean, or *shrāddha* are also performed at *tirthas*. Some go to holy places to meet an enlightened guru and listen to his discourses or seek his spiritual guidance and blessings.

India is a land of thousands of sacred places that owe their sanctity to the avatars of God and holy sadhus who were either born there or had visited them. Many holy places lie in the mountains, on the seashore, in caves or on the banks of sacred rivers.

HOLY PLACES

The seven ancient holy cities of India are Ayodhyā, Mathurā and Vrundāvan, Haridwāra, Vārānasi, Dwārakā, Ujjayini or Ujjain, and Kānchipuram.

The four holy *dhāmās* (abodes) are Badarinātha (North), Jagannātha Puri (East), Rāmeshvaram (South) and Dwārakā (West).

The four main Kumbh Mela sites are Prayāga (Allahabad in Uttar Pradesh), Haridwāra (Uttarakhand), Ujjain (Madhya Pradesh) and Nāsik (Maharashtra).

Given below is a brief account of the places of pilgrimage. The seven holy rivers of India and other pilgrim places are described in the next chapter.

SEVEN ANCIENT HOLY CITIES

1. Ayodhyā

Ayodhyā is a renowned ancient city on the bank of River Sarayu. It is the birthplace of Bhagwan Rāma. The city of Ayodhyā, in the Faizabad district of Uttar Pradesh, is 130 kilometres from Lucknow and 190 kilometres from Vārānasi. The Atharva Veda describes it as "a city built by devas and as prosperous as *swarga* itself." Manu, the first traditional king of India, is said to have founded the city of Ayodhyā as his capital. Great Ikshvāku kings like Māndhātā, Harishchandra, Bhagiratha, Dilip and Raghu ruled over Ayodhyā. In Tretā Yuga, Bhagwan Rāma was born to King Dasharatha and Queen Kaushalyā in Ayodhyā.

The famous Chinese travellers, Fa-hsien (400 CE) and Hsüan Tsang (700 CE), visited Ayodhyā and have written interesting accounts. During their time it was a flourishing city of Buddhist monasteries. The city of Sāketa, well known during the time of the Buddha, has been identified with Ayodhyā.

Ayodhyā is also a sacred place for Jains because several Tirthankars had lived there.

The sacred city of Ayodhyā on the banks of holy River Sarayu

Ayodhyā is predominantly a city of mandirs. There is a small mandir at the birth spot of Rāma.

Another important mandir in Ayodhyā is the Kanaka Bhavan. Sitā is believed to have lived there. The famous Hanumān Gadhi Mandir attracts thousands of pilgrims daily. Legend has it that Hanumānji lived there in a cave and guarded the city. The Tretā-kā-Mandir stands on the spot where Rāma performed the Ashwamedha Yajna. The Nāgeshawaranātha Mandir has the *murti* of Bhagwan Shiva and was established by Kusha, the son of Rāma. Twenty kilometres from Ayodhyā lies Nandigrāma, from where Bharata lived and ruled on behalf of Rāma while Rāma was in exile for 14 years.

Bhagwan Swaminarayan lived in Ayodhyā from the age of five to eleven years. He was then known as Ghanshyam. There is a mandir dedicated to him on the place where his house was in the Barhattāpur area. On the mandir precincts are shrines commemorating his guru, Ramanand Swami, and parents, Dharmadev and Bhaktimata. Opposite the mandir lies the sweet shop from where Ghanshyam ate sweets. Behind the mandir nearby is a small shrine dedicated to Shiva where Ghanshyam used to go for darshan and have his siesta. From Rāma ghat Nilkanth plunged into the River Sarayu and after crossing it he embarked on a seven-year pilgrimage of India.

The famous Hanumān Gadhi Mandir, Ayodhyā

Shri Rādhā-Raman Dev Mandir, Vrundāvan

Thereafter, he established the Swaminarayan Sampradaya in Gujarat.

2. MATHURĀ AND VRUNDĀVAN

Mathurā is a very ancient city established by Shatrughna, the younger brother of Rāma. It is sacred to the Vaishnavas as the birthplace of Bhagwan Krishna and is situated on the bank of the River Yamunā, about 157 kilometres south of Delhi in Uttar Pradesh. It is believed to be more than 5,000 years old.

Shri Krishna spent his childhood in Gokula, near Mathurā. Vrundāvan is about 11 km from Mathurā and is famous for the childhood *lilā* (play) of Shri Krishna with the *gopis*. The holy land associated with Shri Krishna's birth and childhood activities are Mathurā and twelve main forests – one of which is Vrundāvan. Mathurā and the holy area spread over 32 kilometres around it are known as Vrajabhumi or Vrajamandala. According to a traditional saying, Mathurā is travelled to by pilgrims in pursuit of liberation and Vrundāvan is visited for religious experience by visualizing Krishna's childhood *lilās*.

The renowned mandirs in Mathurā are the Shri Rangaji Mandir and Dwārakādhisha Mandir. In Vrundāvan one finds the Rādhā-Raman Dev Mandir, Govindaji Mandir, Bānke Behāri Mandir, Madana Mohana Mandir, ISKCON Mandir and others. Devotees passionately go for darshan of and offer prayers to the *murtis* of Rādhā and Krishna in these mandirs.

Mathurā has several ghats for the devotees to bathe in the Yamunā, which is considered to be meritorious. Every year Krishna devotees undertake a Vrajamandala *parikramā* – a pilgrimage of mandirs and sacred places in Mathura and its surrounding holy places like Vrundāvan, Nandagrāma, Gokula, Mt. Govardhana, the village of Varsānā (also called Barsānā) sacred to Rādhā, and others. The pilgrimage takes about a month to complete.

Every year hundreds of thousands of devotees come to Mathura and Vrundāvan with an aspiration to have a vision of or experience the divine presence of Rādhā and Krishna. The pilgrims take the dust of Vrundāvan and apply it on their head for sanctification.

Mathurā was a famous centre of art. Its school of sculptors had its heyday between 50 and 1200 CE.

3. HARIDWĀRA

Haridwāra or Haradwāra (Hari means Vishnu and Hara means Shiva; *dwāra* means gateway) is situated on the banks of River Gangā in northern India. It is thus considered to be the gateway to the abode of Vishnu and Shiva. It is also the gateway to the four main pilgrim places of Uttarakhand, namely, Badarinātha, Kedaranātha, Gangotri and Yamunotri.

Haridwāra is 263 kilometres from New Delhi and is situated by the River Gangā at the foot of the Sivālika range of the Himalayas in the Saharanapur district of Uttarakhand. It is here that Gangā leaves the mountains and enters the plains. Haridwāra is the first town on the plains. Taking a bath on its ghats purifies the soul and blesses one with *moksha*.

There are five main holy places in Haridwāra: Gangādwāra, Kushavarta, Balakeshwara, Neela *parvata* and Kanakhala.

The Gangādwāra has a ghat called Harki Paidi. The water

Flowers and cotton wicks for worship of River Gangā

The mahā-ārati of River Gangā at Harki Paidi ghat, Haridwāra

body is called Brahmakunda. Bhagwan Brahmā bestowed his benedictions that whosoever bathed here would be cleansed of his or her sins. Every evening a *mahā-ārati* of River Gangā is performed, after which the *deepas* are set afloat on its waters.

The Gangā flows from the Neela *parvata* and spreads in seven streams called Saptadhārā. At this place the legendary child-devotee Dhruvaji had performed austerities to have darshan of Bhagwan Vishnu.

In Kanakhala lies the Daksha Mandir. The Purānas note that King Daksha Prajāpati performed a *yajna* here. Shivaji, King Daksha's son-in-law, was not invited. Sati, Shiva's wife and Daksha Prajāpati's daughter, went to the *yajna* uninvited. Because of her father's contempt for her husband, she felt insulted and then burnt herself during the *yajna* through her yogic powers. This infuriated Shivaji, who then created Virabhadra to kill Daksha Prajāpati.

There are hundreds of mandirs and ashrams in Haridwāra where pilgrims perform various spiritual sadhanas for self-elevation.

4. Vāranāsi

Vāranāsi is another ancient holy city in the State of Uttar Pradesh. It is closely connected with Bhagwan Shiva. It is

Pilgrims bathe in the River Gangā by the banks of the sacred, ancient city of Vāranāsi

situated on the banks of Gangā and is about 720 km southeast
of Delhi. It is also called Kāshi and Banaras (an anglicised
form of Vāranāsi). It was established by Divodāsa, a human
incarnation of Dhanvantari.

The venerable city is mentioned in the Brāhmana and
Upanishad texts and also in the Mahābhārata with reference
to a festival celebrated in honour of Shiva, which the Pāndavas
attended with their mother. Later, there was a strong Buddhist
influence in Vāranāsi. The holy city is also mentioned in the
Vāmana Purāna and Buddhist texts.

During Shankarāchārya's time (8th century CE) the city
became a renowned centre of learning Hinduism. Vāranāsi
has always been a great centre of learning, and scholars from
all parts of India come to study here. The Banaras Hindu
University (BHU) and the Kāshi Vidyāpeetha are the two most
esteemed academic institutions of recent times.

The renowned Kāshi Vishvanātha Mandir is dedicated to
Bhagwan Shiva, known here as Lord Vishvanātha. It is one of
the twelve *jyotirlingas*.

Vāranāsi is famous for its ghats or steps that lead down
into the River Gangā. It is on the famous Manikarnikā ghat,
associated with Pārvati, that pilgrims bathe and also cremate
bodies. Many ritually scatter after cremation the charred bones

(*asthi*) of loved ones in the Gaṅgā so that the departed souls gain liberation and *punya*. Also, since ages Hindus have believed that death at Kāshi automatically grants them liberation. So many aspirants come in their old age to live and die here.

The Tulasi Mānas Mandir is dedicated to Bhagwan Rāma and built on the spot where Goswāmi Tulasidāsa composed the great Hindi epic *Rāmacharitmānas,* which details the life and deeds of Bhagwan Rāma.

5. DWĀRAKĀ

The town of Dwāraka, also written and known as Dwārika or Dwāravati, lies by the seashore near the port of Okhā in Saurashtra (Gujarat). It is associated with Bhagwan Krishna who established and ruled over it after slaying the evil Kansa in Mathurā. Shri Krishna migrated with the entire Yādava community to the coast of Saurashtra and founded the town known as Swarnadwārikā.

Dwāraka is sacred to all the Vaishnavas. It is believed that the Swarnadwārikā established by Shri Krishna was engulfed by the sea seven days after his earthly departure. Recent excavations have shown that the sea submerged five settlements and the present day Dwāraka is the sixth.

The main mandir in Dwāraka is the Dwārakādheesha or Ranchhodji Mandir. It is a five-storey structure with the main *shikhara* rising to 140 feet in height. The mandir sanctum has a beautiful *murti* of Bhagwan Dwārakādheesha or Ranchhodarāi (Shri Krishna), who is the presiding deity of the town. The image of Krishna is made of black stone, which is three feet in height with four arms. Krishna Janmāshtami is the biggest festival celebrated in the mandir.

The Rukmini Devi Mandir is dedicated to Rukmini, one of the eight main queens of Shri Krishna. The confluence of River Gomati with the sea is also a holy place, and bathing here endows one with liberation. The Dwārakādheesha Mandir is

Tilak Bisht

Dwārakādheesha Mandir, Dwārakā

located nearby. The Nāgeshvara Mahādeva is one of the twelve *jyotirlinga* mandirs of Shiva. It is only 10 km from Dwārakā. Not far from Dwārakā is the Gopi pond, where Shri Krishna met the *gopis* when they came to see him from Vrundāvan. The sacred clay from Gopi pond is called *gopi-chandana* and it is used by Vaishnavas to make the *tilaka* mark on their bodies.

In addition to the mandirs, Dwārakā is also one of the four seats established by Ādi Shankarāchārya. The seat is known as Shārdā Peetha.

6. UJJAIN

Ujjain is also known as Ujjayini or Ujjaini. It lies on the bank of the River Kshiprā, 80 kilometres to the north of Indore in Madhya Pradesh. It is one of the four places sanctified by a few drops of *amruta* (immortalizing nectar) from the holy Kumbha. A Kumbha Mela is held on the spot once every twelve years. Ujjain's other ancient names are Avanti, Ujjaini, Kaushasthali and Amarāvati. The city is one of the fifty-one Shaktipeethas in India. There is a natural self-born *linga* or *jyotirlinga* of Bhagwan Shiva in the Mahākāleshvara or Mahākāla mandir, which is described in glorious terms by the great poet Kālidāsa in his poem *Meghaduta*.

The great King Ashoka was the viceroy of Ujjain. In circa

Darshan Thakker

Shri Dwārakādheesha, Dwārakā

Rāma ghat on River Kshiprā, Ujjain

57 BCE the legendary King Vikramāditya lived in Ujjain and made it the capital of his empire. Nine great gems *(nava ratnas)* among men enhanced the glory of his court; some of whom were Kālidāsa, a poet and playwright, Dhanvantari, a physician, Varāhamihira, an astrologer, and others. For several centuries Ujjain was the cultural capital of India. The celebrated Hindu astronomer and astrologer, Varāhamihira (505-587 CE), lived in Ujjain. He referred to the *Suryasiddhānta,* which is a great *jyotisha* (astrological) work taught by Surya (sun-god) to Maya (the architect of the asuras), to prepare his work called *Panchasiddhāntikā.* He gave the first revised version of the Hindu calendar.

The places of pilgrimage and religious prominence here are the River Kshiprā, Mahākāleshvara Mandir, Siddhvada (banyan tree), cave of Bhartruhari, Harisiddhamātā Mandir, Gopāla Mandir, Mangalnātha Mandir and others. About three kilometres from the Gopāla Mandir lies the Sāndipani ashram where Krishna and Balarāma were educated by Sage Sāndipani. In 1693 the king of Jaipur, Jaisinhji, established an observatory here.

7. KĀNCHIPURAM

Kānchipuram or Kānchi is a sacred city situated on the bank

of River Pālār, 75 kilometres south-west of Chennāi (Madras) in the State of Tamil Nadu. It was built in 6th century CE by the Pallava kings. Later it was ruled by the Chola and Vijayanagara dynasties. It is popularly known as the golden city of a thousand mandirs. It is divided into Shivakānchi and Vishnukānchi.

Kānchipuram is a major town for the worship of Shiva-Shakti and Vishnu. It is one of the most renowned Shaktipeethas. There are three main cities where goddess Shakti is worshipped. The goddess Kāmākshi is worshipped in Kānchipuram, goddess Meenākshi at Madurāi and goddess Vishālakshmi in Koshi.

Ādi Shankarāchārya is said to have set up his *matha* or teaching centre in Kānchipuram known as Kāmakoti Peetham.

The popular holy places in Kānchipuram are: Kāmākshi Amman Mandir where the goddess Kāmākshi is worshipped and the Kailāshanātha Mandir is dedicated to Bhagwan Shiva. The Kāmākshi mandir has a shrine of Ādi Shankarāchārya. The mandir was built in the 8th century CE by the Pallava ruler. It is the oldest structure in Kānchipuram. Another mandir dedicated to Bhagwan Shiva is the Ekambareshwara Mandir. Its tower or *gopuram* is 188 ft high and the mandir shrine has the *murtis* of 63 Nāyanmārs (Shaiva saint-poets of Tamil Nadu), also spelt as Nāyanārs. It was built in the 16th century CE during the Vijayanagara Empire.

The Varadarāja Mandir in the Vishnukānchi part of Kānchipuram is an important place of pilgrimage for the Vaishnavas. The presiding deity is Varadarāja or Bhagwan Vishnu, which is in a standing posture. There are *murtis* of Ālvārs (Tamil Vaishnava saint-poets) and Rāmānujāchārya that are worshipped. Rāmānujāchārya, the founder of Vishishtādvaita philosophy, served the deity in the mandir. There is also a rare mandir dedicated to Chitragupta, the scribe and accountant of Lord Yama, god of death, who records meticulously the deeds of all people for administering justice after death.

Kānchipuram has been associated with many famous people.

Kāmākshi Amman Mandir, Kānchipuram

Chānakya (300 BCE), the author of the Arthashāstra, is said to have been born here. Besides Ādi Shankarāchārya, the Buddha is believed to have visited this place.

FOUR SACRED DHĀMAS

'Dhāma' means abode. The four holy Dhāmas of India are Badarinātha, Jagannātha Puri, Rāmeshvaram and Dwārakā. The four Dhāmas of north India are Gangotri, Yamunotri, Kedarnātha and Badarinātha.

Magnificent mandirs enshrine the *murtis* of Bhagwan Vishnu and Bhagwan Krishna in three of the Dhāmas, namely, Badari, Jagannātha Puri and Dwārakā; and Bhagwan Shiva is the resident deity of Rāmeshvaram. The four Dhāmas are situated like the four points of the compass. In the north lies Badarinātha (Uttarakhand), to the east lies Jagannātha Puri (Orissa), to the south is Rāmeshvaram (Tamil Nadu) and to the west is Dwārakā (Gujarat). Hindus aspire to visit all four Dhāmas at least once in their lifetime. Pilgrims believe that by visiting these places their sins are dissolved and they acquire *moksha*.

1. BADARINĀTHA

Badarinātha lies perched in the Garhwāla mountains in Chamoli district of Uttarakhand State, a part of the Himalayas, at a height of 10,400 feet above sea level. For Hindus the mountains are deemed to be the abode of the devas. Badarinātha lies on the banks of River Alakanandā. In ancient times the two sages Nara and Nārāyana had built their ashram at Badarinātha to perform austerities. It is believed that Veda Vyāsa lived at the place with his disciples. Subsequently Vyāsa got the name Bādarāyana.

The main mandir, called Badarivishāla Mandir, is believed to have been built by Vishvakarmā (the architect of the devas). It houses the *murti* of the principal deity called Badarivishāla

Badarivishāla Mandir, Badarinātha

(or Bhagwan Vishnu), made of *shālagrāma* (black stone). It is
seated in *padmāsana* and has four arms, holding the *shankha*
(conch), *chakra* (disc), *gadā* (mace) and *padma* (lotus). Besides
the *murti* of Bhagwan Badarivishāla in the sanctum sanctorum
there are also the *murtis* of Nara and Nārāyana. To the right of
Badarivishāla is the *murti* of Kubera (god of wealth) and before
him is the festive *murti (chala* or movable *murti)* of Bhagwan
Vishnu. During the winter months, from October to May, the
mandir doors remain closed because of extreme cold, and so the
festive *murti* of Vishnu is taken down to Joshimatha for worship,
which is 6,150 feet below. During this time, it is believed that
Nāradaji performs the puja of the deities.

Nearby the Badarivishāla Mandir lies the Tapta Kunda, a
natural thermal spring. Devotees take a holy dip in the warm
spring water. The snow-clad Mt. Neelakantha towers above
Badarinātha and appears golden in the morning sunlight. Other
sacred places are huge slabs of stones on which ancient rishis
and devotees had performed austerities, namely, Mārkandeya
shilā, Nrusimha *shilā,* Nārada *shilā* and Garuda *shilā.*

2. Jagannātha Puri

Jagannātha Puri or Purushottama Puri or simply Puri is
a small coastal town in the eastern State of Orissa. It is 477

kilometres from Kolkata. It is one of the holiest places of India, visited by millions of Hindus every year. Puri, also known as Purushottama *tirtha*, is the hallowed seat of Bhagwan Jagannātha (Lord of the world). A pilgrimage to Puri is believed to liberate a person from the cycle of births and deaths. The centre of attraction is the towering Jagannātha Mandir. The Purānas mention that King Indradyumna built the mandir at the command of Bhagwan Vāsudeva (Krishna). Subsequently, Oriya kings, Choda Gangā Deva (1078-1148 CE) and Ananga Bhima Deva (1174 CE) added other structures during their reigns. The mandir's *vimāna* or central pinnacle over the main sanctum is 192 feet high. The mandir has 6,000 pujaris and servitors who worship and serve the mandir deities. The Brahmin cooks prepare 54 food offerings daily for the deity. The sanctified food or *prasāda* is distributed to the devotees and poor. Daily 10,000 people take *prasāda*.

The *murtis* of Bhagwan Jagannātha (Shri Krishna), Subhadrā (sister) and Balarāma (brother) are made of wood, and they are without arms and hands. The *murti* of Bhagwan Jagannātha is five feet tall. Legend has it that God appeared in a dream to King Indradyumna and revealed that Vishvakarmā will come and make the *murtis*. He came as an old man and said that he would carve the *murtis* behind closed doors and that no one should enter till they were finished. If anyone did, then he would leave the *murtis* unfinished. The work began, but after some time the king became impatient. Vishvakarmā had carved the wooden *murtis* up to their elbows and was about to proceed in making their arms and hands when the king entered. Instantly, Vishvakarmā disappeared. Ever since, there is a tradition to carve the *murtis* without their arms and hands.

The murti of Subhadrā flanked by Bhagwan Jagannātha (right) and Balarāma, Jagannātha Mandir, Ahmedabad

During the Ratha Yātrā (chariot festival) in Jagannātha Puri, the main *murtis* of the Jagannātha Mandir are placed on the *rathas*. In most of the other mandirs of India the *ratha yātrā* festival is celebrated by placing *chala murtis* or *utsava murtis* in

Aerial view of the massive Jagannātha Mandir, Jagannātha Puri

a decorated *ratha* for the ritual procession. The wooden *murtis* of Jagannātha Puri are replaced periodically with some relics (believed to be those of Krishna) being transferred into the new ones. The old *murtis* are ritually disposed of.

On the second day of the Indian month of Āshādha (June/July) a grand *ratha yātrā* of the deities is carried out in Jagannātha Puri in giant chariots *(rathas)*. The main *ratha* of Bhagwan Jagannātha is 45 feet high, has 16 wheels with each having a diameter of seven feet. The entire *ratha* is pulled with ropes by thousands of devotees. The two smaller *rathas* have the *murtis* of Subhadrā (43 feet high, having 12 wheels) and Balarāma (44 feet high, having 14 wheels). The *rathas* are taken from Jagannātha Mandir in Puri to the Gundichā Mandir, three kilometres away. Here they are kept for one week, after which they are brought back to the main mandir. The Ratha Yātrā festival attracts multitudes of devotees who come for darshan of the deities and to haul the *rathas*. The former king of Jagannātha Puri inaugurates the *yātrā* by briefly sweeping the road with a golden broom and pulling the *ratha*.

Ādi Shankarāchārya (788-820 CE) established one of his four monasteries in Puri. It is called Govardhana Matha or Govardhana Peetha. Rāmānujāchārya (1017-1137 CE) had visited this place, so too had Kabir (1440-1518 CE) and Chaitanya Mahāprabhu

Ratha Yātrā festival in Jagannātha Puri

(1486-1533 CE) had lived here for quite some time.

Jagannātha Puri also has five other sacred places that pilgrims should visit. They are the lake of Mārkandeya, the Vata tree, Balarāma mandir, the sea and the Indradyumna lake.

3. RĀMESHVARAM

The town of Rāmeshvaram is on an island situated between the Palk Strait and the Gulf of Mannar at the very tip of the Indian peninsula. It is the place from where Bhagwan Rāma built a bridge *(setu)* to Sri Lanka (24 km) to rescue his consort Sitā from Rāvana. Both the Vaishnavites and Shaivites visit this place of pilgrimage and it is known as the Vāranāsi of the south.

The presiding deity is the Shiva *linga* called Rāmanātha, which is one of the twelve *jyotirlingas*. The famous Rāmanātha Mandir or Shiva Mandir was built in the 17th century CE. It is situated near the sea and has four *gopurams* (ornate gate towers), one of which is 138 feet high. The mandir has a grand 1,220 metre (3,700 feet) *parikramā* and 4,000 huge granite pillars (12 ft high). The mandir was built on the site where Shri Rāma made a *linga* out of sand (called Ramanātha) and offered puja prior to his march to defeat Rāvana. The Rāmanātha Mandir is considered to be one of the best examples of Dravidian architecture. The main sanctum has a *linga* named Rāmanātha. On its left is the shrine of Pārvati and near the main *linga* are smaller *lingas*. Behind the Rāmanātha shrine is another shrine dedicated to Bhagwan Vishnu. The *linga* is daily offered *abhisheka* with the waters of River Gangā. The holy water is distributed to pilgrims who come for darshan and worship. The main festival celebrated here is Mahāshivarātri.

The footprints of Shri Rāma are enshrined in a small shrine known as Gandhamādana on a hillock about 2.5 kilometres to the west of Rāmanātha Mandir.

Five kilometres south of the mandir lies the submerged bridge or *setu* built by Shri Rāma to cross over to Lanka.

Grand parikramā of Rāmanātha Mandir, Rāmeshvaram

Rāmanātha Mandir, Rāmeshvaram

4. DWĀRAKĀ

Dwārakā, one of the four holy *dhāmas,* is in Gujarat and was established by Bhagwan Krishna who ruled over his Yādava community (see details pp. 252-253).

FOUR KUMBHA MELA SITES

Kumbha Melas are grand mega festivals where sadhus, sannyasis and householder-devotees gather for a ritual bath in a holy river or confluence of rivers. They also listen to spiritual discourses, chant the name of God and perform austerities. The Kumbha Mela takes place when the sun enters the Kumbha *rāshi* or Aquarius. It is held at four places in India: Prayāga (Allahabad), Ujjain, Haridwāra and Nāsik. Each of the four places was sanctified by the Amruta Kumbha which was acquired by the churning of the ocean by the devas and asuras. The Kumbha Mela is held in turn every three years at each of the four places. The Mela at Prayāga or Allahabad, where the confluence of Gangā, Yamunā and the subterranean Sarasvati occurs, is particularly very popular. Millions belonging to all Hindus *sampradāyas* gather for the ritual bath to wash away their sins and be blessed with *punya*. In 1989, the Kumbha Mela in Allahabad attracted about 15 million pilgrims.

Let us now briefly deal with the holy places of Allahabad

Kumbha Mela, Haridwāra

Pilgrims bathe at the Kumbha Mela, Prayāga

and Nāsik. The other two, Haridwāra (pp. 249-250) and Ujjain (pp. 253-254), have been mentioned before.

1. PRAYĀGA OR ALLAHABAD

The sacred city of Prayāga, also known as Allahabad, is one of the oldest cities in India. It was formerly called Prayāga in commemoration of a *yajna* performed by Lord Brahmā. Prayāga, i.e., *pra* means best and *yāga* means *yajna*. Therefore Prayāga means a place of excellent fire-sacrifice. It is 585 km southeast of New Delhi and 160 km south of Ayodhyā. People mainly visit this pilgrim place to take a holy dip in the Sangama – confluence of the Rivers Gangā, Yamunā and Sarasvati – to become free from all sins.

Prayāga is called Tirtha-rāja, the king of all holy places. Its antiquity is indicated by a verse in the Rig Veda itself (10.75, the Khila part). It is believed that Veda Vyāsa stayed here and wrote the Shiva Purāna.

The most popular Kumbh Mela is held here. It is the largest religious festival in the world.

Allahabad is renowned for the Sangama bath. It also has a Hanumān Mandir where the *murti* of Hanumān is in a reclining posture. Every year the River Gangā rises till the water touches the sleeping Hanumānji's feet and then starts receding. The ashram of Sage Bhāradwāja has now been replaced by Allahabad University. Bhagwan Rāma and Sitā visited the ashram during their exile. The Chitrakuta hill is about 140 kilometres from here, in the Bandā district.

2. NĀSIK

The town of Nāsik, in Maharashtra, lies by the source of the holy River Godāvari. To the north of Nāsik, Rāma and Sita lived in the forest of Panchavati for a long time during their fourteen-year exile. Rāvana abducted Sitā from here.

Nāsik once abounded in mandirs, most of which were destroyed by Aurangazeb (1618-1707 CE). Today, the mandirs of Sunderanārāyana (enshrined with the *murtis* of Nārāyana, Shridevi and Bhudevi), Kālārāma (with the *murti* of Rāma) and others are among the more popular pilgrim places.

Bathing in the River Godāvari, which is believed to have an underground connection with River Gangā, confers *punya*. People who cannot afford to take the ashes of departed relatives to the River Gangā, immerse them in the Godāvari here. A Kumbh Mela is held here once every twelve years.

SUMMARY

1. 'Tirtha' means 'ford' or a place for 'crossing over'. A *tirtha* is a place where the sacred meets the earth, the higher realms meet the lower and the divine meets the human. In brief, it is a holy place where devotees go to on a pilgrimage to wash away their sins and sanctify themselves.

2. India has hundreds of holy places. The seven ancient holy cities in India are Ayodhyā, Mathurā, Haridwāra, Vāranāsi, Ujjain, Dwārakā and Kānchipuram.

3. The four holy *dhāmas* are Badarinātha, Jagannāthā Puri, Rāmeshvaram and Dwārakā.

4. The four Kumbh Mela sites are Prayāga, Haridwāra, Ujjain and Nāsik.

Kālārāma Mandir, Nāsik

13

Sacred Rivers and Places of India

Elegant sculptures of Rivers Gangā, Yamunā and
Sarasvati, formerly located at Swaminarayan Akshardham,
Gandhinagar (Gujarat). (Inset) Kedāranātha Mandir

Seven Holy Rivers, Twelve Jyotirlingas, Other Pilgrim Spots

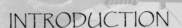

INTRODUCTION

Hinduism has always believed that its holy rivers are goddesses and not merely physical or natural phenomena. Normally on sacred festive days Hindus take a dip in the rivers to wash away their sins and increase their spiritual merit. Thousands go on a pilgrimage to take the customary dip. Such rivers attain their sanctity through association with God, his incarnations or holy persons. Hindus take a dip in the holy rivers to dissolve their sins, and the holy sages bathe to relieve the rivers of their burden of sins.

The seven holy rivers are themselves places of pilgrimage. They are, the Gangā which rises in the Himalayas and flows to the sea in West Bengal; the Yamunā which rises from Yamunotri in the lower Himalayas and joins the Gangā at Prayāga or Allahabad; the Sindhu (formerly in undivided India), now the Indus river, issues from Langa lake near Mānasarovar and empties itself in the Arabian Sea; the Sarasvati (not visible today) originated from the Himalayas; the Narmadā flows from Amarkantaka in central India and through Gujarat to meet the Arabian Sea; the Godāvari originates from Maharashtra and flows through Andhra Pradesh to the Bay of Bengal; and the Kāveri flows from Karnataka and then through Tamil Nadu to meet the Bay of Bengal.

Even today devout Hindus invoke the waters of these seven sacred rivers at the time of their daily bath, during ritualistic worship of the family deity and in all other rituals. The *shloka* recited is *Gange cha Yamunechaiva, Godāvari, Sarasvati, Narmade, Sindhu, Kāveri Jalesmin Sannidhim Kuru.* It means, "O Gangā, Yamunā, Godāvari, Sarasvati, Narmadā, Sindhu and Kāveri please enter (into this *kumbha*)."

The twelve *jyotirlingas,* where Shiva revealed himself in the form of a *linga* (emblem) of light, are of great importance especially to Shaiva devotees.

Some of the other famous pilgrim places are Rishikesha, Kedāranātha, Kailāsa-Mānasarovara, Amaranātha, Vaishno Devi, Pushkara, Tirupati Bālāji, Madurāi, Shabarimalai, Guruvāyur, Nāthadwārā, Somanātha, Kanyākumāri and Chhapaiya.

A brief account of all of them is as follows:

SEVEN HOLY RIVERS

1. RIVER GANGĀ

River Gangā, also known as the Ganges, is one of India's holiest rivers. Of all the rivers of India, no river has captivated the minds and hearts of the pious more than the Gangā. It has been mentioned once in the Rig Veda (*Nadistuti.* 10.75.5-6) and praised in the Purānas.

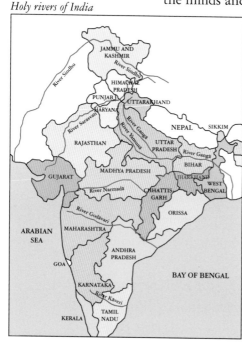

Holy rivers of India

Gangā issues forth from the Himalayas at 13,600 feet from a place called Gaumukh or Gomukha (rock formation shaped like a cow's mouth) near Gangotri. Gangotri is a glacier and the source of Gangā in the Tehri Garhwāl district of Uttarakhand State in northern India. From its source it is known as Bhāgirathi. Thereafter on its journey towards Haridwāra, the River Alakānanda merges with it at Devaprayāga, 64 kilometres before Haridwāra. At this place it enters the plains and is called Gangā hereafter. The different rivers that join it along its course to the Bay of Bengal are Mandākini, Yamunā,

River Gangā at Rishikesh

Sarayu (Ghāgrā), Sone, Dāmodara, Gandaki, Koshi and the Brahmaputra. There are a number of pilgrim centres on the banks of River Gangā and its tributaries, namely, Devaprayāga, Rudraprayāga, Karnaprayāga, Badarinātha, Kedāranātha, Rishikesh, Haridwāra, Kāshi or Vāranāsi and Prayāga. River Gangā is 2,500 km long.

Gangā was born out of the left foot of Bhagwan Vāmana (an incarnation of Vishnu). Thereafter it was confined to the celestial region *(swarga)*. A description of how the Gangā descends from *swarga* to earth is found in the Rāmāyana. She was brought down by the incredible effort of King Bhagiratha to liberate his ancestors. The story begins with King Bhagiratha's ancestor, King Sagara, who conducted a Rājsuya *yajna* to gain more sovereignty. The white horse that was let loose, as part of the *yajna*, was stolen. King Sagara's 60,000 sons went in search of the horse. Eventually, they found it in the ashram of Kapila Muni. Thinking that the Muni had stolen the horse, the king's sons insulted him and accused him of stealing it. Kapila Muni was angered and destroyed all of them with the fire of his austerities. When his sons did not return, King Sagara told his grandson, Anshumān, to go and look for them. Anshumān returned with the white horse and the bad news. King Sagara was saddened and completed the *yajna*. Subsequently, he

Gaumukha, the source of River Gangā near Gangotri

handed over the kingdom to Anshumān and retired to the forest to perform austerities. The king, prior to leaving, told Anshumān to liberate the souls of his ancestors. To accomplish this Anshumān would have to invoke the holy waters of Gangā to flow over the ashes of his ancestors. But Anshumān had no time to perform austerities and please Gangā. When he passed away, his only surviving son, King Dilipa, performed lifelong austerities. But Gangā was not pleased enough to descend from *swarga*. After King Dilipa's demise, his son, Bhagiratha, performed austerities. Finally, Gangā was pleased, and agreed to descend on earth. But she said that only Bhagwan Shiva could bear the force of her fall on earth. Then Bhagiratha resumed his austerities to please Shiva. The latter was pleased and agreed to bear the force of Gangā before it could gently flow to earth. But when Gangā descended with arrogance, Shiva trapped her in his locks to humble her. Again Bhagiratha prayed to Shiva to release her. Then, when Shiva freed Gangā, she started flowing behind King Bhagiratha towards the ashram of Kapila Muni. On the way, Gangāji insulted the austere Rishi Jhanu by washing away his sacrificial platforms. The great rishi was angered, and to teach her a lesson he drank the entire River Gangā like a drop of water. Bhagiratha once again prayed to the rishi, who then released the water from his ear. From then on she also became known as Jāhnavi. Finally when the waters of Gangā touched the ashes of Bhagiratha's ancestors at Kapila ashram, their souls were liberated. The River Gangā is also known as Bhāgirathi because of the immense effort of King Bhagiratha in getting her to earth.

Hindus believe that almost all holy rivers of India have a dual form – physical and divine. In its divine form they are revered as mother goddesses or *lokamātās*. The River Gangā is described as a beautiful, fair lady riding a crocodile and holding lotuses in her two hands.

The holy waters of Gangā are used in ceremonial worship and

River Yamunā flowing through Āgrā

purificatory rites. No religious act can be said to be complete without the use of its water. At Hara Ki Pauri in Haridwāra people bathe in its waters to wash away their sins. Every evening thousands of pilgrims perform *ārati* of the river and then set afloat the *deepas*, creating a spectacular, divine sight. The River Gangā is considered as the Mother in Hinduism.

2. RIVER YAMUNĀ

River Yamunā (also written as Jamunā) is the second most sacred river of India, after Gangā. It is mentioned in the Rig Veda (*Nadistuti*. 10.75.5, 7.18.19.). The river issues forth from Yamunotri, which is renowned for its thermal springs and glaciers, at 3,293 metres (10,801 ft) above sea level. The glacial lake of Saptarishi Kunda on the Kālinda mountain, a part of the Himalayan range, is the source of the River Yamunā. Thus Yamunā is also known as Kālindi. After journeying 1,376 km it merges with the Gangā and the subterranean Sarasvati at Prayāga Allahabad. The point of confluence is called Triveni Sangama.

The river is connected to the childhood *lilās* of Bhagwan Krishna. The divine dance of Krishna with the *gopis* – took place on the banks of River Yamunā at Vrundāvan and Gokula.

New Delhi and the holy towns of Vrundāvan and Mathurā

River Indus or Sindhu

are situated by the Yamunā. Rajapur, the birthplace of Tulasidāsa, is also situated on its banks.

The waters of Yamunā are dark in colour. The River Yamunā also has a divine form as a goddess. She is the daughter of Surya. Yama, god of death, is her twin brother. She is illustrated as a lady with a dark complexion standing on a tortoise, wearing a garland of blue lotuses. She is the presiding deity of the Yamunotri Mandir at Yamunotri. Like Gangā, Yamunā has also been praised profusely as a mother in devotional songs by poets and saints, especially those of the Vallabha Sampradāya. The devout take a dip in its holy waters and feel blessed.

3. River Sindhu

River Sindhu, known today as Indus River, is mentioned several times in the Rig Veda. Sindhu was one of the biggest and longest rivers of southeast Asia. It originates from the northern part of Langa lake near Mānasarovar (now in Tibet-China) called Sing-e-khabab. It enters into India near Leh, the capital of Ladakh (Jammu-Kashmir State), travels westwards through the Himalaya, Gilgit and Punjab regions of Pakistan where it meets five rivers, Jhelum, Chenāb, Rāvi, Beās and Satlaj, and finally merges into the Arabian ocean. In ancient times it flowed through Kutch, Saurashtra and Khambhāt.

The famous ancient cities of Mohenjo-daro, Chanu-daro and others developed on the bank of this river. The Indus (Sindhu) Valley Civilization covered wide swathes of land and reached its peak about four thousand years ago because of the River Sindhu. The region in ancient northwest India, known as Sindh from the River Sindhu, was famous for its excellent war horses. Mahābhārata's famous character, King Jayadratha, the son-in-law of Dhritarāshtra was the ruler of Sindha. According to Kautilya's *Arthashāstra,* Sindha was also connected with Magadha or today's Bihar. In addition, due to the River Sindhu emptying into the Arabian ocean foreign trade flourished to as far as Mesopotamia (now Iraq), as evidenced from the items found there. A dip in the River Sindhu was believed to grant *moksha*. It is now in modern-day Pakistan.

The Government of India annually celebrates the Sindhu Festival at Leh in Ladakh.

4. River Sarasvati

The Rig Veda and other Vedic literature like Aitareya, Panchavimsha and Shatapatha Brāhmana texts (2.41.16 & 7.95.2) describes the River Sarasvati as a mighty river. In some places it is believed to have been eight to thirteen kilometres wide. It had its origin in the Himalayas and flowed parallel to the Sindhu or Indus River towards the Arabian Sea. It was most probably the lifeline of people up to 2000 BCE. It is no longer visible today, having disappeared underground in about 1900 BCE in the Rann of Kutch due to tectonic disturbances. Satellite pictures and geological excavations have proved its existence, though now it is an underground dry bed.[1]

The Mahābhārata declares that many Vedic sacrifices were performed on its banks. The Pāndavas lived on the banks of

---

1. The Vāyu Purāna describes the River Sarasvati to have originated from the feet of the Himalayas and while journeying to the sea divides the land into Sindha and Maru (i.e. Marwad or Rājasthan). Cited in *Bhagavad Gomandal Kosha, Vol.9,* by Maharaja Bhagawatsinhji. Rajkot: Pravin Prakashan, 1986, p.8,537.

River Narmadā with the famous Omkāranātha Mandir on its banks (L)

the river in Kāmayakavana for some time during their exile.[2] The ashram of Sage Dadhichi was also on the banks of the holy river.

5. River Narmadā

The River Narmadā is remembered during worship rituals. It has been eulogized in the Mahābhārata and also in the Matsya, Kurma and Padma Purānas.

The river has its origin in the mountains of Amarkantaka in Madhya Pradesh. It flows towards the west in Gujarat and meets the Gulf of Cambay near Bharuch. It is 1,282 kilometres long. In all there are 238 *tirthas* on its banks like Omkārnātha, Karnāli, Shuklatirtha, ashram of Bhrugu rishi and others. At Omkārnātha there is a mandir enshrining one of the twelve *jyotirlingas*. The mandir is situated on the island of Māndhātā that lies between the Rivers Narmadā and Kāveri (not to be confused with the Kāveri of South India). It is here that Bhagwan Shiva is believed to have destroyed the three evil cities of the demon Tripura.

Along its bank, the devout perform *shrāddha* rites in honour of their ancestors to gain *punya*.

The Narmadā *parikramā* is a sacred deed that includes

---

2. Mahābhārata 1.95.26; 3.12.14; 3.36.41.

River Godāvari, Nasik

traversing by foot from the confluence with the sea up to the source at Amarkantaka and then returning along the other bank to the sea. This generally takes two years. The water of Narmadā is so pure and holy that it is believed that even goddess Gangā comes once in a year as a black cow and returns free from sins as a white cow after bathing in it.

Veda Vyāsa writes highly about the river, "By bathing in the waters of Sarasvati for three days, Yamunā for seven days and a single dip in Gangā purifies the pilgrim. But one becomes pure by mere darshan of River Narmadā."[3]

6. RIVER GODĀVARI

The river originates from the Brahmagiri hill near Tryambakeshwara in the Nāsik district of Maharashtra State. It courses towards the east to join the Bay of Bengal. The total length of the river is 1,465 kilometres.

The Brahma Purāna[4] declares that the Gangā to the south of the Vindhya Mountains is Godāvari or Gautami. A story in the Purāna describes that Sage Gautama, husband of Ahalyā, brought this river (a stream of Gangā) from the matted locks of Shiva to the Brahmagiri hills. Then Sage Gautama requested

---

3. Padma Purāna 13.7.

4. 78.77.

Bhagwan Shiva to reside near his hermitage and the place became known as Tryambakeshwara.

According to the Vālmiki Rāmāyana Shri Rāma lived in Panchavati on the bank of River Godāvari, during his stay in the Dandaka Forest. It was from here that Sitā was kidnapped by Rāvana.

A bath in the River Godāvari is considered to be very holy. *Shrāddhas* offered to ancestors in the River Godāvari bring *punya* and liberation.

The Brahma Purāna mentions 100 *tirthas* on the banks of Godāvari, such as, Tryambaka, Kushāvarta, Janasthāna, Govardhana, Nāsik, Panchavati and others.

7. River Kāveri

River Kāveri is often known as Dakshinagangā or Gangā of the south. It originates from the Brahmagiri Hills in the district of Kodagu (or Coorg) in Karnataka. It flows in the southeasterly direction through the districts of Mysore and Tanjavur (Tanjore) in Karnataka and Tamil Nadu respectively. The river finally merges with the Bay of Bengal near the small town of Kāveripattinam. Its total length is 760 kilometres.

There are several stories in the Purānas about this river and its goddess Kāveri.

A large number of small rivers join it at different places. Several renowned centres of pilgrimage and mandirs on its banks are: Shrirangam in Tamil Nadu, Shrirangpattanam near Mysore in Karnataka and Madhyaranga Mandir near Shivana Samudra in Karnataka State. In all these three places, which are small islands on the river, there are mandirs of Shri Ranganātha in which all the *murtis* of Bhagwan Vishnu are in a reclining posture.

The famous Shiva mandirs on its banks are at Chidambaram and Tanjavur. The Bruhadeshwara Mandir in Tanjavur is the largest and most famous Shiva mandir in India. Tirujnāna

TWELVE JYOTIRLINGAS

Shri Nāgeshvara

Shri Mallikārjuna

Shri Vishvanātha

Shri Bhimashankara

Shri Trayambakeshvara

Shri Vaidyanātha

Shri Kedārnātha

Shri Omkāreshvara

Shri Ghrushneshvara

Shri Mahākāleshvara

Shri Somanātha

Shri Rāmeshvaram

Sambandhar, the renowned Shaiva saint-poet, was born on the banks of Kāveri. The great poet Kamban composed his version of the Rāmayana in Tamil on the banks of this river.

OTHER PILGRIM PLACES

1. TWELVE JYOTIRLINGAS

The Shiva Purāna mentions the twelve ancient places of pilgrimage where Shiva revealed himself in the form of *jyotirlingas* (emblems of light). One finds *lingas* or mainly the holy black rocks shaped in an oval shape enshrined in the main sanctum of Shiva mandirs. *Jyotirlingas* are self-revealed without external human help or agency. The Shaivites undertake pilgrimage to the twelve *jyotirlingas* to please Bhagwan Shiva and gain spiritual merit.

The twelve *jyotirlingas* are: Kedarnātha in the Uttarakhand State in the Himalayas, Vishvanātha in Vāranāsi in Uttar Pradesh, Somanātha in Prabhāsa Pātana in Gujarat, Mahākāleshvara in Ujjayini in Madhya Pradesh, Omkāreshvara on an island in River Narmada also in Madhya Pradesh, Rāmeshvaram at Setubandha in Tamil Nadu, Mallikārjuna at Shrishailam in Andhra Pradesh, Trayambakeshvara near Nāsik in Maharashtra, Bhimashankara near Pune at the source of River Bhima in Maharashtra, Ghrushneshvara near Ellorā Caves in Maharashtra, Nāgeshvara near Dwārakā in Gujarat, and Baijanātha or Vaidyanātha in Deoghara in Jharkhand.

Locations of the Twelve Jyotirlingas

2. RISHIKESHA

Rishikesha is located in the northern part of Uttarakhand State. It is 238 km northeast of Delhi and 24 km from Haridwāra and lies on the banks of River Gangā. It is surrounded by hills on three sides and is an idyllic place.

Ashrams and mandirs dot the town of Rishikesha. Lakshmana Jhulā spans the River Gangā

It is known as *tapo bhumi* – a place where rishis and aspirants performed meditation and austerities.

Legend says that Bhagwan Vishnu vanquished the demon Madhu at Rishikesha.

The Lakshmana Jhulā, a suspended iron bridge over River Gangā, was built in 1939. Near the bridge one finds the Lakshmanaji Mandir. Here Lakshmana, the younger brother of Rāma, performed austerities for twelve years. The mandir has the *murtis* of Lakshmanaji and Dhruvaji.

The renowned Bhārata Mātā Mandir is situated in the heart of the old town on the banks of Gangā. Its main sanctum has the *murti* of Bhagwan Vishnu carved out of a single *shālagrāma*.

An hour's drive from Rishikesha along the River Gangā brings one to the Vashishtha cave where Sage Vashishtha meditated.

The Triveni Ghat is the main ghat where pilgrims take a holy dip and perform the evening *ārati* of River Gangā.

Twelve kilometres from Rishikesha lies a mandir of Nilkantha Mahādeva. It is believed that here Bhagwan Shiva drank the poison churned from the ocean.

3. KEDĀRANĀTHA

Kedāranātha is located in the Garhwāl district of Uttarakhand at a height of 3,600 metres (11,760 ft), above sea

Lakshmanaji Mandir, Rishikesha

Kedāranātha Mandir with the Himalayas in the background

level. It is a small hamlet with the ancient Shiva Mandir of Kedāranātha as the main attraction. After reaching by road from Rishikesha to Gauri Kunda pilgrims travel 14 km by foot, mule or in a palanquin to cover the height of 5,550 feet to reach Kedāranātha. Between May and October thousands of pilgrims make the pilgrimage from Gauri Kunda to Kedāranātha Mandir.

Kedāranātha Mandir is a majestic sight surrounded by lofty snow-capped peaks. The River Mandākini flows behind it. The present mandir was built by Ādi Shankarāchārya in the 8th century CE. The main sanctum has a conical *linga*. In front of the sanctum there is a *mandapa* (hall) where one finds a large stone image of Nandi (the bull) and many images of devas and devis, including those of the Pāndavas.

According to legend, the Pāndavas came here at the word of Shri Krishna to perform penance in atonement for having killed their kin in the Mahābhārata War and to please Bhagwan Shiva. But Shiva did not wish to give them darshan, so he went away and stayed at Guptakāshi. When the Pāndavas came to know of this they went there. But Shivaji left for Kedāra. The Pāndavas followed closely behind. To remain elusive Shivaji took the form of a bull. Sahadeva, the youngest of the Pāndavas, recognized him and told Bhima. Then Bhima tried

Hinduism

Mount Kailāsa, believed to be the abode of Bhagwan Shiva

to catch the bull. The bull rapidly dug the ground with its horns to disappear underground. But Bhima was able to get hold of the bull's hump. Bhagwan Shiva then appeared before the Pāndavas because of their devotion and penance. He told them to perform oblations upon his hump with ghee (clarified butter) and their sins would be dissolved. Ever since, the *jyotirlinga* at Kedāranātha Mandir is conical like a bull's hump. Devotees worship it by offering balls of ghee. In all, there are five Kedāra Mandirs (Pancha Kedāras): Madhyamaheshwara, Tunganātha, Rudranātha, Kāleshwara and Badari-Kedāra.

Behind the Kedāranātha Mandir lies the memorial shrine or samadhi of Ādi Shankarāchārya.

4. KAILĀSA-MĀNASAROVARA

Mount Kailāsa is mentioned in the Rāmāyana, Mahābhārata and some Purānas as the abode of Bhagwan Shiva. It is one of the northern peaks of the Himalayas in Tibet, 22,028 feet high. It is believed that Shiva resides here with his wife, Pārvati, and children, Ganesha and Kārtikeya. Rāvana had tried to uproot Kailāsa with his hands, but was severely punished by Shiva who just pressed his big toe and trapped him. Mt. Kailāsa is revered by Hindus, Buddhists, Jainas and the Bonpas of Tibet.

Kailāsa-Mānasarovara are among the most sacred places of

Holy Mānasarovara, Tibet

The sacred cave of Amarnātha with the ice Shivalinga, Kashmir

Raj Patel

pilgrimage for Hindus. Both are in Tibet (China).

Legend says that Mānasarovara, also written as Mānasa-sarovara, was created by Brahmā out of his mind while he was performing austerities in the Himalayas. Hence the name, 'lake that emerged out of (Brahmā's) mind'. Mānasarovara is 14,950 feet above sea level and is 32 km from Mount Kailāsa. Its actual circumference is 89 kilometres, but the *parikrāma* route is 113 kilometres. Visitors also circumambulate Mount Kailāsa which takes two to three days.

The Rivers Sindhu (Indus), Satlaj, Brahmaputra and Sarayu originate from this lake or a nearby area. The lake water is crystal clear. A dip in its holy waters is highly meritorious.

There is a twin lake called Rākshasatāla, where Rāvana performed austerities to please Bhagwan Shiva.

5. AMARNĀTHA

Ice Shivalinga, Amarnātha

The Amarnātha (Shiva) cave in Kashmir is situated in the Himalayan ranges at a height of about 13,000 ft. It is situated 138 kilometres northeast of Srinagar, the capital of Kashmir. It is a big natural cave about 150 feet high, 100 feet wide and 200 feet long. There are two holes in the cave from which water trickles and freezes into ice. Beneath the bigger hole a huge *linga* of ice forms annually, which is the famous Amarnātha

Vaishno Devi Mandir
with goddess Durgā in
her three aspects: (L to R)
Mahāsarasvati, Mahālakshmi
and Mahākāli

linga. It is eight to twelve feet high. Flanked on either side are two more ice formations known as Ganesha and Pārvati.

Pilgrims travel in groups from Srinagar during June, July and August. The Shrāvana Purnimā day (in July/August) is considered most auspicious because according to legend Shiva appeared in the cave on this day. Since Shiva made the devas eternal by giving them *amruta*, he is known by the name Amarnātha – Lord of the immortals.

6. Vaishno Devi

The pilgrim centre nestles in the Himalayan ranges of the Jammu region. It is a cave-shrine (Vaishno Devi Mandir) dedicated to goddess Durgā in her three aspects: Mahāsarasvati, Mahālakshmi and Mahākāli. The sanctum has three bulbous forms in stone *(pindis)*. Mahāsarasvati is fair in shade, Mahālakshmi is yellowish-red in colour and Mahākāli is black. The Vaishno Devi Mandir is at a height of 5,200 feet above sea level. The cave is 93 feet long and 5 feet high.

The whole shrine is in a natural rock formation. Its origin according to a local story says that a pious Brahmin called Pandita Shridhara lived at the base of Trikuta (mountain where the shrine is now located) about 700 years ago. Due to his devotion and prayers the Divine Mother manifested herself

Raj Patel

Pilgrims arrive at Katrā to
embark on their pilgrimage to
Vaishno Devi Mandir

The Pushkara lake and city, Rajasthan

as a little beautiful girl and fed a very large crowd invited by Shridhara. The mandir built at this place is called Bhumikā Mandir.

Pilgrims begin their 12 km journey to the cave from the small town of Katrā, which is 48 km from Jammu. On the way are the Bāna Gangā Mandir, Charanapādukā Mandir and the cave, Garbh Joon (where the Divine Mother as a girl had meditated for nine months).

A *deepa* is always kept burning in the Vaishno Devi cave shrine. Pilgrims have to wade through ankle or knee-deep icy water for darshan of the *pindis*.

7. PUSHKARA

Famous mandir and murti of Lord Brahmā, Pushkara

The town of Pushkara is located on the banks of the holy lake of the same name. It is 12 kilometres from Ajmer in Rajasthan. There are 400 mandirs in Pushkara. The mandir dedicated to Lord Brahmā, the creator, is the centre of pilgrimage for devotees. It is one of the only two well-known Brahmā Mandirs in India. The other famous mandir is at Khed-Brahmā in North Gujarat.

The *murti* of Brahmā is in the main sanctum and that of his two spouses, Sāvitri and Gāyatri, are to his right and left. The mandir also has the *murtis* of Sanaka, Sanandana, Sanatkumāra

284

Hinduism

Venkateshawara Mandir, Tirupati

and Sanatsujāta.

Other mandirs in Pushkara are dedicated to Nārada, Badarinārāyana, Varāha, Shiva, Rāma-Vaikunthaji or Shri Rangaji, Venugopāla and Shri Rāma.

Some pilgrims undertake a *parikramā* of Pushkara.

8. TIRUPATI BĀLĀJI

Tirupati is a small town in the district of Chitturu (Chittore) in Andhra Pradesh. Tirumala is a range of seven hills forming a part of the Eastern Ghats. The Tirupati Bālāji Mandir is on the seventh hill at a height of 2,800 feet above sea level. The town of Tirupati is at the foot of the hill. The hill has several names, one of which is Venkata. So the deity on the hill also came to be known as Venkatesha or Venkateshawara, i.e., Vishnu. Bālāji is another name for the deity. Apart from a good driveable road from Tirupati town there are also about 4,000 steps by which some devotees climb the hill to reach the mandir. Tirupati Bālāji is one of the most popular Hindu mandirs of India.

Bhagwan Venkateshawara, Tirupati

The stone *murti* of Bhagwan Venkateshawara is believed to be self-manifested and not man-made. It is assumed to be the sacred image of Hari (Vishnu) and Hara (Shiva). It is believed that the mandir functioned as a Shaiva shrine for several centuries before Rāmānujāchārya categorically declared the image to be that of Vishnu, and introduced a mode of worship following the example of Shri Rangam Mandir in Tamil Nadu. Swami Harshananda writes, "Some other aspects of the image like long hair, the peculiar conical crown, *nāgavalaya* (snake-shaped ornaments) as also certain ritual procedures like offering of *bilva* leaves, decorating [the image] with saree on Fridays have made it an image of Vishnu, Shiva, Devi, Subrahmanya or Harihara. As mentioned before, it is Rāmānuja who is said to have finally settled the disputes by declaring that it is that of Vishnu."[5]

Two pious souls, Rangadāsa and Gopinātha, discovered the *murti* of Venkateshawara, which was partly buried in the ground. The *murti* is made of black stone and is about eight to nine feet tall. It has four hands; two at the back have a *chakra* (disc) and a *shankha* (conch). The front right hand is postured in the *varadamudrā* (boon giving gesture) and the left hand rests on the waist. On either side are the *murtis* of his consorts, Shridevi and Bhudevi. Other *murtis* in the sanctum are Maleyappā (or *utsava murti* meant for processional purposes), Koluvu-Shrinivāsa (used ceremonially like a king), Krishna, Rāma and Sudarshana (disc-deity).

The main festival celebrated is Brahmotsava during Navarātri festival (September/October) for nine days.

9. MADURĀI

Madurāi means that which is sweet like honey. It is a popular place of pilgrimage on the bank of River Vaigai in South India, 461 kilometres southwest of Chennāi. It is renowned for its majestic mandirs like Minākshi Mandir dedicated to Pārvati and Sundareshvara Mandir dedicated to Bhagwan Shiva.

Legend says that Indra experienced peace and happiness at this spot after being defeated by Vrutrāsura. He found a Shiva

---

5. Swami Harshananda. *A Concise Encyclopaedia of Hinduism, Vol.3.* Bangalore: Ramakrishna Math, 2008, p.406.

Meenakshi Sundareshwara Mandir, Madurāi

linga and worshipped it. He got a vision of Shiva who gave him back his royal throne. The local king built his capital city at this spot after he had a dream about *amruta* drops falling over the place.

The Minākshi Mandir has two main shrines. One dedicated to Minākshi (Pārvati) and the other to Sundareshwara (Shiva). It has twelve *gopurams* (ornate towers), a water tank and halls or *mandapas*.

The main festivals celebrated are the marriage of goddess Minākshi with Shiva in April or May, coronation of Bhagwan Sundareshwara during August or September and the Teppotsav or float-festival in January or February.

10. SHABARIMALAI

Shabarimalai lies on a hill 190 kilometres to the north of Thiruvananthapuram (Trivandrum), the capital of Kerala State. The hill is 3,100 feet above sea level. The holy place derives its name from Shabari, the lady saint devotee of Rāma, who lived here and attained *moksha*. The centre of attraction is the Ayyappan Mandir.

Local legend says the mandir was built by Vishvakarmā, the divine architect. The *murti* of Ayyappan (means the Ruler) is 18 inches high. Ayyappan is the son of Bhagwan Shiva and

Teppotsav, float festival, at Minākshi Mandir

Srinivas Fine Arts

Ayyappan Mandir, Shabarimalai

Srinivas Fine Arts

Mohini (the female form assumed by Bhagwan Vishnu). So he is called Harihara-putra – son of Vishnu and Shiva. The mandir has eighteen steps, each of which are six feet long and eight inches wide and very steep. They represent 18 things, namely, the five sense organs: eyes, ears, nose, tongue and skin, eight base instincts like ego, lust, greed, envy, anger, etc., three *gunas: sattva, rajas* and *tamas*, and *vidyā* and *avidyā*. They have to be transcended to reach God.

The pilgrimage is allowed to be done by men, pre-pubescent girls and post-menopausal women. Strict vows have to be observed for 41 days prior to darshan of the mandir: the pilgrim has to wear black, blue or ochre dress, a *rudrāksha* or tulsi garland, observe strict celibacy, and abstain from meat, alcoholic drinks and drugs. The pilgrim carries an Irumudi on his head, similar to a bag with two compartments. In one compartment is a coconut filled with ghee and some puja items. In the second compartment one carries food needed for the journey. Another aspect of this pilgrimage is taking a bath in the River Pampā which was specially brought to earth by Shiva himself to purify a pilgrim of Ayyappan.

The pilgrimage season is from November to March. Hundreds of thousands of devotees perform the pilgrimage to be blessed by Ayyappan.

Srinivas Fine Arts

Lord Ayyappan

Shri Swaminarayan Mandir, Chhapaiya

11. CHHAPAIYA

Chhapaiya is a small village 20 kilometres from Ayodhya. It is the birthplace of Bhagwan Swaminarayan (1781-1830 CE). There are two Swaminarayan mandirs – large and small. The smaller mandir, which has been built on the spot of the birthplace, is behind the main big *shikharabaddha* mandir. The central sanctum of the main mandir has the *murtis* of Dharma, Bhakti and Ghanshyam (the childhood name of Bhagwan Swaminarayan), the right sanctum has the *murtis* of Baldeva-Revati and Harikrishna Maharaj, and the left sanctum has the *murtis* of Kunjavihari (Krishna), Radhika and Vasudeva Narayan. Adjacent to the mandir one finds the *murti* of Ghanshyam Maharaj.

Shri Ghanshyam Maharaj in mandir shrine

The birth spot is a small room that lies beneath the smaller mandir sanctums. The many holy places in the village where Ghanshyam Maharaj bathed, played and performed miracles are intact, namely, Narayan Sarovar, Meen Sarovar, Trikoniyu (triangle-shaped) farm, Khampā Talāvadi (a small lake), Moksha Peepal tree and others.

Even today the village has a rustic but divine ambience and is visited annually by thousands of Swaminarayan followers.

Birthplace of Bhagwan Swaminarayan, Chhapaiya

Guruvāyur Mandir, Kerala

12. GURUVĀYUR

Guruvāyur is a very popular pilgrim centre for Krishna devotees in Kerala State. The name means a town established by the Guru, i.e., Brihaspati. It is a small town 30 kilometres to the west of the city of Trichur. It is renowned for its mandir of Shri Krishna, where the deity is known as Guruvāyurappan – it means the master of Guruvāyur town.

The history of its origin is found in the Sthala Purāna, and local legends based on the Nāradiya Purāna. It describes that the image of this mandir was being worshipped by Shri Krishna himself at Dwārakā (Gujarat). Prior to the submergence of Dwārakā in water, Shri Krishna gave the *murti* to Uddhava telling him to install it in a suitable place. With the help of Brihaspati, Vāyu and Parshurāma the *murti* was installed in a mandir in Kerala. The mandir is believed to be 5,000 years old.

Shri Guruvāyur

King Janmejaya, the great grandson of the Pāndava hero Arjuna, is said to have worshipped this deity to rid himself of leprosy which he had contracted after performing the *sarpa-yajna* to exterminate all snakes and serpents. The mandir has been renovated from time to time.

The presiding deity in the mandir is that of Nārāyana, also called Shrikoil, in a standing position. The four arms are

Somanātha Mandir, Gujarat

adorned with *shankha, chakra, gadā* and *padma*. Nārāyana is also adorned with tulsi garlands and a pearl necklace.

The main mandir is small and it has been built in a typical Keralan style of architecture. It has a main entrance and a gold-plated *dhvajasthambha* 110 feet high. On either side of it are two *dipastambhas*, 22 feet high for lighting lamps. The mandir follows a system of rituals introduced by Ādi Shankarāchārya. There are five main pujas performed daily from 3.00 a.m. to 10 p.m. The *utsava murti* is taken around the mandir in a procession twice a day. Festivals like Gitā Jayanti, New Year's Day (generally 15 April), and Brahmotsavam (February/March) during which an elephant race is held, are the popular attractions. The other festivals celebrated here are Krishna Janmāshtami (birthday of Bhagwan Krishna) in August-September and the Navarātra festival in October.

13. SOMANĀTHA

The Somanātha Mandir, also spelt as Somnāth, is situated in the small town of Prabhāsa-Pātana in Saurashtra, Gujarat. It lies on the bristling shores of the Arabian Sea. The mandir is dedicated to Bhagwan Shiva and it is the first of the twelve *jyotirlingas* mentioned in the Purānas. The original sacred image, called the Sparshalinga, nearly the size of a hen's egg,

One of twelve jyotirlingas, Somanātha Mandir

was given to Soma, the moon deity, by Shiva, who was happy with his intense austerities. Hence the *linga* got the name of Somanātha (Lord of Soma or Moon, i.e., Shiva).

According to legend the first mandir was built by the moon-god over the *linga*. It was in gold. Through time it deteriorated. It was rebuilt by Rāvana in silver, by Krishna in wood and by Bhima in stone.

Historically, one of the first mandirs might have been built by the Vallabhi kings of Saurashtra, some time during 500 CE. The Somanātha mandir was the wealthiest at that time before it was plundered by Mohammed Ghazni in 1026 CE. The mandir is believed to have received the earnings of 10,000 villages that were under it. One thousand Brahmins were engaged in performing the worship rituals. A very heavy chain of gold was used to ring the mandir bell. The mandir hall *(rangamandapa)* had 56 gem-studded pillars, each covered in gold sheets. The *linga* in the *garbha-gruha* was 10 feet high and 6 feet in diameter. The sanctum was grand. It was because of such opulence and wealth that Mohammed Ghazni plundered and then destroyed the mandir. Thereafter, reconstruction by local kings and destruction by the Muslim invaders went on for several centuries. The last destroyer was Aurangazeb in 1706 CE. Another mandir was built near the ruins of the old mandir in 1783 by Ahalyābāi Holkar.

After India's independence in 1947, the mandir was rebuilt on the instruction of Sardar Vallabhbhai Patel (1875-1950), the deputy Prime Minister of India. The Shiva *linga* was consecrated on the original spot. The mandir was inaugurated by the President of India, Dr Rajendra Prasad, on 11 May 1951. The *shikhara* of the new mandir is 164 feet high. It has intricate carvings. Other mandirs and significant places in Somnātha are the Gita Mandir, Lakshmināāyana Mandir, Baldeva Gufā (cave), Triveni *sangama*, Surya Mandir and others.

*Vivekananda Rock Memorial
is a sacred monument off
the coast of Kanyākumāri
that commemorates the visit
of Swami Vivekananda in
December 1892 for meditation
and enlightenment*

14. KANYĀKUMĀRI

Kanyākumāri, also known as Kanyātirtha, has been revered as a place of pilgrimage since 2,000 years. It is dedicated to the Divine Mother or Pārvati in her aspect as a virgin.

The holy town is located at the southernmost tip of India in the Kanyākumāri district of Tamil Nadu. It lies 87 kilometres from Thiruvananthapuram (Trivandrum), the capital of Kerala State. It lies on the seashore where the Indian Ocean, the Bay of Bengal and the Arabian Sea meet.

There are several accounts of how the goddess came to be established here. One of these describes that Punyakeshi, the daughter of Mayāsura (the chief architect of the asuras), performed austerities here to marry Bhagwan Shiva. The Lord promised to marry her at the end of the *kalpa* or aeon but advised her to continue with her austerities. While she was doing so, the terrible demon, Bānāsura, insisted that she marry him. She used her *chakra* to kill him. After this she resumed her austerities, and is believed to be still waiting for her final union with Shiva.

The *murti* of the virgin goddess is in the standing position. The carved figure of a lion suggests that she is Durgā. The mandir has four pillars, when struck they produce the sound of *mrudanga, vinā,* flute and *jaltaranga*.

Another recently constructed beautiful and prominent

*Vivekānanda Rock Memorial,
Kanyākumāri*

mandir nearby has an impressive image of Swami Vivekananda. It lies on the large rock in the sea. A regular ferry service carries visitors from the coast to the mandir.

15. NĀTHADWĀRĀ

Nāthadwārā is a small town by the banks of Banāsa River in the State of Rajasthan. It lies 48 kilometres northeast of Udaipura. Nāthadwārā means 'the gate leading to the Master' (God). It is renowned because of the 17th century Shrināthaji Mandir. The presiding deity is Shrināthaji (a form of Bhagwan Krishna). It is a popular pilgrim place for the Vaishnava disciples, especially of Shri Vallabhāchārya, and is the main centre of the Pushti *mārga*.

According to legend, the *murti* of Shrināthaji was found by Shri Vallabhāchārya on Mt. Govardhana in Vrundāvan. To protect it from being destroyed by Aurangzeb, the *murti* was being carted away to a safer place. While the cart was passing through Nāthadwārā the wheels sunk to its axles. Despite efforts to proceed ahead the cart remained stuck. The priests took it as a sign from Krishna that he in the form of the *murti* did not want to travel further. Thereafter a grand mandir was built at that very spot.

The mandir structure is simple, and the beauty of the *murti* of Shrināthji attracts countless Vaishnava pilgrims every year. The life-size *murti* is carved out of a single black stone. One of the arms is held up as if it is holding the Govardhana mountain. The other rests on the waist apparently in a dancing posture and granting blessings to all. According to the Pushti *mārga* tradition the pujaris change the vestments and ornaments of Shrināthji daily and offer only fleeting darshan (*jhānkhi*) to the visitors by opening the curtains and then closing them shortly thereafter. The *bhoga* offered to the *murti* is sold at a minimal price by the shopkeepers outside the mandir.

During Holi, Diwāli and Janmāshtami the mandir overflows

Shrināthaji, Nāthadwārā

with devotees. The *annakuta* festival is celebrated on the first day of the Hindu Year with great devotional fervour, attracting thousands of devotees.

The town of Nāthdwārā is also famous for its *pichhwāi* paintings, savoury sweets and souvenir articles.

CONCLUSION

Only a few of the many hundreds of places of pilgrimage have been mentioned. There are many other holy places, small and great, where pilgrims and tourists visit in large numbers, namely, Muktinātha (Nepal), Gayā, Kataragāma, Māyāpuri, Bhuvaneshwara, Sākshi Gopāla, Dakshineshwara Mandir, Belur Matha (Kolkatā), Konārka, Kumbakonama, Chitrakuta, Pandharapura, Dākora, Ambāji, Kurukshetra, Naimishāranyakshetra, Kumārikākshetra and others.

SUMMARY

1. The seven holy rivers of India are, Gangā, Yamunā, Sindhu, Sarasvati, Narmadā, Godāvari and Kāveri. Hindus believe that rivers have two forms: (1) physical and (2) divine. They are divinities or mother goddesses. Thus they are revered as deities.

2. The Shiva Purāna notes the twelve ancient pilgrim places where Shiva revealed himself in the form of a *linga* (emblem) of light or *jyotirlinga*. The 12 *jyotirlingas* are in Kedārnātha, Vishvanātha, Somnātha, Mahākāleshvara, Omkāreshvara, Rāmeshvaram, Mallikārjuna, Trayambakeshvara, Bhimashankara, Ghrushneshvara, Nāgeshvara and Vaidyanātha or Baijanātha.

3. Other popular pilgrim places include Rishikesha, Kailāsa-Mānsarovara, Amarnātha, Vaishno Devi, Pushkara, Tirupati-Bālāji, Madurāi, Shabarimalai, Chhaipaiya, Guruvāyur, Kanyākumāri.

14

Holy Festivals

The Ratha Yātrā festival is one of the grandest and largest of Hindu celebrations held in Jagannātha Puri, Orissa. (Inset) Ganesha Utsav.

Mahā-Shivarātri, Pushpadolotsava,
Guru Purnimā, Rakshābandhana,
Onam, Vijayā Dashami...

INTRODUCTION

India is a land of holy festivals and celebrations that rejuvenate and relieve its people from the monotony of daily life and its burdens. Its social and predominantly spiritual content make its people vibrant and religious. For devout Hindus festivals provide a mystical connection with God and their own atman. Festivals also lighten the burden of bad karma and help integrate devotion and knowledge in their lives. Festivals provide a beautiful and joyful mosaic of colour, pageantry, beauty, music, dance and rituals.

Hindu festivals reinforce the innate fundamentals of each individual's existence, both spiritual and temporal, which are otherwise overshadowed by mundane and rational activities. The spiritual fervour inspired through festivals convinces one that life is worthwhile, and that it is possible to live happily, religiously and righteously in the midst of an increasingly materialistic and indulgent society. Before we briefly explain how some of the main festivals are celebrated by Hindus in India and abroad, let us consider the Hindu calendar system.

THE HINDU CALENDAR

India, like many other countries, bases its business life, travel, social activities, national holidays and other activities on the universally applied Gregorian calendar. This system rests upon the movement of the sun through the 12 signs of the zodiac (constellations), which gives us our 12 solar months. However

Hindus celebrate and observe their festivals and sacraments according to their own calendar based on lunar months. The Hindu calendar uses the solar year but divides it into 12 lunar months. One lunar month is the time the moon takes to travel around the earth, which comes to 29½ days. It is divided into two halves: the bright half or Shuklapaksha in which the moon waxes and the dark half or Krishnapaksha in which it wanes. Each lunar day is called *tithi,* and it is counted from sunrise to sunset and not from midnight. Different times and different lunar days are considered auspicious or inauspicious for worship, fasting, travelling, getting married and inaugurations, etc. They are determined by Hindu astrologers. In north India, the lunar month ends on the day of the full moon *(purnimā)*, while in Gujarat it ends on the new moon day *(amāvāsya)*.

Hindus generally follow the Vikrama Samvat era which began in 57[1] BCE. Thus, 1900 CE in the Gregorian calendar corresponds to the year 1957 of the Vikrama Samvat era. The New Year begins in different months for different parts of India. In North India, it begins on the first day of Chaitra (April) because they follow a different calendar era to that of Vikrama Samvat. Gujarat and the central regions of India follow the Vikrama Samvat in which the New Year begins on the first day of Kārtika (October or November).

The twelve lunar months are: Kārtika (Oct.-Nov.), Mārgashirsha (Nov.-Dec.), Pausha (Dec.-Jan.), Māgha (Jan.-Feb.), Phālguna (Feb.-Mar.), Chaitra (Mar.-Apr.), Vaishākha (Apr.-May.), Jyeshtha (May-June), Āshādha (June-July), Shrāvana (July-Aug.), Bhādrapada (Aug.-Sept.) and Āshwina (Sept.-Oct.). Each month is named after a constellation in which the full moon is sighted. Twelve lunar months make a total of 354 days, which amounts to 11 days less than the solar year. To avoid the deficit with the solar year of 365 days, the

Seasons and months in the Hindu Calendar

---

1. Sometimes 56 years is added to the Gregorian Year depending on the beginning of the New Year which is different in various regions of India.

Indian year includes an extra month or *adhika-māsa* every 2½ years. Though it is lunar based it remains in consonance with the solar year.

The seven days of the week are named after celestial bodies and planets: Ravivāra (Sun) is Sunday, Somavāra (Moon) is Monday, Mangalavāra (Mars) is Tuesday, Budhavāra (Mercury) is Wednesday, Guruvāra (Jupiter) is Thursday, Shukravāra (Venus) is Friday and Shanivāra (Saturn) is Saturday.

In the Hindu calendar there are six seasons, each of two months. They are Vasanta (spring), Grishma (summer), Varshā (rain), Sharada (autumn), Hemanta (late autumn) and Shishira (winter).

The celebration of festivals is mainly a response to the presence of the Divine. The devout respond to the Divinity by fasting, singing devotional songs, worshipping in mandirs, seeking blessings from holy people and reading the sacred texts. The Hindu festivals in the Indian calendar have a spiritual content, celebrating the birth or victory of God and his avatars. Not all of them are commonly celebrated by every Hindu — some have a special regional meaning; some are observed by devotees of a particular deity; some are family-based; others are occasions related to mandir-visiting and pilgrimage. In Hindu festivals the Hindus worship, celebrate and also interact socially with family, relatives, friends and the community in general. The spiritual, social and psychological impact of celebrating festivals is immense because it has a positive and elevating effect.

A brief account of some of the festivals is as follows:

1. MAKARASANKRĀNTI-UTTARĀYANA AND PONGAL (January)

Makarasankrānti-Uttarāyana is a very popular festival celebrated on 14 January in the Indian month of Pausha. Every year on this day when the earth routinely changes its

Sadhus and the poor are given alms on Uttarāyana

Gujaratis flying kites on Uttarāyana, Ahmedabad

orbital path, the sun moves toward the northern direction and enters in Capricorn (Makara). Since the northerly direction is considered holy, this festival is a call for all to follow the path of righteousness. From this day onwards all auspicious occasions and rituals are allowed. It also traditionally marks the end of the harvest season and Hindu farmers thus express their gratitude by worshipping cows and oxen.

Uttarāyana is a day of charity when Hindus give alms to mandirs, Brahmins, sadhus, sannyasis and needy people. In Maharashtra and Gujarat, the householders offer balls of sesame seeds and gur as a symbol of goodwill. The young and old, mainly in Gujarat, gather on terraces and in open spaces to fly kites all day. The kite festival brings great excitement. It also conveys a spiritual message that as long as one is bound to God with the thread of obedience, then one shall savour the bliss of his divine form by always remaining attached to him.

The Pongal festival celebrated in Thiruvananthapuram, Kerala

The people of Tamil Nadu celebrate the Pongal festival on this day. They feast on boiled rice offered to the sun. The rice is gathered from their new harvest. They express with gratitude God's generosity through worship, songs and prayers. It also marks the Tamil New Year's day.

A decorated Shivalinga for Shivarātri festival. Devotees offer milk and bilva leaves to smaller Shivalingas on the occasion

2. MAHĀ-SHIVARĀTRI

(February/March)

Mahā-Shivarātri is the great night in honour of Bhagwan Shiva that falls in the Indian month of Māgha. A festival that celebrates the birth, glory and power of Shiva – a great ascetic steeped in prayer and austerity. It celebrates the day of origin of the famous 12 *jyotirlingas* in India. The devout rejoice in taking a holy dip in the Gangā because it had issued from the locks of Shiva.

The Shiva Purāna narrates how a hunter stayed awake all night by dropping *bilwā* leaves on a Shivalinga. The merits of his act purified his heart. Hence, devotees keep vigil on this night by singing bhajans to Shiva, listening to discourses on his life and teachings and bathing the sacred Shivalinga with water, milk, honey, saffron water and offering *bilva* leaves while chanting the *Shatarudriya* (Yajur *vedic* hymns to Shiva). Large gatherings and fairs are customarily held on this day at nearly all the Jyotirlinga pilgrimage centres, Girnār (Junāgadha, Gujarat) and other holy Shaiva mandirs.

3. HOLI AND PUSHPADOLOTSAVA

(February/March)

Holi and Pushpadolotsava are spring festivals celebrated

Wood piled up at crossroads in Ahmedabad for the Holi fire. Coloured powder in the foreground for sprinkling on the people

with fire and colour in the Indian month of Phālguna. On the day of Holi, all Hindus celebrate the victory of the devout Prahlāda over his evil father Hiranyakashipu. The joy of sprinkling coloured powder and water makes the Holi festival immensely popular.

Hiranyakashipu tried to have Prahlāda killed many times because of the latter's faith in God. But he failed. The story of his last attempt says that he asked his sister, Holikā, who was immune to the power of fire, to take Prahlāda in her lap and then set fire to the pyre of wood that she was sitting on. Prahlāda, however, remained unscathed, whereas Holikā was burnt to ashes.

To commemorate this victory of good over evil, giant bonfires are traditionally lit in the evening of Holi day. People circumambulate the fire, pouring a trickle of water from small pots on the ground and throwing coconuts into the fire. When the fire dies down they take the holy ash and apply it as a round mark on their forehead. On this day Kāmadeva (lord of love) was burnt to ashes by Shiva because he tried to arouse Shiva's passion while engrossed in meditation.

The next day the Vaishnavas celebrate Pushpadolotsava. On this day, the *gopis* of Vrundāvan prepared a swing decorated with fragrant flowers for Shri Krishna, performed his puja and

Bonfire lit to mark Holi

Devotees celebrating Holi in Mathurā

Hinduism

Pramukh Swami Maharaj celebrates Pushpadolotsava by spraying sanctified coloured water on devotees, Sarangpur, Gujarat

rocked him with intense joy and bhakti. The devotees celebrate this day by decorating a swing with flowers and rocking the *murti* of God. Then they spray the coloured water and throw coloured powder on each other.

The sentiments of making a bonfire of one's evil nature, colouring one's life with the hue of bhakti and swinging God in the swing of one's heart are the spiritual messages of these celebrations.

4. RĀMA NAVAMI & SWAMINARAYAN JAYANTI

(April)

On this day India rapturously celebrates the legacy of two great divine figures that graced its holy soil – Bhagwan Shri Rāma and Bhagwan Shri Swaminarayan.

Hailed as Maryādā-Purushottama, Shri Rāma, the seventh avatar of Bhagwan Vishnu, is an icon of familial obedience and discipline for all Hindus. His noble life and the Rāma *rājya* he established have always remained beacons of inspiration and hope for Indian society. The holy name of Rāma has pulsated in the hearts of countless for millennia as an incarnation of God.

Shri Rāma was born on the ninth day of the lunar month of Chaitra (April). Devotees celebrate on this day by chanting his holy name and reciting the *chopāis* (verses) about his life from

Ārati at Rāmaji Mandir

the *Rāmacharitmānasa* of Tulasidāsa. In the evening, crowds attend the Rāmalilā – a colourful stage performance on Rāma's life. People observe a fast or take only fruits and liquid on this day.

The second guiding light that blessed India was Purna Purushottam Bhagwan Shri Swaminarayan (1781-1830 CE). Born in Chhapaiya, near Ayodhyā, he left home at the age of 11 and travelled the length and breadth of India for seven years. He established the Swaminarayan Sampradaya in Gujarat and spearheaded a moral and spiritual renaissance, eradicating the sati custom, violent *yajnas*, addictions and superstitions. He fostered the bhakti tradition by establishing six mandirs and initiating over 3,000 sadhus and *paramhansas* of high spiritual calibre.

He preached the ideals of Sanātana Dharma, namely, faith, truth, compassion, non-violence, self-control and others. Through his divine personality he revealed his supreme glory, liberated countless people from ignorance and blessed them with divine joy. His work was continued by his successor and ideal devotee Gunatitanand Swami and thereafter by Bhagatji Maharaj, Shastriji Maharaj, Yogiji Maharaj and now by Pramukh Swami Maharaj.

*Enactment of Rāmalilā,
New Delhi*

Grand Ratha Yātrā festival in Jagannātha Puri, Orissa

5. RATHA YĀTRA

(June/July)

Jagannātha Puri, Orissa, is one of India's holiest places of pilgrimage. Every year it is transformed into a sea of spectacular devotion on Ratha Yātrā day, celebrated on the second day of Āshādha that occurs in June-July. A mammoth gathering of more than one million devotees line the streets of Puri in Orissa to have darshan of the *murtis* of Bhagwan Jagannāthaji (Shri Krishna), his sister Subhadrā and brother Balarāma ceremoniously drawn in three grand chariots from Jagannātha Mandir to their country home. The festival is also celebrated in many cities and towns of India, especially in Ahmedabad, Gujarat.

The devotees enthusiastically receive *prasāda* of mung, *jāmbu* fruit and cucumber.

Together with this vibrant manifestation of devotion, the Kathopanishad metaphorically teaches that the body is like the chariot, intellect the driver *(sārathi)*, mind the reins, senses the horses, atman the master and the road the material objects (1.3.3-4). The festival inspires one to give God or the God-realized guru the reins of one's life-chariot to secure *moksha*.

Devotees pulling the giant chariot

BAPS devotees on Guru Purnimā, Bochasan, Gujarat

6. GURU PURNIMĀ

(July)

Hindus throughout the world congregate in large numbers to honour their spiritual guru on the full moon day of Āshādha in the month of July. They honour him with garlands, gifts (guru *dakshinā*) and prayers to express their love and gratitude. They renew their pledges to abide by the guru's teachings and guidance for the whole year. The disciples sing his glory in an assembly, perform *pujan* by applying a round mark of kumkum on the guru's forehead and seek his blessings for enlightenment.

This day is also known as Vyāsa Purnimā because Veda Vyāsa is revered as the first guru by all Hindus and also as an incarnation of God. He is adored for having contributed to the immense wisdom and glory of Hinduism. He classified the Vedas and authored the Brahmasutras, Mahābhārata and 18 Purānas.

7. RAKSHĀBANDHANA

(August)

Pramukh Swami Maharaj blesses devotees on Guru Purnimā, Bochasan

Rakshābandhana commemorates the 'freeing' of Bhagwan Vishnu from King Bali's service. The 'freedom' was secured when goddess Lakshmi tied a *rākhi* (a decorated thread)

Hinduism

A sister tying rākhi on her brother's wrist to mark Rakshābandhana

around Bali's wrist. Ever since, on this day, sisters tie *rākhis* on their brothers' wrists to wish them well and to seek their protection.

The festival is celebrated on the full moon day in the month of Shrāvana (August). In response to the tying of *rākhi* to his wrist, the brother gives gifts, clothes or cash to his sister. She prays for his welfare, and the brother pledges to protect her.

Originally a *rākhi* was a handspun cotton thread dyed yellow with turmeric, but now it comes in different materials of various shapes, sizes and colours. Three knots in the thread signify protection in thought, word and deed.

This day is also celebrated as Nārikela Purnima because fishermen offer coconuts to appease Lord Varuna (sea-god). The day also marks the changing of the sacred thread *(upavita)* among Brahmins and others. This tradition dates back to Vedic times when the academic New Year commenced on this day.

8. KRISHNA JANMĀSHTAMI
(August/September)

Janmāshtami, on the eight lunar day of the dark half of Shrāvana (August/September), marks the birth of Bhagwan Shri Krishna. A festival of national celebration, Janmāshtami is an occasion of joy, worship and singing the glory of Bhagwan

Bhagwan Krishna

Stage performance of Krishna Lilā by BAPS youths on Janmāshtami festival, Toronto. The photo shows Krishna (right) as an emissary appealing for peace in the court of the Kauravas

Shri Krishna's divine *lilā* (incidents). From his childhood adventures of stealing curds and butter and destroying Kāliya, the serpent, to his divine moonlight dance with the *gopis* on the banks of the Yamunā, Shri Krishna has fascinated and charmed devotees and poets for thousands of years.

The eternal song of the Gitā imparted to Arjuna and his superb statesmanship and skilfulness during the Mahābhārata battle are signatures of Shri Krishna's profound wisdom and divinity. He fulfilled his mission to establish dharma and destroy evil.

Shri Krishna's fond association with the cow, flute and Rādhāji reveal a unique bond of divine love and compassion. For millennia, his glorious life has shaped the social, spiritual and cultural life of India.

On Janmāshtami day the devout observe a fast and teenage boys and youths form human pyramids to break pots of curds hung high across streets. The mandirs resound with the reading and enactment of Krishna's pastimes from the Shrimad Bhāgavata and performance of puja rituals.

At midnight, *ārati* of Lālji, the child *murti* of Shri Krishna, is performed in mandirs and homes. The *murti* is rocked in a decorated, silver *hindolā* (swing) and bhajans are sung in his praise. A variety of food items like curds, sweets, fried foods

Teenage boys break a pot of curds strung across a street in Mumbāi on Krishna Janmāshtami

The unique snake-boat race is a thrilling part of Onam, the harvest festival of Kerala

and *panchājiri* (a special baked mixture of five ingredients: dry coriander *(dhaniā)*, seeds of dill plant *(suvā)*, dry ginger *(suntha)*, ground sugar crystals and ghee are offered to God and distributed to devotees as *prasāda*.

9. ONAM
(August/September)

It is the most important harvest festival of Kerala. The people of Kerala believe that when Lord Vāmana exiled King Bali to the *pātāla* region the latter prayed to Bhagwan Vishnu to allow him to visit his citizens once a year. Vishnu permitted him to do so on the day of Onam, which falls in August or September. The whole of Kerala celebrates the reception of King Bali to make him rejoice at seeing his subjects happy. The festivities last for ten days, which include giving away presents, dancing to songs in praise of Bali and snake-boat racing.

10. GANESHA CHATURTHI
(August/September)

The fourth day of the bright half of the lunar month of Bhādrapadā (August/September) is celebrated as the birthday of Shri Ganeshaji or Ganapatiji – the god of auspiciousness, remover of obstacles and bestower of happiness and liberation.

After the ten-day celebration of Ganesha Utsav thousands of devotees join the ceremonial procession for the immersion of Shri Ganeshaji in the sea, Mumbai

This festival is celebrated for ten days.

As with other festivals, the homes, mandirs and canopied shrines on streets, especially in Andhra Pradesh, Karnataka, Maharashtra and Gujarat, are elaborately decorated. For ten days, colourful clay images of Ganeshaji are installed and worshipped with rituals of *pujan, ārati* and offerings of laddus. Devotees beseech him to grant them intellect, riches and enlightenment. Bal Gangadhar Tilak (1856-1920), a renowned freedom fighter, introduced the festival to rouse the nationalistic fervour of the Indian people. After ten days the *murtis* of Ganeshaji are ceremoniously carried to rivers, lakes or oceans for immersion.

11. NAVARĀTRI AND VIJAYĀ DASHAMI (DASHAHARĀ)
(September/October)

Giant murti of Ganesha worshipped in a canopied shrine in Mumbai during Ganesha Utsav

The purpose behind celebrating Navarātri lies in the victory of goddess Durgā, a benign form of goddess Pārvati, in a battle against the demon, Mahishāsura. The latter had appeased Brahmā by performing austerities and obtained a boon that he would never die at the hands of a human being. The demon subsequently started ravaging the three worlds. To counter the demon, Durgā was given weapons, namely, *vajra* by Indra, *chakra* by Vishnu and *trishula* by Shivaji. Durgā created eighteen

On Dashaharā giant effigies of Rāvana, Kumbhakarana and Meghanād are burnt to commemorate the victory of Rāma, New Delhi

arms for herself and fought with Mahishāsura who attacked her in the form of a snorting bull. The fierce battle lasted for nine days, with Durgā destroying the demon on the tenth day.[2]

In Bengal and certain parts of India the festival of nine nights honours the goddesses Durgā, Lakshmi and Sarasvati, starting with the first day of the lunar month of Āshwina (September/October). Three days are dedicated each to Durgā (goddess of valour and Shiva's consort), Lakshmiji (goddess of wealth and consort of Nārāyana or Vishnu) and Sarasvati (goddess of knowledge and consort of Brahmā). In Bengal the festival is known as Durgā Puja where huge decorated clay images of goddess Durgā are consecrated in large canopies on plain grounds and streets. The *murtis* are worshipped for ten days and then ceremoniously immersed in rivers like Gangā, lakes or seas.

In Gujarat the traditional *garbā* dance and *dāndiyā rāsa* (traditional stick dance) are performed for nine nights. The tenth day, known as Dashaharā (Dasarā or Dasherā) or Vijayā Dashami, is celebrated as a day of valour and triumph. On this day Bhagwan Rāma vanquished the demon Rāvana and liberated his consort Sitādevi from her confinement in Lankā. To commemorate this day, gorgeous stage performances of

Navarātri, nine nights of devotion and dance, Ahmedabad

2. Devi Bhagavat 5.16.

Rāma Lilā depict the heroism and divinity of Rāma in northern India. The episodes climax with the burning of giant effigies of Rāvana and Kumbhakarana to salute the victory of Rāma.

Vijayā Dashami is also the birthday of Bhagwan Venkateshwar, the presiding deity of Tirupati Bālāji Mandir in Andhra Pradesh.

On this day students seek to earn the blessings of Sarasvati Devi – the goddess of learning – by performing puja, and placing books and quills before her image. The Kshatriyas perform puja of their weapons on this day.

12. DEEPĀWALI & ANNAKUTA UTSAVA
(October/November)

The four-day spectacular Deepāwali (Diwāli) festival is popularly known as the festival of lights. It is variously associated with Bhagwan Rāma, Krishna, goddesses Lakshmi and Sarasvati and Hanumānji. Deepāwali is the grand finale to the annual festivals of India. It is one of the most festive and auspicious of all celebrations in the Hindu calendar and celebrated by all Hindus throughout the world. Deepāwali is celebrated on the last day of the final month of Āshwina (October/November). The traditional rituals of worship and prayer in the five-day Deepāwali festival start with Lakshmi Pujan on the thirteenth day (Dhanatrayodashi or Dhan Teras) of the dark half of Āshwina month, when everyone performs puja of wealth in the form of gold and silver coins to purify them and pray for their benevolent use. On the fourteenth day (Krishnachaturdashi or Kāli Chaudasha) Hanumānji is worshipped to protect one from evil spirits. And on the next day, on Deepāwali, the last day of the year, the account books of devotees are sanctified with the ritual *mahāpujā* or popularly known as Shārdā (Chopdā) Pujān.

Deepāwali or Deepa Utsava is celebrated by placing *deepas* (lamps) on windows and doors of homes and in mandirs.

Opposite: Diwali and New Year's celebrations in Gujarat include ritual sanctification of account books, preparing rangoli, lighting firecrackers, offering prayers and a feast to God

Hinduism

Holy Festivals

Sometimes they are floated on rivers. Colourful designs, portraits or scenes *(rangolis)* are created with different coloured powders to decorate the entrance to homes and buildings *(rangolis)*. A display of fireworks celebrates Shri Rāma's return to Ayodhyā after his 14-year exile and victory over the evil Rāvana. The day also marks the birth of Lakshmiji as she emerged out of the ocean during the Samudra Manthana or churning of the ocean.

New Year's Day or Nutan Varsh is the day after Diwāli in the Vikram calendar.[3] It falls on the first day of Kārtika month. It is celebrated in a spirit of bonhomie with personal visits to homes of relatives and friends. Family bonds are renewed and forgiveness is asked for from others to whom one may have hurt in any way in the previous year.

New Year's Day is also marked with an offering of a grand feast or *annakuta* to God with devotion and in appreciation of his abundant generosity for the new harvest.

The second day of the New Year is celebrated by sisters who honour their brothers (Bhāi *bija*) by inviting them for a celebratory lunch. The brothers rejoice with and offer gifts to their sisters.

In this way the five-day celebration of Deepāwali inspires devotion and love for God and one's family and friends.

13. KUMBHA MELA

Every three years a mammoth festival called the Kumbha Mela is held when the sun enters in Aquarius or the Kumbha constellation. It is held at one of four pilgrim places: (1) at the confluence of Rivers Gangā, Yamunā and Sarasvati in Allahabad, also called Prayāga, in North India, Uttar Pradesh, (2) at the River Godāvari in Nāsik on the west coast, Maharashtra, (3) at River Kshiprā in Ujjain in central India,

---

3. In some states of India New Year's Day falls on different months of the year. Chaitra *sud* 1 – New Year's Day in north India, Maharashtra and Tamil Nadu. Vishu – New Year's Day in Kerala. Nutan Varsh – Kartik *sud* 1, New Year's Day in Gujarat and Rajasthan.

Kumbha Mela in Haridwāra, the biggest religious celebration in the world

Madhya Pradesh, and (4) at the River Gangā in Haridwāra in north India, Uttarakhand. Every three years a Kumbha Mela is held at one of these four places, and once in twelve years a *purna* or mega-Kumbh Mela is held in these places by turns. Millions of devotees, sadhus and sannyasis of various denominations and *sampradāyas* congregate to bathe in the holy water on the auspicious hour to be blessed with *punya* and to dissolve their sins. They live in tents by the river bank, practising austerities, living on simple food, doing *japa* and meditation and giving gifts to deserving persons. The spiritual leaders of different Hindu *sampradāyas* also hold meetings to discuss various issues relevant to the practice of Hinduism.

The Kumbha Mela at the confluence of three rivers in Prayāga (Allahabad) is the biggest spiritual gathering. The Uttar Pradesh State government puts up a city of tents in which pilgrims live free of cost. Spiritual heads of all *sampradāyas* hold satsang and bhajan during the six-week-long festival. Seventy million people attended the Kumbha Mela in 2001 at Prayāga. Prior to the ritual bath each of the heads of various *sampradāyas* and his followers take out a procession, chanting and singing God's holy name to the accompaniment of musical instruments.

Kumbha Mela at Ujjain

The origin of the Kumbha Mela can be traced to the story of the *kalasha* (pot) of *amruta* (nectar) obtained after the devas (gods) and asuras (demons) churned the ocean. The asuras grabbed the pot and started quarrelling as to who should take the first sip. So, Bhagwan Vishnu assumed the form of a very charming damsel called Mohini. The asuras were overwhelmed by her beauty and charm and gave the *amruta* to her to distribute. Mohini started distributing *amruta* to the devas. When the asuras realized that the *amruta* was almost finished, they became furious at the deception. On perceiving this, Mohini disappeared. Jayanta, one of the sons of Indra, took the pot and ran away with the remaining *amruta*. The asuras followed hastily to retrieve it. Jayanta, placed the pot at four places while taking rest, namely, on the banks of River Godāvari in Nāsik, Maharashtra; River Kshiprā in Ujjain, Madhya Pradesh; River Gangā in Haridwāra, Uttarakhand; and at the Triveni-sangam in Prayāga (Allahabad), Uttar Pradesh. When the *amruta kumbha* was lifted at each of the four places, some drops of nectar fell on earth, permanently sanctifying the river water and places. The devout therefore visit these holy places to take a ritual bath for purifying themselves.

CONCLUSION

Other important holy festivals and celebrations are Hanumān Jayanti, Vāmana Jayanti and Nrusimha Jayanti. There are other holy days celebrated at regular intervals, namely, Ekādashi and Purnimā. On these days, devotees generally observe a fast, visit mandirs and read or listen to religious discourses of their choice. Most of these festivals vary from region to region, depending on local traditions, deities and sacred sites and auspicious times. Connectivity with the Divine by humans seeking inner purification and spiritual liberation is the common thread that runs through all the holy festivals.

SUMMARY

1. India is a land of festivals and celebrations that are held to worship and honour God and his manifestations. Hindu festivals dissolve bad karma, consolidate devotion and knowledge, and bring joy and freshness in the lives of people of all backgrounds.

2. The Hindus have a lunar calendar that divides the solar year into twelve lunar months. Each month is further divided into the bright and dark halves as per the waxing and waning of the moon. Each lunar day is called *tithi* and any secular or religious enterprise or project is expected to be performed at an auspicious time. The time when such ventures are started is very important. There are six seasons, each having two months in the Hindu calendar.

3. The celebrations of festivals like Makarasankrānti, Mahā-Shivarātri, Holi and Pushpadolotsava, Rāma Navami and Swaminarayan Jayanti, Ratha Yātrā, Guru Purnimā, Rakshābandhana, Janmāshtami, Ganesha Chaturthi, Onam, Navarātri and Vijayā Dashami, Deepāwali, Annakuta Utsava and Kumbha Mela usher in joy and devotion to millions of Hindu.

15
Devotional Rituals

ISKCON, Ahmedabad

A pujari performs arti of murtis of Bhagwan Rāma, Sitā, Lakshmana and Hanumānji, ISKCON Mandir, Ahmedabad. (Inset) A sadhu performs pujan of a replica of Bhagwan Swaminarayan's holy footprints

Pranāma, Puja, Mahāpujā, Darshan,
Ārati, Dandavat Pranāma, Pradakshinā,
Naivedyam, Nāma Japa,...

INTRODUCTION

Hinduism has hundreds of brief and elaborate rituals. Formerly, the mandir used to be the nucleus of almost every village and town in India. Mostly all activities were centred in and around the mandir. So, the rituals of darshan, *ārati, sevā* and celebrating festivals became an intrinsic part of a Hindu's life. From the simple *pranāma* and the chanting of God's names to the elaborate *yajna* rituals, all were focused on worshipping and appeasing the Divine. The general articles of worship include water, leaves, flowers, fruits, kumkum, milk, yogurt, rice grains, *deepa*, bell, spoon *(sruva)*, plate *(pātra)*, small metal water-pot *(kalasha)*, etc.

Rituals form an integral part of worship and have been practised from generation to generation in countless homes and mandirs. They are deeply embedded in the Hindu culture. Initially, one who is disinterested or is an outsider may consider them to be tedious, abstruse and unexciting, but the impressions and vibrations produced through daily rituals evoke divine feelings, noble thoughts, peace and faith. Through personal action involved in rituals, the devotee experiences a participatory feeling and connection with the Divine. Such rituals, performed with a spiritual mindset and feeling, become acts of bhakti or devotion to God, which gradually purify, strengthen and soothe the senses and mind of the devotee. They also dissolve and lighten the devotee's burden of frustrations and resolve his or her moral lapses. They further serve in dissolving *dehabhāva* and in leading the individual towards *moksha*.

Pranāma expresses reverence to the image of God

The various rituals include *pranāma*, puja, *mahāpujā,* darshan, *ārati, naivedyam, nāma japa, dandavat, pradakshinā, yajna* and others.

1. PRANĀMA

A Hindu expresses reverence to the image of God by joining the palms and bowing the head. This ritual is called *pranāma. Pranāma* is also a gesture used for greeting guests, showing respect to seniors and conveying farewell to friends, relatives and others.

Pranāma, when offered to God, shows one's obeisance to him. A devotee also bows to God with humility and submission – *pranipāta*. The palms held together by the heart and the bowed head convey deep reverence from the heart and total surrender of the mind. Furthermore, by offering *pranāma* to God, who is the creator, sustainer, destroyer and possessor of infinite powers, one acknowledges his supreme greatness, glory, refuge and protectorship.

Children show respect to their teacher

So briefly, by offering *pranāma* to God, guru, parents and elders, one offers respect and seeks their blessings for happiness and protection in this world and beyond.

The other related gestures of reverence to the Divine are *panchānga pranāma* and *shāstānga dandavat pranāma.* Prostrating

The daily puja ritual cleanses the mind and fills one's heart with divinity, peace and faith in God

and touching the five or eight specified parts of the body to the floor is called *panchānga pranāma* (mainly offered by female devotees in mandirs and personal puja; also offered by children to their parents and elders) and *shāstānga dandavat pranāma* (mainly offered by male devotees) respectively.

Many times while offering *pranāma* the devotee says a personal prayer to God or chants his name. Offering *pranāma* soothes and rejuvenates the body and mind. The feeling of respect and humility in the devotee lingers and grows with daily practice. The practice of *pranāma* is also prevalent all over Southeast Asia.

2. DAILY PERSONAL PUJA

The puja of a deity performed on a personal level is done in two ways. Some devotees worship a small *murti* of their chosen deity *(ishtadevatā)*, made either of *panchadhātu* or stone, and others worship printed images. In the former case, devout Vaishnavas engage themselves in the daily morning ritual of awakening the deity (called Bālamukunda, Lālji or Thākorji), bathing the *murti* in water, dressing and adorning him with ornaments and a flower garland. Thereafter, they worship the deity with kumkum, sandalwood paste, incense, *deepa,* etc. Then they apply a sacred mark on their own forehead,

Deities, sages and devotees are worshipped in the mahāpujā

arms and chest. This is followed by meditating, turning *mālā* (rosary), offering prostrations and prayers and singing bhajans before the deity. The personal ritual worship may last from half an hour to one hour or even more. In the second practice of worshipping hand-painted or printed images of the deity and guru *paramparā,* the devotee invokes the deity, meditates, applies a sacred mark on his own forehead, arms and chest, turns the *mālā* while chanting a mantra, performs *pradakshinā* and *dandavat,* offers prayers and finally briefly reads a portion of a shastra or holy text. The daily puja ritual may have different forms in various *sampradāyas*.

Many devotees drink water, have breakfast and engage in their worldly duties only after performing personal puja. This daily ritual cleanses the mind and imbues the individual with divinity, peace and faith in God.

3. MAHĀPUJĀ

Sadhus and youths performing mahāpujā

This is a ritual wherein all the main deities, sages and devotees are worshipped. *Mahāpujā* is performed in many Swaminarayan mandirs for the spiritual progress, peace, fulfilment of desires and solutions to the problems of devotees. As an act of devotion it means service to the deity and a way to please him and win his favour for both *bhukti* (worldly success) and *mukti* (liberation).

Hinduism

Darshan means beholding the deity with devotion and respect

It is also performed to sanctify a home or office prior to living or working there. The ritual is conducted by a sadhu or Brahmin priest. It begins with the chanting of Vedic peace prayers (called *shānti pātha),* and thereafter the deities are invoked in oval-shaped betel nuts. Then the *nyāsa vidhi* is performed in which the participant invokes the Divine in each part of his or her body by chanting appropriate Vedic mantras. This makes one pure and eligible to worship the deities, which one performs thereafter. Firstly, one bathes the deities with *panchāmruta*[1] and sacred water while chanting mantras. Then one adorns them with clothes, applies sandalwood paste, offers food and *ārati* and performs circumambulations and prostrations. Finally, prayers are offered to the deities for forgiveness for any lapses during the ritual ceremony and for the fulfilment of wishes and solutions to problems.

4. DARSHAN

Darshan literally means beholding the deity, guru or the place of pilgrimage with devotion and respect. It is a central and important religious activity of all practising Hindus. When they go to a mandir they say, "I am going for darshan," but they do not say, "I am going for worship." Since the Hindus believe

---

1. A mixture of five things: milk, curd, ghee, sugar and honey.

Ārati is a ritual of profound devotion, love and respect for God

that the deity is present in the sacred *murti* the act of darshan is charged with religious meaning. To "see" and to be "seen" by the deity, holy person or sacred place *(tirtha)* is the essence of darshan. The devotees gain the blessings of the Divine.

While doing darshan of the deity in a mandir, devotees offer *pranāma* by joining their palms together and bowing their head in respect. Then a detailed darshan of the deity involves "seeing" the *murti* from head to toe along with the adornments and attire. The ritual of darshan calms the mind and fills the person with divinity and joy.

Devotees generally go for darshan to mandirs during *ārati* (morning and evening), festive days, *ekādashi, punam* (full-moon day), birthday or any socially important day of their life.

5. ĀRATI

Ārati is the most popular ceremony in Hinduism. It is a ritual that expresses devotion and respect to a deity. *Ārati* is performed by circling *deepas* before the *murti* of God or guru while chanting a prayer. It is one of the sixteen steps *(shodasha upachāra)* of the puja ritual. It is often called "the ceremony of lights" during which the devotee seeks protection, benediction and *moksha* by singing God's glory. In some mandirs the pujari performs *ārati* with camphor, a three or a five-wick lamp,

A pujari offers ārati to Bhagwan Jagannātha

incense, a flower, water and other items. The ceremony is mostly performed standing and by ringing a small hand bell. It is accompanied by playing a drum and a pair of gongs, and blowing a conch shell.

The ritual originated many centuries ago when the *murti* of a deity was illuminated for the darshan of devotees. The pujari in the dark sanctum sanctorum of mandir circulated the *deepa* from head to foot while chanting mantras or singing a prayer. Gradually the practice developed into *ārati*. When the *ārati* is over it is circulated among devotees who cup their down-turned hands over the flame and raise their palms to touch them to their eyes and head. This helps the devotees to absorb and be blessed with the sacred light of the *deepas*. *Ārati* is performed not only in mandirs and home shrines but also after a religious ceremony or prior to or after a spiritual discourse. In *shikharabaddha* Vaishnava mandirs (big pinnacled temples) there is a tradition of performing *āratis* five times[2] every day, whereas in *hari* mandirs (small temples) or home mandirs it is done twice daily, in the morning and evening.

6. DANDAVAT PRANĀMA

Dandavat pranāma is a gesture of reverence to the deity or spiritual guru in which a devotee prostrates on the ground. *Dandavat* means "like a stick lying on the ground."

Shāstānga dandavat means prostration, in which eight parts of the body touch the floor:

Oorasā shirasā dhrustyā manasā vachasā tathā padabhyām
karābhyām jānubhyām pranāmo-shtāngam muchyate.

- Āhanik Sutrāvali

The eight parts are chest, head, eyes, mind, speech (mouth), feet, hands and thighs. The reason why eight parts should touch the floor is that a person performs all activities with body,

Panchānga pranāma

---

2. Five-time *āratis* performed in most mandirs are *mangalā* (early morning at 6.00 am or earlier), *shanagāra* (between 7.00 am and 7.30 am), *rājabhoga* (around 11.15 am), *sandhyā* (time of sunset) and *shayāna* (between 8.00 and 8.15 pm.)

Dandavat pranāma or prostration is a gesture of reverence to the deity in which eight parts of the body touch the ground

mind and speech, therefore all the three should be offered or surrendered to God. Only males perform *shashtānga dandavat pranāma*.

Panchānga pranāma is a gesture of offering respect in which five parts of the body touch the ground, namely, head, hands, feet, mind and speech. Males offer *ashtānga* or *panchānga pranāma* to the *murti* of God, parents, seniors and sadhus. Females offer only *panchānga pranāma* to God and parents.

The ritual of *pranāma* is a gesture of reverence and humility. It's daily practise dissolves one's ego.

7. PRADAKSHINĀ

The practice of circumambulating around the deity, mandir, sacred mountain, lake or river is called *pradakshinā*. It is performed to show respect to the deity and to absorb the divine vibrations of the deity or holy place. The devotee performs *pradakshinā* after having darshan of the deity or sacred site. While so doing he or she chants God's holy name and remembers him. The devotee also performs *pradakshinā* while doing daily puja at home.

The ritual of *pradakshinā* helps consolidate and realize God to be the centre of one's activities.

Pradakshinā means circumambulating a shrine or deity with reverence

Naivedyam is the ritual offering of food and drink to the deity

8. NAIVEDYAM

Naivedyam is a bhakti ritual in which a devotee offers food to the *murti* of God. It is done to express appreciation to God as the provider and sustainer and to sanctify the food.

While visiting mandirs, devotees partake of the *prasāda* – food offered to the deities – and feel blessed. In addition, in their home shrines, devotees offer their breakfast, meals or whatever they eat or drink to the deities first. When the breakfast or meal is placed in the home mandir the *thālas* (songs supplicating the Lord to accept the offering) are sung by members of the family.

The annual *annakuta* offering of thousands of vegetarian food items to the deities in mandirs on the Hindu New Year's Day is an overwhelming experience of dedication and bhakti. There have been many occasions when the deities have eaten the offered food items.

9. NĀMA JAPA

Repeating God's name (mantra *japa*) aloud or in one's mind is both a sadhana and a religious ritual. It is called *nāma japa.*

There is an innate tendency for the mind to dwell upon worldly objects. As a result, the meditation or concentration on anything divine becomes extremely difficult. The moment

Repeating God's name is called nāma japa

one closes one's eyes to meditate upon God, the mind becomes filled with worldly thoughts. To provide an inward focus, our ancient rishis had created certain mantras or holy syllables whose vibrations have the power to create an ambience that enables one to concentrate and meditate. The mantras or holy names of God are chanted repetitively *(japa)* to purify one's mind and surroundings.

It is believed that mantras and their sounds contain an image of the deity they represent. When chanted, they produce images of the respective deities. So a Rāma mantra will produce an image of Rāma within the consciousness of one who chants it. But initially, the image will form only for the time that the person chants the mantra. Later on, as the impressions of the mantra become implanted within one's consciousness, the image of the deity remains for longer periods and then one reaches a point where the deity actually becomes present forever *(sākshātkār)*.

Japa should be done after completing one's ablutions and in a clean, quiet place. It is mainly done with the aid of a *mālā*. The devotee turns the *mālā* with his or her thumb chanting God's name loudly or silently in the mind. One must try to keep one's body as still as possible during the ritual.

A mālā with 108 beads

Nāma japa is the easiest and surest way to purify and elevate

Hinduism

The fire ritual (yajna) is performed to please God and acquire worldly happiness

the mind, and relieve oneself from worries and tensions. It creates divine vibrations within and without and is believed to increase one's concentration. It is done while performing one's morning puja, in mandirs, in holy pilgrim places or anywhere and at any time. The ritual should be performed with the remembrance of the deity in one's mind.

Nāma japa is the most important means in the Gaudiya Vaishnavism of Mahāprabhu Chaitanya and the Vārkari Sampradāya of Maharashtra, whose devotees spend hours singing aloud bhajans and the name of Vitthala or Vithobā.

In the Vibhuti Yoga chapter of the Bhagavad Gitā (10.25), Bhagwan Krishna states, *"Yajnānām japa yajno'smi"*. It means, "Among the *yajnas* (fire sacrifices), I am the chanting of the holy names."

10. YAJNA

The word *yajna* is derived from the Sanskrit root word *'yaj'*, which means to 'give'. *Yajna* is generally translated as sacrifice or offerings in which one offers the best objects to God.

There are two scriptural sources of *yajna* rituals – Vedas and Āgamas. The early Vedic era placed great importance on *yajna* (fire ritual) as a means to appease the devas and earn their favour. The Āgamic rituals are mainly related to fire rituals performed to please deities in *murti* form in mandirs and elsewhere. Basically, according to the Vedas and Āgamas, *yajnas* are performed to gain worldly prosperity, fame, good health, progeny and liberation.

In the Bhagavad Gitā, Bhagwan Krishna describes the system of 'giving' as the *yajna chakra* (cycle):

Annād bhavanti bhutāni parjanyād annasambhavaha,
Yagnād bhavati parjanyo yagnaha karma samudbhavaha.[3]

"Through food life forms come into existence, through rain food is formed; through *yajna* there is rain and the *yajna* is produced through karma (effort)."

The life cycle mentioned by Shri Krishna in the Bhagavad Gitā is called the *yajna bhāvnā*. In it each element produces or nourishes the other. This concept of sacrifice is also found in nature's food cycle and the oxygen and water cycles in our ecosystem.

The *yajnas* prescribed by the Vedas include the offering of grains and ghee in the sacrificial fire or altar *(vedi)*. The fire is the medium that conveys the sentiments and prayers of the aspirants to the devas in *swarga*. However with time the Brahmin priests started sacrificing animals to appease the devas. They interpreted the popular Vedic verse, *ajena yajeta*, in which *aja* means both barley and goat, by sacrificing goats and other animals and then cooked them to eat it as *prāsada*.

The Mahābhārata ratifies the tradition of non-violent *yajnas*, "Yajnas should be performed with seeds – this is the Vedic tradition. *Aja* is barley seed. Therefore it is not proper to slaughter goats. Wherever there is animal slaughter in *yajnas*, it is not the way of righteous men."[4]

The Mahābhārata instructs, "*Na hinsyāt sarvabhutāni...*" – "Do not kill any living creature."[5]

A yajna vedi or altar

---

3. B.G. 3.14.
4. Shānti Parva 324. 4-5; 337. 4-5.
5. Vana Parva 213. 34.

FIVE TYPES OF YAJNAS

The five principal kinds of *yajnas* to be performed by householders in accordance to the shastras are: 1. *Deva-yajna*, 2. *Rishi* or *Brahma-yajna*, 3. *Pitru-yajna*, 4. *Manushya-yajna* and 5. *Bhuta-yajna*. The *runa* (obligation) mentioned in Chapter 3 is similar to that of the five types of *yajnas* explained below.

1. Deva-yajna

The devas sustain and nourish all life on earth. They are Varuna (water-god), Agni (fire-god), Surya (sun-god), Chandra (moon-god), Prithvi (goddess earth) and others. Man performs *deva-yajna* through chanting of appropriate mantras and offerings of ghee and grains in the *yajna* fire to appease the devas and to appreciate them for their contributions to the welfare of mankind and all living things.

2. Rishi or Brahma-yajna

The objective of performing this *yajna* is to repay one's debt to the rishi or guru who imparts knowledge during one's stay as a student in the *gurukula*. It is also performed to attain *moksha*. The *Brahma-yajna* involves the disengagement of the ten senses and mind from material pleasures to focus on God. It is done by meditating on God, listening to spiritual discourses, having darshan of God, reading the shastras, partaking of food that has been offered to God, and by contemplating on and praying to God.

Deva Yajna: Rituals to appease the devas

3. Pitru-yajna

Pitrus mean one's forefathers or ancestors. They are believed to live in a higher realm as one's guardians or custodians. *Pitru-yajnas* are performed to appease them and to fulfil the debt one owes to them for one's birth and existence. Householders daily pray for the happiness and *moksha* of their ancestors. During the 15-day *shrāddha* period in Bhādrapada (October) they

Rishi Yajna: Prayer, meditation and other spiritual endeavours

offer special rituals, prayers and a meal of *khir* (cooked rice in sweet, thick milk), *puri* and other food items to Brahmins, cows, crows, pigeons, etc. They believe that their forefathers come and accept their offerings through them. Subsequently, the ancestors shower their pleasure and blessings upon them for progress and happiness.

4. Manushya-yajna

This is a sacrifice performed to fulfil one's debt to humanity. It includes all acts of charity and donation for serving and loving others in order to rid of one's ego, greed, cruelty, violence, anger and other base instincts. *Manushya-yajna* also includes serving the poor, sick and needy. It should be done selflessly, and without harbouring any desire for fame, name or returns. The only sentiment one should have is to please God through serving humanity or Daridranārāyana (Nārāyana in the form of poor and helpless people).

5. Bhuta-yajna

This sacrifice expresses thanks to the contributions of all life forms (*bhutas*) to humanity. Every living organism contributes to the development and nourishment of life on earth. The intricate web of life is connected with and interdependent on all its members. Man's existence is dependent on other life forms, so he should not destroy or upset the fragile and dynamic balance in our ecosystem. Instead, he should conserve and help nourish all life forms. Since Vedic times the rishis of India have been chanting prayers (*shānti pātha*) for peace and harmony in all life forms. A vegetarian diet is important as a mark of respect and preservation of animals. Hindus also generally serve a portion of their meals daily to nourish animals.

CONCLUSION

The heart of the *yajna* rituals lies in selfless sacrifice and

Pitru Yajna: Rituals to fulfil the debt to one's ancestors

Manushya Yajna: Serving the poor, sick and needy

Bhuta Yajna: Service to animals

offering of gifts and food to God, devas, *rishis,* forefathers, teachers, birds, animals and all those who are in need. What is important during the sacrifice are the sentiments of detachment and selflessness expressed through the mantra *idam na mama* (this is not mine). Hinduism has a living *yajna* tradition that seeks to preserve, serve and foster all life forms.

When a devotee performs the rituals of *pranāma,* puja, *mahāpujā,* darshan, *ārati, dandavat pranāma, pradakshinā, naivedyam, nāmā japa* and *yajna* with the sole aim of pleasing God, then these acts are transformed into bhakti. And these seemingly small acts of devotion to God liberate the devotee from his or her mundane attachments and tendencies. The devotional rituals are in fact a spiritual practice which uproot an aspirant's desires for mundane things and join him or her to the divine form of God.

SUMMARY

1. In ancient times the mandir was generally the centre of the village and town. The devotional rituals associated with the mandir played an important role in integrating spiritual faith in the lives of people.

2. The various rituals that engage people in worship and devotion are *pranāma,* puja, *mahāpujā,* darshan, *ārati, dandavat pranāma, pradakshinā, naivedyam, nāma japa* and *yajna.* The five types of *yajna* are:

   i. *Deva-yajna*: Performing *yajnas* by offering grains in a sacred fire to appreciate and please the devas.

   ii. *Rishi* or *Brahma-yajna*: Focusing the ten senses and mind on God through meditation and reading of shastras, darshan, listening to spiritual discourses, etc.

   iii. *Pitru-yajna*: Pleasing one's ancestors through *yajna, tarpana,* and *shrāddha* ceremonies.

   iv. *Manushya-yajna*: Serving mankind selflessly.

   v. *Bhuta-yajna*: Caring for and nourishing all life forms.

16

Sacred Symbols and Objects

The auspicious pot, coconuts, wheat grains, betel leaves and nuts on a bājoth (wooden platform) for a ritual ceremony. (Inset) Deepa, symbol of knowledge and enlightenment

Aum, Swastika, Shālagrāma, Shivalinga, Deepa, Purna Kalasha, Shankha...

INTRODUCTION

The human mind and senses cannot perceive the Infinite or God directly, but they can grasp what is concrete, finite or tangible. This is why it becomes easy to see or think of God through any of his physical forms and symbols (*pratikas*). The Shālagrāma and Shivalinga, which are the forms of Nārāyana and Shiva respectively, are worshipped by Hindus. Many other symbols used in worship and prayer draw the mind away from material objects and direct it towards God. Hinduism has many sacred symbols and *murtis* of deities that inspire the transformation and elevation of the human mind. For example, the simple *tilaka* or *chandraka* applied on the forehead by men and women is not only a mark of their religious affiliation, but it also helps them develop self-awareness that they are devotees of God, and must therefore abide by his moral and spiritual commands. Furthermore, it is also a personal reminder that one must see the world not only with one's physical eyes, but with the mind's eye, the third eye, the eye of the soul.

There are also many gestures and symbols that have both religious and social significance like namaste, Aum and *swastika*. All these and others ultimately proclaim the core of the individual – the resident God within.

1. AUM OR OM (First Sound and Form of God)

Aum, also written as Om, is also called *pranava*. It is the cosmic sound of the creator. Hindus believe it to be the first mantra and sound from which creation issued forth. It is the monosyllabic form of God. It is made up of the letters A (phonetically as in 'around'), u (as in 'put') and m (as in 'mum'). The three letters stand for the three states of consciousness, namely, A for waking, 'u' for dream and 'm' for deep sleep, and according to the Māndukya Upanishad chanting Aum as a whole makes one conscious of the fourth or *turiyā* state (God-realization). Aum also represents the three main devas (Brahmā, Vishnu and Shiva), three Vedas (Rig, Yajur and Sāma) and the three worlds (Pruthviloka, Devaloka and Pātālaloka). Aum is the divine sound and therefore pervades all life. It is considered to be the mystical syllable containing the entire Universe.

Aum is chanted as a prayer and for an auspicious beginning in all tasks.[1] It is also used to conclude an act of worship, a religious work or an important task.

2. SWASTIKA (Symbol of Auspiciousness)

It is a symbol of auspiciousness and knowledge, representing the sun. It is a graphic representation of the sun's rays, energy and munificence spreading in all four directions. The word *swastika* means 'all well'. It is derived from the Sanskrit word '*swasti*' which means 'let there be goodness everywhere'. The symbol epitomizes continuous motion, meaning progress. It also represents the world-wheel, the eternally changing world around a fixed, unchanging centre or God.

The four vertical right-angled arms denote four directions; the four Vedas; the four varnas; the four ashramas and the four human aims or *purushārthas*, namely, dharma (righteousness), *artha* (wealth), *kāma* (desires) and *moksha* (liberation). The *swastika* is a revered symbol of auspiciousness in Sanātana Dharma. It is also a symbol of the *mulādhara chakra,* one of the centres of consciousness at the base of the spine.

Hindus use the auspicious *swastika* symbol to get all-round

Aum is the cosmic sound of the creator. It is the first mantra and sound after creation

Swastika is a Hindu symbol of auspiciousness and knowledge

1. B.G. 17.23-24.

prosperity by drawing it on the entrance doors, thresholds, opening pages of account books, invitation cards, and social and religious functions. No ceremony is complete without the *swastika*. It is also believed to have the power to destroy negative forces and misfortune. Finally, it must not be confused with the Nazi Swastika, which was represented in a tilted manner and came to acquire a sinister meaning altogether.

3. SHĀLAGRĀMA (A Form of Bhagwan Vishnu)

It is a sacred oval-shaped black stone that is worshipped as an aniconic form of Bhagwan Vishnu. The *shālagrāma* is found in abundance on the banks of and in the River Gandaki in Nepal. Generally, it has a golden streak inside its cavity. Vaishnava devotees worship the *shālagrāma* by bathing it in milk, curds, honey and saffron water, then offer clothes and food to it. Worship of *shālagrāma* is praised profusely in the Pāncharātra Āgamas.

The *murtis* of Nārāyana at the Badarinātha Mandir and that of Shri Krishna at Udupi (Karnataka) are said to be carved out of the *shālagrāma* stone. Unlike *murtis* made of other stones wherein the presence of God has to be invoked through elaborate consecration ceremonies called *prāna-pratishthā*, *shālagrāmas* have His presence eternally by their very nature. They are believed to possess an inherently divine power *(sahajavibhuti)*.

The shālagrāma is a form of Bhagwan Vishnu

4. SHIVALINGA (A Form of Bhagwan Shiva)

The Shivalinga is generally an elliptical aniconic black stone that represents Bhagwan Shiva. Literally, Shiva means 'auspiciousness' and *linga* means an 'emblem', therefore Shivalinga means 'emblem of auspiciousness'. There are two types of *lingas* – natural and man-made – and *chala* (moveable) and *achala* (immovable). The *linga* is in two parts: the pedestal *(pitha)* and the *linga* proper. The base of the Shivalinga is called

Bhagwan Shiva is worshipped as a Shivalinga

the Brahmabhāga which refers to Brahmā, the creator, the middle part is known as Vishnubhāga which represents Vishnu, the sustainer, and the uppermost portion is called Rudrabhāga representing Shiva, the destroyer. It is this uppermost cylindrical portion that is visible and worshipped. Therefore it is called *pujābhāga*. Sometimes the face of Shiva is carved on the *pujābhāga*. Such a *linga* is called Ishwaralinga. But if the whole figure of Shiva is carved then it is known as Rudralinga. Shaiva devotees worship the Shivalinga by performing *abhisheka* (ceremonial pouring) of water or milk and offering of *bilva* leaves. The twelve *jyotirlingas* of Shiva in India are believed to have come into existence without human agency or intervention. A Shaiva Sampradāya, called Lingāyata or Virāshaivism, insists that all its members wear a small Shivalinga on their body to remind them of their innate Shiva-like nature.

5. DEEPA (Lamp)

Light symbolizes knowledge and enlightenment. The *deepa (diyā)* is a symbol of divine light. All worship rituals or auspicious beginnings commence by igniting a *deepa*.

Philosophically the oil or ghee in the *deepa* represents the material desires *(vāsanās)* and the wick the ego. When lit by the light of spiritual knowledge the *vāsanās* become extinct and the ego perishes.

Every Hindu aspires for the divine light of knowledge and freedom from the darkness of ignorance. This is reflected in a popular Vedic and Upanishadic prayer, *Tamaso mā jyotir gamaya...*[2] which means "Lead me from darkness to light."

The deepa (diyā) is a symbol of God's divine light

6. PURNA KALASHA (Auspicious Potful of Water)

A husked coconut circled with mango or *āsopālava* leaves placed on a pot filled with holy water is called a *purna kalasha*. It is a symbol of perfection and auspiciousness. Through

Purna kalasha is a symbol of perfection and auspiciousness

2. Shatapatha Brāhmana 14.4.1.30-31; Bruhadāranyaka Upanishad 1.3.30-31.

chanting of Vedic and Paurānik mantras the holy rivers and the god of water, Varunadeva, are invoked into the pot of water. The sacred water from the pot is then sprinkled in all directions and on the devotees for sanctification, prosperity and peace.

The *kalasha* is used during religious worship, in *yajnas,* weddings, inaugural functions and sanctification rituals of a building or land. It is placed near the home entrance as a sign of welcome, and held in one's hand while receiving holy persons. The ceremonial *kalasha* is a replica of the Amruta Kalasha and therefore it also symbolizes immortality – the Amruta Kalasha was brought by Sage Dhanvantari during the churning of the ocean *(samudra manthana)*.

A *kalasha* is either made of gold, silver, copper or even clay. While performing rituals it should be filled with water. Other things that may be put inside it are precious stones, flowers and herbs. Brahmā, Shiva, Vishnu and Devi are believed to reside in the *kalasha's* mouth, neck, bottom and middle respectively.

7. SHANKHA (Conch)

The conch or *shankha* is a product of Varunadeva (the ocean-god). It is one of the common objects in the hands of *murtis* of many Hindu deities, especially those associated with Vishnu, and sometimes with the Devi. The conch is placed at the feet of God's *murti* in mandirs as a symbol of *nāda* Brahma or Aum, dharma, victory and auspiciousness. The sonorous sound of the *shankha* or conch is made to honour and please the Lord. It is also a victory call of good over evil. The sound of the conch elevates people's minds to a prayerful attitude. It is often filled with water or milk and used in ritualistic worship of the deities.

The *shankha* is held to be extremely important, like the Sudarshan Chakra, in Shri Vaishnavism. The famous *shankha* of Bhagwan Krishna in the Gitā is called Pānchajanya.

The sound of shankha or conch honours and pleases the deities

8. GHANTĀ (Bell)

The ringing sound of the *ghantā* or bell is considered auspicious because it is associated with mandir and worship rituals like *ārati*, puja and *mahāpujā*. The *ghantā*, generally made of bronze, is always used in ritualistic worship. The sound of the bell is considered to be *pranava* or Omkāra. The body of the bell represents Ananta (god of time), the tongue symbolizes Sarasvati (goddess of speech) and the handle signifies *prāna-shakti* or the energy of prana (vital breath). The top of the handle is usually adorned with images of Hanumān, Garuda, Nandi (the bull-mount of Shiva), *chakra* (disc) or *trishula* (trident).

The bell is rung during worship as an invitation for the deities to come, especially during the *ārati* ceremony, and dispel evil spirits. The sound of the bell is also believed to awaken the power of the mantras chanted during worship rituals. Hence it is called *mantramātā* or mother of mantras.

The pujari or a devotee rings the bell prior to having darshan of or offering prayer to the deity and during the ritual *ārati*.

It is the usual practice to hang a bell or a few bells in a mandir or in front of the main shrine. The ringing of bells in a mandir is a call to prayer. The ringing sound facilitates the senses and the mind to focus on God, and it also drowns away irrelevant noises and other sounds.

The sound of ghantā or bell is considered auspicious

The lotus symbolizes beauty, truth and auspiciousness

9. PADMA (Lotus)

The *padma* or lotus symbolizes truth, auspiciousness and beauty *(Satyam, Shivam* and *Sundaram)*, which are the essential virtues of God. Also, many parts of his body are compared to the lotus: lotus eyes, lotus feet, lotus hands and the lotus of the heart. Furthermore its sacredness is associated with the fact that the lotus rose from the navel of Vishnu and is the seat of Brahmā, the creator, Mahālakshmi and Sarasvati.

The lotus, though born and rooted in mud, blossoms unaffected by it. Similarly, a person may be born in a low caste, but like a lotus he or she can blossom beautifully in character through his or her own good actions, like Viduraji and Shabari. The lotus also symbolizes a person of wisdom or enlightenment, who is untainted by the mud and muck of base instincts. Many Indian deities are closely connected with the lotus: Bhagwan Vishnu holds a lotus in his hand, his consort Lakshami is seated on a lotus; and Bhagwan Shiva is worshipped by offering lotus flowers. There are many colours of lotus, i.e., white, red and blue, that suggest many splendours of the Divine.

Kundalini Yoga describes that our body has energy centres *(chakras)*, and that each one has a lotus with different numbers of petals. The Sahasrāra Chakra at the top of the skull has a 1,000-petalled lotus which opens when the yogi realizes God.

10. TILAKA AND CHANDRAKA (Holy Marks)

The *tilaka* and *chandraka (chāndlo)* are symbols of one's affiliation to a specific Hindu tradition or organization. Vaishnava worshippers apply a U-shaped *(urdhvapundra)* white or yellow *tilaka* of *chandana* with a streak of *chandana* or kumkum or a round-shaped red *chandraka* in the middle of the forehead. Shaiva worshippers apply three horizontal streaks of holy ash on their forehead.

The devout also apply the *tilaka* and *chandraka* on his or her arms, chest and other parts of the body while chanting the various names of God. The U-shaped *urdhvapundra* represents the holy feet of God and the *chandraka* the ideal devotee of God. The *chandraka* also symbolizes a devotee's fidelity to God. The application of both the *tilaka* and *chandraka* gives a devotee feelings of sanctity, connectivity and allegiance to God. When marked on the forehead of the deity it may signify the power of that deity to uplift the devotees spiritually. And when applied on the forehead of devotees it reminds them of the need to take a spiritually upward path.

The tilaka and chandraka denote a Vaishnava devotee of the Rāmānanda Sampradāya

Shiva worshippers apply a *tripundra* (three horizontal markings) of *bhasma* or holy ash and Devi worshippers apply only a red *chandraka* of kumkum.

The *tilaka* covers the area between the eyebrows, which is the seat of memory and thinking (the *ājnā chakra*) in yoga. Applying the *tilaka* and *chandraka* daily restrains one from wrong action and protects one from bad influences.

11. BHASMA (Holy Ash)

Bhasma or holy ash is generally applied by some devotees on their forehead, and some ascetics rub it all over their body. *Bhasma* is the ash from the *homa* (ritual fire), in which special wood along with ghee and other herbs have been offered in a *yajna*. Fire is believed to reduce all substances to their primal state of purity. *Bhasma* therefore purifies the body. The application of *bhasma* signifies destruction of evil and remembrance of the Divine. *Bhasma* is believed to give glory and protection to one who applies it.

Bhasma is especially associated with Bhagwan Shiva and Shakti. Bhagwan Shiva applies it all over his body, signifying renunciation and total eradication of ego.

12. JAPAMĀLĀ (Rosary)

A *japamālā* or *mālā* (rosary) is used in chanting (*japa*) God's name. It generally consists of 108 beads, made of *rudrāksha* or tulsi or *bilva* wood. The *mālā* is used by placing it on the middle finger of the right hand, and turning the beads in a clockwise direction with the thumb. The forefinger or index finger is kept away from the *mālā*. The *mālā* is usually turned in a cloth-bag. When it is turned without the cloth-bag, care is taken that it does not touch the ground in order to preserve its sanctity.

One may wonder why a *mālā* has 108 beads. The Hindu shastras instruct that one should chant God's name all day

A devotee of Shiva with holy ash on his forehead

Mālā (rosary), used in chanting God's name

together with each breath. So, if we consider twelve hours for the waking state, a person breathes 15 times every minute and 900 times in one hour. For twelve hours of the day one breathes 10,800 times. So in 24 hours a person breathes 21,600 times (Chudāmani Upanishad 32-33). Because it is not possible to chant a mantra with each breath, the shastras state that the fruit of chanting it with each bead of a *mālā* will be 100 times more. So, after chanting 108 beads of a *mālā* it all adds up to 10,800 – which is equal to the number of times one breathes in 12 hours.

Another reason for having 108 beads in a *mālā* is that it is related to the number of configurations of stars in the universe. The ancient rishis divided the sun's motion into 27 *nakshatras* or constellations (a group of stars). Each *nakshatra* has four sub-sections called *charans* (parts). So the 27 *nakshatras* have 108 *charans* altogether. Therefore the number of beads in a *mālā* are 108. Where the two ends of the *nakshatras* meet, that region of the cosmos is called "Mount Sumeru". Similarly, the largest bead that joins the two ends of the *mālā* is called the *sumeru*. While turning the *mālā* one should not cross the *sumeru*, but reverse the direction and resume chanting.

13. KANKANA-SUTRA-BANDHANAM (Auspicious Thread)

As part of any religious or auspicious occasion a *kankana-sutra-bandhanam* or a string of red and yellow cotton thread is tied on the wrist of a participant or guest. It symbolizes a divine promise of protection and freedom from obstacles. The priest sings the mantra of *kankana bandhanam* that says, "O Lord, protect him (the host) from obstacles and guard him from evil influences. Grant him long life and bless him with the fruits of good deeds." The *kankana-sutra* is also tied for the same purpose by a mother or sister to her son or brother respectively.

Tying a nādā chhadi protects one from obstacles and evil influences

14. UPAVITA (Sacred Thread)

Upavita or sacred thread is invested to a Brahmin, Kshatriya and Vaishya child at the age of eight, eleven and twelve respectively. The *upavita* ceremony, called *upanayana*, is one of the 16 sacraments performed in the life of a Hindu boy. After receiving the *upavita* the child becomes a student and eligible to go to the *gurukula* to study and receive spiritual and temporal knowledge from the guru. During his period of study he observes *brahmacharya* or celibacy.

The *upavita* is worn from the left shoulder to the right waist. It has three cotton threads tied together. The three threads represent Gāyatri (goddess of mind), Sarasvati (goddess of wisdom) and Sāvitri (goddess of virtues). Also, one who wears the *upavita* is reminded to be pure in thought, word and action. The three threads further signify the debt one owes to the guru, parents and society. The three strings are tied by a knot, which represents God – who is the creator, sustainer and destroyer. When one gets married one wears an *upavita* with six threads – the three more strings are on behalf of one's wife.

Darshanam

Sacred Thread Ceremony: After this ritual the child becomes a student

Dhvaja or flag is a common feature of Hindu mandirs

15. DHVAJA (Flag)

Dhvaja is a flag or a banner fixed on a post or *dhvaja-danda*. It is a common feature of Hindu mandirs. The *dhvaja* is either made of a metallic plate, (i.e., copper or brass) or of cloth. The metallic *dhvaja* is attached to a staff placed in front of the *garbha-gruha* or in the compound before the mandir. The metallic flag is engraved with the figure of the *vāhana* (carrier mount) of the presiding deity in the mandir. For example, a Vishnu mandir will have the figure of Garuda (eagle) engraved on its *dhvaja,* in the case of a Shiva mandir one will find a bull on its banner and if it is a Devi mandir one will find the figure of a lion.

The *dhvajas* made of cloth flutter on top of the *shikharas* or pinnacles. The orange, red or white *dhvajas*, or a combination of the three colours, flutter from the flagstaffs of mandirs, and during festivals. They symbolize peace, sacrifice and victory of dharma. They also symbolize the presence of the Divine.

The sannyasis of some Hindu *sampradāyas* also carry a *dhvaja* on their staffs as a symbol of their tradition and designation.

17. NAMASKAR

The traditional Hindu form of namaskar is a gesture of friendship, respect and reverence. Hindus join their two palms together, placing them by the heart, and bow their heads while saying namaste, namaskar or *pranāma*, which means "We bow down to you."

When a person greets another with namaskar it means may our minds meet like the folded palms placed before the heart. Bowing of the head is a gracious gesture that symbolizes respect, friendship and humility.

The spiritual meaning reflects the sentiment that God residing in the other person is the same God within oneself. Therefore, namaskar is a symbolic recognition and gesture of reverence and humility to the Divine in the person one meets. That is why one usually closes one's eyes while offering namaskar to a holy person or deity, as if to look within. The gesture is often accompanied by saying Jai Shri Krishna, Jai Siyā Ramā or Jai Swaminarayan.

CONCLUSION

Hinduism has a wide array of sacred symbols and sacred objects that are applied or used during a religious ritual, celebration or in mandirs. Only a few of them were elaborated upon in this chapter. Some of them are specific to any one *sampradāya,* while others are applicable to all. However, in general they all enhance the spiritual consciousness of the devotee. The sacred symbols and objects also protect the devotee from evil and negative influences and actions. Their

Namaskar is a traditional mode of greeting or showing reverence

profound meaning and power to imbue devotees with spiritual faith reflects upon their importance and value in Hinduism.

SUMMARY

1. The human senses and mind cannot perceive the divine form of God directly. They require a concrete, finite or tangible form. *Pratikas* or symbols in Hinduism represent the Divine. The sacred symbols and *murtis* of deities help in transforming and elevating the human consciousness and the soul.

2. Some of the many sacred symbols and objects in Hinduism include Aum, Swastika, Shālagrāma, Shivalinga, Deepa, Ārati, Purna Kalasha, Conch and many others.

3. In some cases the sacred symbols reflect the *sampradāya* to which one belongs to, but in general they increase spiritual awareness and protect the devotee from evil influences and actions.

GLOSSARY

A

abhangas	bhajans composed by saint-poets of Maharashtra
abhayamudrā	hand posture of deity, promising protection
abhisheka	a ritual pouring of water on *murti* of a deity for worship
āchāra	code of conduct
Achintyabhedābheda	philosophy of Inconceivable Difference and Non-Difference
achit	non-sentient
adharma	unrighteousness
ādhibhautika	one of three types of miseries faced by man, inflicted by living beings and humans
ādhidaivika	one of three types of miseries faced by man, due to natural forces controlled by devas
adhika-māsa	intercalated month. The twelve lunar months of the Hindu year fall short of the solar year by about eleven days. In order to synchronize the lunar year as closely as possible with the solar year and the cycle of the seasons, one lunar month is added every two-and-a-half years. This extra month is called Adhika *māsa* or Purushottama *māsa*
adhikāra	spiritual eligibility
adhikāri	competent person
adhvaryu	special priest of Yajur Veda
ādhyātamika	one of three types of miseries faced by man, due to one's mind
ādikāvya	first poem, namely the Rāmayana
Advaita	'non-dual'. The monotheistic doctrine propounded prominently by Shankarāchārya which states that the Ultimate Reality is only one (i.e., 'non-dual') principal substance – *nirgun* Brahma – and that all else is merely an illusion.
advaitic	related to Advaita
agni	fire
agni deva	the fire-god
ahamkāra	1. ego, one of the four aspects of the *antahkaran* characterized by its function of giving rise to the sense of self. 2. On a cosmic level, a product of Mahattattva.
ājnā chakra	one of six subtle centres of consciousness in yoga situated in the middle of the eyebrows. It is a seat of memory and thinking
ākāsha	space
akrodha	absence of anger
akshamālā	rosary with 108 beads in the hand of a deity
Ālvārs	twelve god-immersed saint-poets of south India, who lived between the sixth and ninth century CE

āmalaka	stone ring on mandir *shikhar* or pinnacle
amāvāsya	'no-moon' day signifying the last day of a lunar month, i.e., the 15th day of the dark half of an Indian calendar month. New moon
amruta	'without death'. The nectar churned from the ocean by the deities and the demons, known to grant immortality to those who drink it
amsha	parts
amshāvatāra	partial incarnation
anāhata chakra	one of six subtle centres of consciousness described in yoga. Located in the heart, it is a centre that controls the sense of touch and the genitals
andaja	'born from egg'. Category of life forms born from eggs, i.e., all birds, reptiles, etc
ankusha	a small sharp weapon to control an elephant. To restrain
annakuta	offering of many food items before the *murti* of God
antaryāmi	'inner knower'. Power of God to reside within *jiva, ishwara* and Brahman
antaryāmin	inner controller – Paramātmā
antyeshti	death rites
Anubhāshya	Vallabhāchārya's commentary on the Brahmasutras
anugraha murti	image of deity in a blessing form
anumāna	inference
anupalabdhi	non-perception
aparā	mundane
aparigraha	non-possession
apaurusheya	not man-made (normally referring to Vedas)
apavarga	concept of *moksha* in Vaisheshika and Nyāya Darshanas. It is a state of freedom from all pain and suffering
āptavākyas	words of a spiritually enlightened person
ārati	Hindu ritual of waving lighted wicks before the *murti* of God as an act of worship
archā	ritual of smearing a *murti* with sandalwood paste
Archajyotisha	a 36-verse book on astrology available from the early sections of the Rig Veda
arghya	offering of water in a ritual
artha	one of the four human endeavours allowing for the fulfilment of desires for material objects, in particular wealth
arthāpatti	'postulation' – one of the basic sources or means of valid knowledge in Hindu philosophy
Arthashāstra	writings dealing with economics and politics. One such work is Kautilya's *Arthashāstra*
asana	yogic postures
ashtachhāpa	eight great poet-devotees of Vallabhāchārya
Ashtādhyāyi	Sanskrit grammar text by Pānini
ashtānga yoga	'eight-limbed yoga'; the eight steps or stages of yoga: *yama* (restraint), *niyama* (observance), asana (seat or posture), pranayama (mastering life force), *pratyāhāra* (withdrawal), *dhāranā* (concentration), dhyana (meditation) and samadhi (contemplation and God-realization)

āsopālava	type of tree whose leaves are used in rituals and on auspicious occasions as decoration
asteya	non-stealing
asthi	charred bones after cremation
āstika	1. 'Believer'. Person who believes in the existence of God, or more generally, one who is religiously inclined. 2. Person or shastra that accept the authority and authenticity of the Vedas
astra	a missile. It is presided over by a particular deva and when invoked it empowers the missile with destructive capability
Atharvajyotisha	a book on astrology from the Vedic period
ātmā	pure soul
ātmabhāva	feeling or experience that one is *ātmā*
ātmabuddhi	intense affection
ātmajnāna	knowledge of one's self as *ātmā*
Avadhutagītā	a famous Advaita Vedānta work attributed to Dattātreya (an avatar of Vishnu)
avatāravāda	one of the fundamental beliefs of Hinduism that God manifests on earth in human and other forms to destroy evil and accept the devotion of devotees
avatāri	the supreme God who is the cause of all divine incarnations
āveshāvatāra	a temporary entry of the Divine, as in Bhagwan Nrusimha
avidyā	synonymous with *māyā*. False understanding of the nature of reality. Ignorance

B

baddha jivas	*jivas* bound to *māyā*
Bhaja Govindam	devotional hymn by Shankarāchārya
bhakta	disciple
Bhaktisutras	aphorisms on bhakti by Nārada and Shāndilya
bhāshya	commentary or intepretation of the Hindu shastras
bhasma	holy ash
bhoga	food offering to Bhagwan
bhukti	worldly success
bhuloka	earth
bhuta-runa	debt to all living beings including birds, animals, etc.
bhuta-yajna	caring for and nourishing all life forms
bhuvarloka	sixth realm in the 14-realm system of a *brahmānda*
bilva	a sacred tree also known as *bel* tree or the wood-apple tree. It is dear to Shiva. The tree is worshipped during Durgāpujā. Its leaves are used in the worship of Shiva and Shakti
brahmachāri	celibate
brahmacharya	practice of eight-fold celibacy and being immersed in Brahman (Paramātmā)
brahmānda	individual 'cosmos' comprising a system of 14 realms, of which there are countless millions on various planes. The 14 realms of each *brahmānda* are, in descending order: Satyaloka, Tapaloka, Janaloka, Maharaloka, Swargaloka, Bhuvaraloka, Mrutyuloka, Atala, Vitala, Sutala, Talātala, Mahātala,

	Rasātala, Pātāla
brahmanishtha	God-realized
brahmarup	form of Brahman (i.e., Aksharbrahman). Possessing qualities similar to those of Brahman
brahmasambandha	a ritual ceremony to become a devotee in the Vallabha Sampradāya where a person gets the mantra of dedication from a guru
brahmavidyā	spiritual knowledge
brahma-yajna	repaying one's debt to the rishi or guru by meditating on God, listening to spiritual discourses, having darshan of God, reading the shastras, partaking of food that has been offered to God, and by contemplating on and praying to God.
buddhi	intellect

C

chakra	a disc which is the weapon of Shri Krishna. According to yoga it is a centre of consciousness in the human body
chakshu	eye
chandana	sandalwood
chandas	prosody
chāndlo/chandraka	auspicious vermilion mark applied on the forehead
charanāmruta	water made holy by washing feet of deity or guru which is drunk by devotees
chit	consciousness
chopāi	verses in a shastra that are mostly sung, like in Rāmāyana

D

Daivata Kānda	book that explains names of deities
dakshinā	donation given to Brahmins at the end of a religious ceremony
damaru	small hand-held drum of Shiva
dāna	donation in cash or kind
danda	form of punishment
dandavat	prostration
dāndiyā rāsa	traditional stick dance of Gujarat
darshan	seeing God and the God-realized Sadhu with reverence and devotion
darshana	philosophical system
dāsa	servant of God
dāsa bhāva	feeling of servitude
dashāvatara	ten principal incarnations of Bhagwan Vishnu
dāsya	devotion as a servant
dayā	compassion
deepa	a traditional Indian lighted lamp
dehabhāva	attachment to the physical body. Misidentification of one's self with the body
devālaya	mandir
deva-runa	debt to devas (gods)
devatā	deva

deva-yajna	fire sacrifice to appease the devas
dhāma	abode of God
Dhanvantari Nighantu	ayurvedic text
dhāranā	sixth step of *ashtānga* yoga that involves practice of concentrating one's mind on God
dharma	righteousness, responsibility, duty
dhvaja	flag
dhvaja-danda	staff for flag on mandir *shikhara*
dhvajasthambha	tall flag post in mandir premises
dik	eight quarters or directions. Each direction is protected by a deity *(dikpāla)*
dikshā	initiation
dipastambha	lamp post in a mandir
divya	divine
divya dampati	divine couple
Divya Prabandham	'divine compositions'. Songs written in Tamil by the Ālvārs, sung during worship of the deity in Shri Vaishnava mandirs
diyā	see *deepa*
drashtās	seers of truth. Sometimes also refers to God as the observer within each *ātmā*
dravya	substance
dukha	existence of suffering in this world
Dvaita	'dual'. Philosophical doctrine propounding the eternally distinct natures of the *jiva* and God, as opposed to the monistic doctrine of the Advaita school propounding their non-duality
dvipa	island, or a landmass resembling an island
dwāra	gateway
E	
ekāntika dharma	dharma or religion that comprises four aspects, namely, dharma, *jnāna*, *vairagya* and bhakti
ekantiki bhakti	bhakti combined with dharma, *jnāna* and *vairāgya*. Synonymous with *ekāntika* dharma. See also: *ekāntika* dharma
ekeshwaravāda	belief in one supreme God
G	
gadā	mace
gana	a group of servants or members of Shivaji's army
gandha	smell
gandharva	class of celestial deities whose occupation is music and singing; musicians of heaven
garbā	traditional dance of Gujarat
garbhādhān	one of 16 samskaras in which prayers are offered to God to help the wife conceive a good child
garbha-gruha	the inner shrine of a mandir where the *murtis* are consecrated

gavākshas	windows
ghantā	bell
ghrāna	nose
gopis	women of the cowherd class who were devotees of Shri Krishna
gopuram	ornate entrance gates to mandirs in South India
grantha	a shastra, a text
gruhasthāshrama	the householder stage, one of four stages of life
guna	qualities
gurukula	residential school
guru-shishya	master-disciple
guru-shishya paramparā	master-disciple tradition

H

halāhala	deadly poison that emerged from churning of the ocean
hari mandir	type of temple
hansa	swan
hasta mudra	hand gestures that refer to position of hands of *murtis* of deities
hindolā	swing
homa	ritual fire
hotā	priest of the Rig Veda who recites mantras during fire sacrifice or *yajna* to invoke the devas for receiving the oblations

I

ishtadevatā	one's chosen deity
ishtāpurta	cumulative result of performance of sacrificial rites and good works for others
ishwara	devas or one of the five eternal realities
itihāsa	epics like the Rāmāyana and Mahābhārata

J

jagat	world
jagati	side wall of mandir
jal	water
jaltaranga	musical instrument containing water
Janaloka	one of 14 realms of each *brahmānda* or cosmos
japamālā	rosary used for *japa* or repetition of mantra
jarāyuja	born from the womb, i.e., mammals
jhānkhi	momentary *darshan* of deity
jihvā	tongue
jiva	self or soul
jivan mukti	spiritual liberation in this life
jivātmā	see *jiva*
jnāna	knowledge
jnāna-kānda	knowledge section

jnāna-mārga	path of knowledge for *moksha*
Jnāneshvari	Marathi commentary on the Bhagavad Gitā by Sant Jnāneshvar
jnāni	a wise person
jyotirlinga	*linga* (pillar) of light that is symbolic of Shiva. There are twelve *lingas* that are self-manifested and worshipped today
jyotisha	ancient Indian science of astronomy and astrology

K

kaivalya	state of liberation
kāla	time
kalasha	small water-pot made of copper used in rituals
kalpa	the day and night of Brahma, the creator, which amounts to 8,640,000,000 human years
Kalpa	science of sacrificial rites and rituals
kāma	one of the four human endeavours allowing for the regulated fulfilment of one's personal and social desires
kānda	section
kankana-sutra	auspicious thread
kanthi	necklace made of tulsi beads or other wooden material given when a person is initiated into a *sampradāya*
kapha	phlegm
kārana	cause
kārya	effect, generally defined to mean the world
kārya-kārana	effect-cause
kathā	spiritual discourse
kaustubha	jewel
khadaga	sword
khir	cooked rice in sweet, thick milk
kriyā	movement or activity
kriyamāna	karma or action performed every moment
kshirasāgara	ocean of milk
kumbha	pot
kumkum	vermilion powder used for applying *chāndlo*
kundalini shakti	basic power in a human being which is likened to a coiled serpent lying dormant at the *mulādhāra* until it is roused by appropriate yogic exercises

L

lilā	divine actions or play of God
linga	an oval-shaped stone symbolic of Bhagwan Shiva
loka	world, region, realm; usually *triloka* – three worlds – Swargaloka, Mrityuloka, Pātālaloka

M

madhura bhāva	sentiment of intense love
madya	wine
mahāpujā	special worship offered to Bhagwan Swaminarayan, Gunatitanand Swami, *muktas*, incarnations and deities
Maharloka	one of 14 realms of each *brahmānda* or cosmos
maithuna	sexual intercourse
mālā	rosary
mana	mind
mānas putra	Brahma's 'mind-born' children
manavantara	time ruled by one Manu, which is 308 million human years
mandala	book or group
mandapa	hall
manushya-yajna	acts of charity and donation in the form of serving and loving others; performed to fulfil one's debt to humanity
mārga	path
matha	hermitage
matsya	fish
māyā	ignorance, material universe, darkness. One of the five eternal realities. Anything that deviates one from the worship of God
māyā-shakti	God's external power responsible for creation of the material universe
Mimāmsāsutras	book of aphorisms on Mimāmsā philosophy by Sage Jaimini
moha	excessive attraction or attachment to people, relatives and objects
moksha	liberation from *māyā* and cycle of birth and deaths, leading to experience of divine bliss
mrudanga	traditional Indian percussion instrument played to provide rhythm in singing of devotional songs
mrutyuloka	mortal realm or earth. One of 14 realms of each *brahmānda* or cosmos
mudra	hand gesture
mukta	liberated soul
mukti	liberation
mulādhāra chakra	one of six subtle centres of consciousness at the base of the spine. It is the centre that controls the sense organs of smell and the feet
murti	sacred image of God or a deity that is revered and worshipped
murti-pujā	worship of the *murti*

N

nāda	sound
naivedyam	food offered to a deity
nakshatra	cluster of stars or constellation. It is the name of 1/27th part of the path of the moon round the earth (13.33 degrees of the sky). Some names of *nakshatras* are Ashvini, Rohini, Ārdrā, Revāti, etc. *Nakshatras* are related to the *rāshis* (the twelve zodiacal signs). In naming a newborn baby the *nakashatra* in which it was born is taken into consideration

nāma japa	chanting God's holy name
nāmaghara	special prayer hall
naraka	hell
Nāsadiyasukta	hymn of creation in the Rig Veda
nāstika	non-believer. Person who does not believe in the existence of God, or more generally, one who is not religiously inclined
Nighantu	dictionary of difficult Vedic words, now extinct
nimitta kārana	efficient cause (of world)
nirakāra	formless
nirguna	without *gunas*. Not possessing any attributes of the three *gunas* – *sattvaguna*, *rajoguna* and *tamoguna* – i.e., transcends all *māyik* qualities. Divine
nirlobha	non-covetousness
nirmāna	humility
nirukta	oldest Indian treatise on etymology, philology and semantics. One of the six Vedāngas
nishedha	prohibitions or don'ts
nishkāma	absolute celibacy
nishkāma karma	selfless action in accordance with the shastras
nissneha	detachment
nisswāda	non-taste
nitya mukta	eternally liberated soul
niyama	moral and spiritual disciplines, and religious codes of conduct prescribed by God, the Satpurush, or the shastras
nru-runa	debt to human beings
nyāsa vidhi	ritual chanting of appropriate Vedic mantras to invoke the Divine in each part of the person performing special puja
Nyāyasutras	book of aphorisms on Nyāya philosophy by Sage Gautama

P

pād	feet
pāda	chapter
padma	lotus
padmāsana	lotus posture, one of the eighty-four asanas of yoga
pādukā	wooden slippers
pancha jnāna indriya	five cognitive senses
panchabhutas	gross elements: earth, water, fire (light), air and space
panchadhātu	five metals, namely: gold, silver, copper, lead and iron, used to mould a metallic *murti*
Pānchajanya	name of *shankha* used by Bhagwan Krishna
panchājiri	roasted mixture of five ingredients: dry coriander (*dhaniā*), seeds of dill plant (*suvā*), dry ginger (*suntha*), ground sugar crystals and ghee offered to God, and distributed to devotees as *prasāda*
pancha-mahāyajna	five *yajnas*: *deva-yajna*, *rishi-yajna*, *pitru-yajna*, *nru-yajna* and *bhuta-yajna*

pancha-makāra	Vāmāchāra or left-hand path promotes the ritual use of "five Ms", namely, wine (*madya*), fish (*matsya*), meat (*māmsa*), parched grains and gestures (mudra) and extra-marital sexual union (*maithuna*).
panchāmruta	A mixture of five things: milk, curd, ghee, sugar and honey.
panchānga pranāma	a gesture of offering respect in which five parts of the body touch the ground, namely, head, hands, feet, mind and speech. Mainly offered by female devotees in mandirs, personal puja and to guru; also offered by children to their parents and elders
pancha tanmātras	five subtle elements related to their cognitive senses, namely, sight, sound, smell, taste and touch
pāni	hand
para	transcendental form of Vishnu in Vaikuntha *dhāma*
parā	spiritual knowledge
paramhansas	'supreme swan'. A male sadhu of the highest order, characterized by his ability to discriminate between *sat* and *asat* – just as swans were traditionally considered to be able to separate milk from water
paramparā	tradition or succession of gurus
parashu	battle axe
parikramā	circumambulation of deity, guru, holy place or river
pariprashna	questioning the guru and asking for clarification of spiritual principles
parva	chapter in shastra. Celebration
parvata	mountain
pāsha	noose of impurities
pātāla	one of 14 realms of each *brahmānda* or cosmos
pati	husband. Lord
paurānik/purānic	related to the Purānas. Ancient
pāyu	organ of excretion
phala pradāta	dispenser of the fruits of one's karmas
pichhwāi	traditional art of painting native to Rajasthan
pinda	rice ball
Pingala	shastra that deals with versification or the rules for the metres in which Vedic mantras and poems were composed
pitha	pedestal
pitru	forefather
pitru loka	abode of forefathers
pitru-runa	debt to ancestors
pitru-yajna	yajna performed to please one's ancestors
pitta	bile
pradakshinā	practice of circumambulating around the deity, mandir, holy place or river
prajnā	wisdom
prakat	to present on earth
prakruti	primordial matter. World or person's nature
pramāna	valid means of knowledge, like perception, inference, etc.

prameya	objects of true knowledge to be known like atman, body, senses, etc.
pranāma	obeisance offered with folded hands
prāna-pratishthā	Vedic ceremony of image consecration
pranava	Om. Cosmic sound of the creator
pranayama	the process of controlling one's breath
pranipāta	surrendering to guru
prapatti	total surrender of self to God or guru
prārabdha	portion of one's accumulated karma *(sanchita)* that one is presently experiencing in this birth
prāsāda	king's palace. Huge mandir
prasāda	food sanctified by offering it to God
pratika	symbol
pratimā	*murti* or image
pratisarga	dissolution and re-creation *(pratisarga)* of the universe
pratyāhāra	fifth step of *ashtānga* yoga that involves the withdrawing of senses from worldly objects in order to tame the mind
pratyaksha	before one's eyes; manifest
prāyashchitta	atonement for moral lapses
preyas	path of sensual pleasure
pruthivi	earth
pujan	ritual of worship
punarjanma	rebirth
punya	merit
puri	a fried delicacy made of wheat flour
purna kalasha	auspicious pot filled with water
purnāvatāra	complete manifestation of the Divine in human form
purnimā	full moon day
purushārtha	pursuits. Collective term for the four goals legitimately pursued by all Hindus, namely: dharma (duties), *artha* (material wealth), *kāma* (desires), and ultimately, *moksha* (liberation)
Purushasukta	hymn of the Ultimate Reality in the Rig Veda
Purushottama	'Supreme Person'; God
pushti	nourishment; encouragement; support

R

rāga	tune, mode of music
rajas	one of the three *gunas,* having attributes of activity, restlessness, anger, violence, desire to satisfy the *indriyas* and extravagance
rājya	kingdom
rākhi	a decorative, strand-like wristlet traditionally tied by sisters to their brothers on the day of Raksha-bandhan on Shravan *sud* Punam (August), affirming the loving bond between each other, and in particular, the brother's vow to protect his sister

rasa	taste
rāsa	a traditional folk dance of Gujarat
rāsalilā	divine dance of Krishna with the *gopis*
rāshi	the twelve zodiacal signs
ratha	chariot
ratha yātrā	chariot festival
rishi-yajna	indebtedness to the rishis or sages, who gave us the legacy of spirituality, culture and education. This debt can be repaid by studying the sacred texts, teaching them to the next generation, practising their principles, and performing the samskaras and austerities prescribed by the sages. Also known as *brahma-yajna*
roopa	form
ruchās	hymns
rudrāksha	the berry of the tree *Elaeocarpus ganitrus,* used to prepare Shaiva rosaries
ruks	verses
runa	obligation
runa-traya	three-fold debts or obligations, namely, *deva-runa* (debt to gods), *rishi-runa* (debt to sages) and *pitru runa* (debt to ancestors)
ruta	cosmic order

S

sādhaka	a person endeavouring on the spiritual path. An aspirant or a novice on the spiritual path
saguna	having a form and personal qualities
saguna upāsanā	worship of the Supreme Reality having a form and qualities
sahasrāra chakra	one of six subtle centres of consciousness in yoga situated at the top of the head
sakāma	having specific material desire or purpose
sākāra	having a physical form
sakhā bhāva	feeling of friendship
samkirtanam	singing of God's name
sampradāya	a tradition handed down from a founder through successive spiritual gurus
samudra manthana	churning of the ocean
sanchita karma	accumulation of karmas; the sum total of all karmas done in one or many lives
Sānkhya	fundamental belief of the Sānkhya doctrine; i.e., all that evolves from *maya* is perishable and vainglorious. Thoughts that make us realize the perishable nature of everything except God, his abode and the liberated souls
Sānkhyakārikā	*Sānkhyakārikā* of Ishwarakrishna (circa 350 to 450 CE) is the most important and probably the earliest basic work of the Sānkhya philosophy
Sānkhyasutras	text which contain the aphorisms of Sānkhya philosophy. The one available today is believed to have been written later in the name of Sage Kapila
sannyastāshrama	complete renunciation of worldly activities and responsibilities to fully engage

	oneself in meditation and other spiritual sadhanas; the fourth stage of life
sant	sadhu. God-realized guru
santosha	contentment
sārathi	driver
sarva kartā	God as the all-doer
sarva shaktimān	attribute of God as being all-powerful
sarva vyāpaka	attribute of God as being all-pervading
sarvajna	attribute of God as being all-knowing
sarvopari	attribute of God as being supreme
sat-chit-ānanda	eternal, consciousness and bliss are attributes of God and *ātmā*
satpurusha	spiritual guru
sattva	used in several senses such as purity and strength. The first of the three *gunas* responsible for knowledge and happiness
sāttvika	a person or thing that has the quality of *sattva*
satya	truth
satyaloka	first realm in the 14-realm system of a *brahmānda*
Satyam	truth
shaucha	purity
setu	bridge
sevā	service
shabda	word. Testimony
shabda pramāna	verbal testimony
shakti	power. Ability
shālagrāma	a round petrified ammonite pebble from the Gandaki River in Nepal that is worshipped as a form of Bhagwan Vishnu
Shānkarabhāshya	commentary by Ādi Shankarāchārya to establish his own school of Kevalādvaita Vedānta
shankha	conch
shānti pātha	Vedic peace prayers
sharira-shariri	body-soul relationship between God and *jivas* and *maya*
shāstānga dandavat pranāma	prostrating to deity, guru or holy shrine by touching eight specified parts of the body to the floor. The eight parts are head, mind, eyes, speech (mouth), chest, hands, thighs and feet
shastravidyā	science of weaponry
Shatarudriya	hymns from Yajur Veda in honour of Shiva
shayana	reclining
shikhā	tuft of hair
shikhara	mandir pinnacle or tower
shikharabaddha	big pinnacled mandir
shilā	stone
Shivam	auspiciousness
shloka	Sanskrit verse
shodasha upachāra	sixteen steps of *mahāpuja* ritual

shrāddha	rites to propitiate one's ancestors
shreyas	paths of *moksha*
Shribhāshya	Rāmānujāchārya's commentary on the Brahmasutras
shrotra	ear
shrotriya	one who knows and has realized the true meaning of the shastras
Shruti	'that which is heard' or revealed. Refers to Veda
siddhānta	doctrine
sinhāsana	throne
Smārta	a *sampradāya* whose followers worship all five deities, namely, Vishnu, Shiva, Devi, Surya and Ganesha, or one of them with highest devotion
Smruti	'that which is remembered'. Refers to Smruti Shastras, namely, Dharma Shastras, Purānas and Itihāsas, etc.
sruk	ladle
sruva	spoon
sthambha	pillar
sthānaka	standing posture of *murti*
sthapati	architect
sthāpatya	style of architecture
sudarshana chakra	disc of Vishnu
sukshma	subtle
sukta	hymn
sumeru	the largest bead that joins the two ends of the *mālā*
Sundaram	beautiful
Surasāgara	bhajans on Krishna by Surdās
sutala	tenth realm in the 14-realm system of a *brahmānda*
sutra	aphorism
swabhāva	inner nature or base instincts
swādhyāya	self-study
swarga	abode of the devas
swasti	'let there be goodness everywhere'
swastika	symbol of auspiciousness
swedaja	born from sweat, i.e., bugs

T

tamas	one of the three *gunas,* responsible for indolence, sleep and evil
Tantra	literature predominantly devoted to Shakti or the Divine Mother and Shiva
tapa	austerity
tapaloka	second realm in the 14-realm system of a *brahmānda*
tarka	logic
Tarkasangraha	work on Nyāya by Annambhatta
tarpana	standing in water after bathing (in a river or tank) to offer water thrice from palms of hand, with appropriate mantras, to devas (gods), *pitrus* (ancestors) and rishis (sages)

teja	light
thāla	plate of vegetarian food for offering to God. Also, song sung while offering food to deity
tilaka	holy mark applied on forehead
tirtha	holy place
tirtha yātrā	pilgrimage
Tirumurāi	collection of Tamil poems and songs compiled into twelve books. They contain fervent invocations of Shiva
tithi	each lunar day
tripundra	a *tilaka* in the form of three horizontal markings on the forehead
trishula	trident
turiyā	state of God-realization
tvak	skin

U

udbhija	category of life forms born of seed, i.e., all forms of plant life
udgātā	special priest of Sāma Veda
upādāna kārana	material cause (of world)
upamāna	analogy
upanayana	one of the 16 sacraments performed for beginning of formal education in the life of a Hindu boy, where he is given the sacred thread (*upavita* or *yajnopavita*)
upāsanā	mode of worship. Philosophical beliefs regarding God. Knowledge that God is supreme, the all-doer, always a divine personality and ever present on earth in flesh and blood
upastha	organ of procreation
upavita	sacred thread
urdhvapundra tilaka	U- or Y-shaped mark on forehead
utsava murti	*murti* used for procession in celebration

V

Vachana	holy text of Vira Shaivism in the Kannada language. The *Vachanas* are little pieces of rhythmic prose sermons meant for common people. They inspire bhakti towards Shiva.
vāda	argument to find truth
vāhana	vehicle; usually an animal carrying a deva
vairagya	detachment from material objects and pursuits
Vaisheshikasutras	book of aphorisms on Vaisheshika philosophy by Sage Kanāda
vajra	thunderbolt weapon of Indra deva
vāk	speech
vānaprasthāshrama	third of the four stages of life, when one withdraws to some extent from social duties and serves merely as an elderly advisor. Literally implying 'taking to the forests'
varadamudrā	boon-giving gesture

varna	social order of Brahmin, Kshatriya, Vaishya and Shudra
varnāshrama	stage and duties of life
varnāshrama dharma	duties and responsibilities of Hindus in relation to their varnas (classes) and ashramas (stages of life).
vāsanās	material desires
vāta	air in body
vātsalya	parental love
vāyu	air
Vedāntasutras	book of aphorisms on Vedānta philosophy by Sage Bādarāyana
vedi	altar for fire sacrifice
vibhava	avatars of God
videha mukti	when *ātmā* of a deceased devotee ascends to the supreme divine abode of God
vidhi	ritual act. The 'do's' codes of conduct
vidyā	knowledge
vimāna	divine chariot
vinā	musical stringed instrument
vitandā	destructive criticism
viveka	discernment
vrutti	mental inclination
vyavahāra	social and financial dealings
vyuha	emanations of Vishnu

Y

yajna	fire ritual
yajnopavita	sacred thread
yajus	Yajur Veda
yama	one of the eight steps in *ashtānga* yoga. Restraint
yantra	'that which holds and protects'. Consecrated geometrical diagram engraved or drawn on metal, paper or palm leaf that represents a deity. Used for worship, protection and control of one's passions
yati	celibate
yoga	art and science of concentration of mind which helps the spiritual aspirant to ultimately realize Paramātmā
Yoga Darshana	philosophy by Sage Patanjali
yoga nidrā	contemplative light sleep
Yogasutras	book of aphorisms on Yoga philosophy by Sage Patanjali
yuga	era

BIBLIOGRAPHY

1. Flood, Gavin. *An Introduction to Hinduism*. Cambridge: Cambridge University Press, 2004.

2. Flood, Gavin. *The Blackwell Companion to Hinduism*. Massachusetts: Blackwell Publishing, 2005.

3. Johnson, Linda. *The Complete Idiot's Guide to Hinduism*. Indianapolis: Alpha, 2002.

4. Klostermaier, K.K. *Hinduism: A Short History*. Oxford: Oneworld Publications, 2000.

5. Knott, Kim. *Hinduism, A Very Short Introduction*. New York: Oxford University Press Inc., 2007.

6. Prakash, Satya. *Founders of Sciences in Ancient India*. New Delhi: The Research Institute of Ancient Scientific Studies, 1965.

7. Sadhu Brahmadarshandas. *Vachanamrut Rahasya Pt.3*. Ahmedabad: Swaminarayan Aksharpith, 2001.

8. Sadhu Mukundcharandas. *Rishis, Mystics and Heroes of India*. Ahmedabad: Swaminarayan Aksharpith, 2006.

9. Shastri, Dr Yajneshwar S. *Foundations of Hinduism*. Ahmedabad: Yogeshwar Prakashan, 1993.

10. Swami Harshananda. *A Concise Encyclopaedia of Hinduism*. Bangalore: The Ramakrishna Math, 2008.

11. Swami Nirvedanand. *Hinduism At A Glance*. Calcutta: The Ramakrishna Mission, 2003.

INDEX

Entries followed by an asterix (*) indicate reference to a photo or illustration.